工商管理专业英语

第三版

主编◎李桂华　郑　琦

ENGLISH FOR BUSINESS ADMINISTRATION

华东师范大学出版社
·上海·

图书在版编目(CIP)数据

工商管理专业英语/李桂华,郑琦主编. —3 版. —上海:华东师范大学出版社,2023
ISBN 978 - 7 - 5760 - 3869 - 9

Ⅰ.①工… Ⅱ.①李…②郑… Ⅲ.①工商行政管理—英语—高等学校—教材 Ⅳ.①F203.9

中国国家版本馆 CIP 数据核字(2023)第 088940 号

工商管理专业英语(第三版)

主　　编　李桂华　郑　琦
责任编辑　皮瑞光
特约审读　李兴福
责任校对　林小慧　时东明
封面设计　俞　越

出版发行　华东师范大学出版社
社　　址　上海市中山北路 3663 号　邮编 200062
网　　址　www.ecnupress.com.cn
电　　话　021 - 60821666　行政传真 021 - 62572105
客服电话　021 - 62865537　门市(邮购)电话 021 - 62869887
地　　址　上海市中山北路 3663 号华东师范大学校内先锋路口
网　　店　http://hdsdcbs.tmall.com

印 刷 者　常熟市文化印刷有限公司
开　　本　787 毫米×1092 毫米　1/16
印　　张　15
字　　数　369 千字
版　　次　2023 年 7 月第 3 版
印　　次　2023 年 7 月第 1 次
书　　号　ISBN 978 - 7 - 5760 - 3869 - 9
定　　价　45.00 元

出 版 人　王　焰

(如发现本版图书有印订质量问题,请寄回本社客服中心调换或电话 021 - 62865537 联系)

第三版前言

时间过得很快，《工商管理专业英语》(第二版)修订出版一晃已经 8 年了。自该教材出版以来，承蒙各位专家和广大读者的偏爱、喜欢或习惯，教材经过多次印刷，修订再版也是自然而然的事情。最近些年，由于作者接近退休，所以要完成的作业和总结性工作很多，包括清华大学出版社的教材《营销管理》、经济管理出版社的专著《品牌价值评估理论与方法研究》和《要素品牌研究》等都在此期间先后出版。《工商管理专业英语》一书本来计划 2020 年再版，但由于新冠疫情影响，直到现在才完成任务。

考虑到读者对工商管理专业英语类教材的实际需要和意见，本次修订变化的部分主要包括：(1)为每一个单元的最后部分(Supplemental Reading Material)增加了思考练习题，以便于广大教师和读者使用时有复习的参考，也使该教材体例整体结构趋向更完整。(2)对第二版中的有些课文标题根据内容和读者及编辑的反馈意见进行了调整，例如将"Unit 1 The Evolution of Management"修订为"The Evolution of Management as a Field of Study"；"Unit 11 Human Resource Management"修订为"Human Resource Management：An Overview"。(3)对教材的查漏补缺。(4)融入二十大精神，尽可能反映一些新的内容，帮助学生了解国际社会的发展动态，从而增强学生的国际意识和全球视野，深化"推动构建人类命运共同体"的理念。

本次修订工作主要由李桂华教授完成。由于水平有限，不妥之处，敬请指正。

在《工商管理专业英语》(第三版)出版之际，要特别感谢对本书进行多次审校的专家，特别感谢责任编辑皮瑞光先生，他们在疫情的中后期就开始了审校工作，非常辛苦。

编　　者

2023 年 4 月

第二版前言

《工商管理专业英语》(第一版)于 2007 年由华东师范大学出版社出版发行。本书出版以来受到同行专家、读者,特别是广大师生好评与厚爱,进而被各财经类和管理类大中专院校广泛采用,累计销售 3 万多册,这是编者没有预计到的,编者表示万分感谢。

在教材的使用过程中,众多同行专家在表示赞赏的同时,也提出了许多宝贵意见。在吸取专家反馈意见的基础上,考虑到市场环境和需求的变化,编者和出版发行单位决定对原教材进行修订。

《工商管理专业英语》(第二版)修订编写的主要目的与第一版一样,旨在帮助工商管理及相关专业的研究生、MBA、大学本科生和在职自学人员,提高阅读理解管理专业英语的水平以及运用英语进行业务交流和洽谈的能力。

本次修订没有打破原有框架,而是在坚持原来教材"既全面又重点突出"的风格基础上,进行了比较大的修改,并选用了最新的范文:一是重新调整全书的单元顺序,其中的第 3、4、5、8、9、10、15、20 单元是新增单元,替换了第一版中比较陈旧的内容;二是内容范围在原来涵盖管理学原理、营销管理、广告促销、财务管理、人力资源管理和国际营销等领域的基础上,增加了电子商务和网络营销的内容,使教材更加适应工商管理发展现状;三是对各章练习题的第 V 题"英译中"全部补充了参考答案,并对部分习题中的语句或表述进行了适当修改,使习题中的语句更为通顺。

本次修订由第一版主编李桂华教授、郑琦副教授完成,其中新增单元的工作主要由李桂华完成。在本教材修订过程中,编者查阅和借鉴了欧美近年新出版的文献资料,尽量选用有代表性的、专业性强的文献。

本次修订工作得到了美国马萨诸塞大学市场营销系教授托马斯·布拉希尔(Thomas Brashear Alejandro)的大力支持,在此表示感谢。

由于水平和时间所限,错误和疏漏在所难免,敬请广大读者和专家继续提出宝贵意见和建议。

编　　者

2015 年 11 月于南开园

第一版前言

本书旨在帮助工商管理及相关专业的大学本科生(专科生)、研究生、MBA 和在职自学人员,提高工商管理专业英语阅读理解水平以及运用英语进行业务交流和洽谈的能力。全书共分 20 单元,内容涵盖管理学原理、市场营销管理、广告促销、财务管理、人力资源管理、国际营销等领域,使学生熟悉并掌握尽可能多的专业英语词汇和术语。在着重训练学生阅读专业英语文献的同时,帮助学生熟悉专业英语文体结构、风格特征及修辞技巧,为将来的工作实践打下较为坚实的专业英语基础。

本书内容具有以下特点:

● 选材新颖,语言地道,参考了大量最新原版教材。

● 内容涵盖范围广泛,包括管理学原理、市场营销管理、广告促销、财务管理、人力资源管理、国际营销等领域。

● 课后习题备有参考答案,有助于学生熟悉和掌握尽可能多的专业英语词汇和术语,有利于提高阅读专业文献的能力,同时适合学生自学。

本书是由南开大学商学院部分教师共同编写。其中郑琦副教授编写 1—8 单元,刘建华、张巍博士编写 9—13 单元,李桂华教授编写 14—17 单元,赵路老师编写 18—20 单元。全书由郑琦、李桂华进行校对、统纂并配以习题和答案后定稿。编者在本书编写过程中参阅了大量相关的英文专业书籍、文献和工具书,并得到华东师范大学出版社的大力支持和帮助,在此一并表示衷心感谢。

参加本书编写工作的老师曾经翻译出版了该领域的大量著作并有国外进修经历,有多年专业外语教学经验。这为我们编写出适用的高质量教材提供了保证。虽然我们竭尽全力,但恐错漏之处难免。恳请专家及使用本书的老师和同学指正。

编 者

2007 年 8 月于南开大学

目录

Unit 1

The Evolution of Management as a Field of Study

Text

The modern era of management began early in the 20th century when classical theorists, economists, and industrial engineers offered a **classical approach** to increase the productivity of individuals and organizations. Both organizational growth and its increasing influence on our economy and standard of living are relatively recent in history; thus the study of management is relatively new. Many of the first individuals to study and write about management were practicing managers. They described their own experiences and tried to **generalize** the principles they believed could be applied in similar situations. Even today, a great deal of what we know about management comes from the **autobiographies** and **memoirs** of men and women who are or have been practicing managers.

Now, however, other individuals also are interested in management for scientific reasons. Social and behavioral scientists view the management of organizations as an **extremely** important social phenomenon worthy of studying through scientific inquiry. As scientists, these men and women make no value judgments regarding good or bad management practices. Their objective is to understand and explain the practice of management.

Between the two extremes of management practice and management science are many individuals who have contributed to the study of management. They include engineers, sociologists, psychologists, **anthropologists**, lawyers, economists, accountants, mathematicians, political scientists, and philosophers.

Such differing **perspectives** on the same subject cannot be neatly classified. Thus, as a manager, you will have at your disposal many ways of looking at management's tasks. Each may be more useful for some problems than for others. For example, a management theory that emphasizes employee satisfaction may be more helpful in dealing with a high employee **turnover** than with delays in production. Because there is no single, universally accepted management approach, you should be familiar with the various major theories.

The three well-established approaches to management thought are: the **classical approach**, which focuses on the task of managing work and organizations; the **behavioral approach**, which focuses on the task of managing people; and the **management science approach**, which focuses on the task of production and operations. Although these approaches evolved in historical sequence, later ideas have not always replaced early ones. Rather, each new approach has added to the knowledge of the previous ones. At the same time, each approach has continued to develop on its own.

During the last 30 years or so, there have been attempts to integrate the three approaches to management—classical, behavioral, and management science. One of these attempts, the systems approach stresses that organizations must be viewed as total systems, with each part linked to every other part. Another, the **contingency approach**, stresses that the correctness of a managerial practice is contingent on how it fits the particular situation in which it is applied.

The systems approach to management is really a way of thinking about management problems. It views an organization as a group of interrelated parts with a single purpose. Because the action of one part influences the others, managers cannot deal separately with individual parts. In solving problems, managers using the systems approach must view the organization as a **dynamic** whole and must try to anticipate the intended as well as unintended impacts of their decisions. Such managers do not solve individual problems. Rather, they intervene in a total system of integrated parts, using the management functions of planning, organizing, coordinating and controlling.

The age-old **confrontation** between the production objective of low costs and the marketing objective of a broad product line is a good example of the interrelated nature of management problems. Each objective conflicts with the other. For example, to **incur** the lowest production costs, a firm would produce only one color and one style. To achieve the marketing objective, however, several models and several colors would be required but at a higher cost. In this situation, a **compromise** is necessary for the overall system to achieve its objective. The objectives of individual parts must be compromised to meet the objective of the entire firm.

The systems approach forces managers to recognize that organizations are systems made up of **interdependent** parts and that a change in one part affects other parts. It seeks to identify the **characteristics** of jobs, people, and organizations, allowing managers to see the interdependence between the various segments of an organization. The basic idea of the contingency is that there is no best way to plan, organize, or control. Rather, managers must find different ways to fit different situations. A method highly effective in one situation may not work in other situations. In other words, the contingency approach seeks to match different situations with different management methods.

Actually, the idea of contingency, or situational thinking is not new. During the 1920s, an early writer in the classical approach mentioned the "law of situation". One scholar and writer in management noted that "different situations require different kinds of knowledge, and the man possessing the knowledge demanded by certain situation tends in the best managed businesses, other things being equal, to become the leader in the moment".

The contingency approach has grown in **popularity** over the last two decades because research has found that, given certain characteristics of a job and certain characteristics of people doing the job, specific management practices tend to work better than others. For example, rigid plans, clearly defined jobs, autocratic leadership, and tight controls have at times resulted in high productivity and satisfied workers. At other times, the opposite characteristics (general plans, vaguely defined jobs, democratic leadership, and loose controls) have produced the same results.

If, for instance, productivity needs to be increased, the manager should not automatically assume a new work method is needed (a classical solution) or that a new motivational approach needs to be tried (a behavioral solution). Instead, the manager should study the characteristics of the workers and the nature of the job, and his own leadership approach before deciding on a solution.

Managers around the globe use more of a contingency approach to survive. **Sole reliance** on a classical or a behavioral or a management science approach is not **sufficient** for organizations. The approaches that worked for Procter & Gamble for 50 years and the start-up of Haier or Legend Computer during the first few years must be modified to fit the changing global environment. Thus, the contingency view has become more relevant and prominent because of the following factors:

1. Increased globalization of enterprises and the need for more government-business **alliances** to compete internationally.

2. Demands for ethical and socially responsive leadership.

3. Changing **demographics** and skill requirements of the workforce.

4. The emergence of new organizational structures that emphasize speed in reacting to environmental changes.

5. Changing needs, preferences, and desires of employees for job security, participation, ownership, and personal fulfillment.

As the contingency approach suggests, the student of management preparing for the 21st century must learn multiple ways to compete, innovate, create, motivate, and lead. Both the systems approach and the contingency approach can provide valuable insights and **complement** the classical, behavioral, and management science approaches.

Glossary

evolution *n.* the process of developing 发展

generalize *v.* to infer from many particulars 概括

autobiography *n.* the biography of a person written by that person 自传

memoir *n.* an account of the personal experiences of an author 回忆录,自传

extremely *ad.* being in or attaining the greatest or highest degree 极度地

anthropologist *n.* someone who studies anthropology (the scientific study of the origin, the behavior, and the physical, social, and cultural development of human beings) 人类学家

perspective *n.* the way in which a situation or problem is judged so that proper consideration is given to each part 合理观察,视角

turnover *n.* the number of workers hired by an establishment to replace those who have left in a given period of time 人员更替数

approach *n.* the method used in dealing with or accomplishing something 方法

contingency *n.* a possibility that must be prepared for; a future emergency 可能事件,可能出现的情况

dynamic *a.* characterized by continuous change, activity, or progress 不断变化的

confrontation *n.* discord or a clash of opinions and ideas 观点或思想的不和或冲撞

incur *v.* to acquire or come into (something usually undesirable); sustain 获得

compromise *n.* something that combines qualities or elements of different things 折中

interdependent *a.* mutually dependent 互相依存的

characteristic *n.* a feature that helps to identify, tell apart, or describe recognizably; a distinguishing mark or trait 特性

popularity *n.* the quality or state of being popular, especially the state of being widely admired, accepted, or sought after 普及

sole *a.* of or relating to only one individual or group; exclusive 单独的

reliance *n.* the act of relying or the state of being reliant 依赖,依靠

sufficient *a.* being as much as is needed 充足的

alliance *n.* the act of becoming allied or the condition of being allied 结盟

demographics *n.* data of or relating to demography 人口统计数据

complement *v.* to add to, make complete 补足

Key Terms and Concepts

Classical approach(**to Management**):Also called classical school. A body of literature that represents the earliest attempts to define and describe the field of management. The approach's main focus is on formally prescribed relationships. Its primary means for acquiring knowledge are personal observation and case studies.（管理学）古典（研究）方法

Behavioral approach（**to Management**）:Also called behavioral school to management. Here it refers to a body of literature characterized by its concern for human behavior in the work environment. The school's primary means for acquiring knowledge is scientific method，with emphasis on research. Chronologically，the behavioral approach to management thought followed the classical approach. Its first phase was identified with human relations theory popular in the 1940s and early 1950s. Its second phase was the behavioral science approach，which came into popular use in the early 1950s.（管理学）行为（研究）方法

Management science approach:Also known as Management Science School. A body of literature characterized by its use of mathematical and statistic techniques to build models for the solution of production and operations problems. The approach's primary means for acquiring knowledge is mathematical deduction. 管理学科学（研究）方法

Contingency（**or situational**）**approach**（**to Management**）:An analysis of management that emphasizes the fact that what managers do in practice depends on a given set of circumstances or the "situation" and that there is no single "best way" to manage.（管理学）权变情境（研究）方法

Exercises

1. What are the three well-established approaches to management? And what are the historical sequences of the development of these approaches to management?

2. Why do management analysis and practice require a systems approach? Give a practical example of this approach.

3. What is the contingency, or situational approach to management? Could any explanation of management be any different? Could any manager operate in any other way?

4. Is management a science or an art according to your understanding? Could the same explanation apply to engineering or finance?

5. What is the essence of the systems approach to management? Give a concrete example of this approach in reality.

6. What kinds of individuals, according to the text, have contributed to the study of management between the two extremes of management practice and management science?

7. In the evolution of management thought, have later ideas always replaced the earlier ones? Please explain.

8. Why is sole reliance on a classical or a behavioral or a management science approach not sufficient for organizations? Please explain.

9. Have you ever managed anything—for example, as part of a job in a social or student organization? If so, did you perform the management functions of planning, coordinating, organizing, leading and controlling without being aware of them?

10. Look up the terms "science", "theory" and "principle" in an acceptable dictionary and determine how they are used. Compare these definitions with the usage of these terms as applied in the text.

contingent	dynamic	conflict	compromise	interdependent	reliance
popularity	sufficient	insights	generalize	memoirs	classic
management	science	behavioral	integrate	sole	

1. The managers described their own experiences and tried to _____ the

5

principles they believed could be applied in similar situations.

2. Even today, a great deal of what we know about management comes from the autobiographies and _____ of men and women who are or have been practicing managers.

3. According to the text, the three well-established approaches to management thought are the _____ approach, which focuses on the task of managing work and organizations; the _____ approach, which focuses on the task of managing people; and the _____ approach, which focuses on the task of production and operations.

4. During the last 30 years or so, there have been attempts to _____ the three approaches to management—classical, behavioral, and management science.

5. The contingency approach, stresses that the correctness of a managerial practice is _____ on how it fits the particular situation in which it is applied.

6. In solving problems, managers using the systems approach must view the organization as a _____ whole and must try to anticipate the intended as well as unintended impacts of their decisions.

7. The age-old confrontation between the production objective of low costs and the marketing objective of a broad product line is a good example of the interrelated nature of management problems. Each objective _____ with the other.

8. The objectives of individual parts must be _____ to meet the objective of the entire firm.

9. The systems approach forces managers to recognize that organizations are systems made up of _____ parts and that a change in one part affects other parts.

10. The contingency approach has grown in _____ over the last two decades because research has found that, given certain characteristics of a job and certain characteristics of people doing the job, specific management practices tend to work better than others.

11. Managers around the globe use more of a contingency approach to survive. Sole _____ on a classical or a behavioral or a management science approach is not _____ for organizations.

12. Both the systems approach and the contingency approach can provide valuable _____ and complement the classical, behavioral, and management science approaches.

1. complement	a. to acquire or come into (something usually undesirable); sustain
2. perspective	b. characterized by continuous change, activity, or progress
3. dynamic	c. the act of relying or the state of being reliant
4. incur	d. to infer from many particulars
5. compromise	e. being as much as is needed
6. sufficient	f. something that combines qualities or elements of different things
7. generalize	g. to add to, make complete
8. reliance	h. the way in which a situation is judged or evaluated

IV. True and False statements.

1. The three well-established approaches to management thought are the classical approach, which focuses on the task of managing work and organizations; the behavioral approach, which focuses on the task of managing people; and the management science approach, which focuses on the task of production and operations. (   )

2. In solving problems, managers using the systems approach must view the organization as a dynamic whole but mustn't try to anticipate the intended as well as unintended impacts of their decisions. (   )

3. In other words, the contingency approach seeks to match different situations with different management methods. (   )

4. The systems approach forces managers to recognize that organizations are systems made up of interdependent parts and that a change in one part affects other parts. (   )

5. Managers around the globe use more of a contingency approach to survive. (   )

6. The systems approach seeks to identify the characteristics of jobs, people, and organizations, disallowing managers to see the interdependence between the various segments of an organization. (   )

7. Between the two extremes of management practice and management science are not many individuals who have contributed to the study of management. (   )

V. Translate the following into Chinese.

Why Study Management?

Learning about management is important for two reasons. First, our society depends on specialized institutions and organizations to provide the goods and services we desire. These organizations are guided and directed by the decisions of one or more individuals designated as "managers". In market-based economy, it is managers who allocate society's resources to various and often competing ends. Managers have the authorities and responsibility to build safe or unsafe products, seek war or peace, build or destroy cities, or clean up or pollute the environment. Managers establish the conditions under which we are provided with jobs, incomes, lifestyles, products, services, health care, and knowledge. It would be very difficult to find any one who is neither a manager nor affected by the decisions of a manager.

Second, individuals not trained as managers often find themselves in managerial positions. Many individuals presently being trained to be teachers, accountants, musicians, salespersons, artists, physicians, or lawyers will one day earn their livings as managers. They will manage schools, accounting firms, orchestras, sales organizations, museums, hospitals, and government agencies. The United States is an organizational society, and its approximately 16 million organizations must have managers.

The future success of any nation in the global village lies in managing productivity, being able to cope with environment changes，and properly managing the workforce. These challenges will require well-educated，knowledgeable，and hard-working individuals deciding that a management career is of value to them personally. We believe that managing is one of the most stimulating and rewarding careers a man or woman can choose.

VI. Translate the following into English.

1. 现代管理学始于 20 世纪早期，当时正统派的理论家、经济学家和产业工程师提出了经典分析法以增强个人和组织的生产力。

2. 强调员工满意度的管理理论，更有助于解决员工流动量大的问题，而不是解决延迟生产问题。

3. 甚至在今天，我们所了解的管理学也都出自那些管理人员的自传和回忆录。

4. 尽管这些方法是按历史顺序发展的，但后者的观念总是会代替前者。

5. 在过去的大约 30 年中，人们试图把古典的、行为的和科学的管理方法融为一个整体。

6. 在这种情况下，为了使整个体系达到其目的，折中的做法是必要的。

7. 严格的计划、明确的分工、集中的领导和严密的控制有时可以提高生产力，并且使员工感到满意。

8. 权变的方法是为了在不同的情况下采用不同的管理方法。

Supplemental Reading Material

Foundations of Managing Work and Organizations

At the beginning of the 20th century，some managers wanting to improve the practice of management began to put their ideas in writing. These managers were particularly concerned with two issues：（1）increasing the productivity of individuals performing work and（2）increasing the productivity of organizations within which work is performed. Directing their attention to finding ways to manage work and organizations so that higher level of output would be produced at lower costs，they created a body of management literature that became known as the classical approach.

The emphasis on rational analysis and application of scientific rigor to facts and information about productivity led to the use of the term *scientific management* to describe the earliest attempts to manage the work of individuals. The first supporters of scientific management were practicing engineers and managers who believed and then demonstrated that work could be done more efficiently and thus more productively. Believing that the most efficient—the best way to do a job could be determined through analysis of data，they urged managers to study the actual performance of work to collect objective data on their observations.

While scientific management ideas were developing，classical organization theory began to evolve. Developers of this theory believed that organizations are the settings within which individuals perform jobs—that organization is a collection of individual jobs— so the organization should also be designed and managed according to principles and practices that stress efficiency and productivity.

The combination of ideas from scientific management's concern for productive work and classical organization theory's concern for efficient organizations creates important body of management knowledge, classical management thought. Managers must know and apply this knowledge to survive both domestic and international competition for resources and products. Today's managers and organizations that make headlines for their high performance stress the importance of rational planning, organizing, and controlling the work of individuals and the organization in which the work takes place. But this recognition of importance of managing did not develop overnight; it took many years to overcome existing management ways.

To appreciate fully the importance of scientific management as a philosophy and practice, you must understand its major contributions. These contributions were in the area of work management, work simplification, work scheduling, and efficiency.

As a supervisor at the Philadelphia Midvale Steel Company in the late 1800s, Frederick W. Taylor became interested in ways to improve lathe work. He began gathering facts and applying an objective analysis that was to typify his entire career. He studied the work of individual lathe workers to discover exactly how they perform their jobs; he identified each aspect of each job and measured everything measurable. His goal was to provide the lathe operator with scientifically based, objective standards that would define a fair day's work.

Taylor's efforts culminated in four principles for managing work:

1. For each element of a person's work, develop a science that replaces the old rule-of-thumb method.

2. Scientifically select, train, teach and develop the worker. (In the past, workers chose their own work and trained themselves as best they could.)

3. Cooperate with the workers to ensure that all the work is done in accordance with the science that has been developed.

4. Recognize that there is almost equal division of work and responsibility between management and the workers. Managers take over all work for which they are better fitted than the workers. (In the past, almost all the work and the greater part of the responsibility were thrown on the workers.)

These four principles became the basic guidelines for managing the work of individuals. Taylor was the first individual to study work in a serious manner. His experiments with stopwatch and word methods inspired others to undertake similar studies in other industries. One result of the efforts of those who followed was the discovery of ways to simplify work.

Principles of Work Simplification. Frank and Lillian Gilbreth, a husband and wife team, combined their talents to produce important breakthroughs in work simplification. An untrained but insightful engineer, Frank Gilbreth was an apprentice bricklayer in his first job. His observations of skilled bricklayers' motions convinced him that many of their body movements (bending, reaching, stooping, troweling) could be combined or eliminated. Bricklaying could be simplified, and production could be increased. By combining and eliminating body movements and increasing the number of bricks laid in a given period, resources (bricklayers' time) are reduced, and output (bricks laid) is increased. The result is an increase in labor productivity.

Principles of Work Scheduling. A close associate of Taylor was a young graduate engineer, Henry L. Gantt. Like Taylor and the Gilbreths, Gantt was concerned with problems of productivity at the shop-floor level. Gantt's major contribution to scientific management is a chart showing the relationship between work planned and completed on one axis and time elapsed on the other. The *Gantt Chart* is still used in industry as a method for scheduling work.

While Taylor and the Gilbreths focused on the workers, Gantt believed that the way managers did their work could be improved and made more productive. He believed that expertise should be the sole criterion for the exercise of authority and that managers have the moral obligation to make decisions by scientific methods, not by opinion. Thus Gantt broadened the scope of scientific management by including the work of managers as appropriate for analysis.

Principles of Efficiency. The public became aware of Harrington Emerson in 1910, when he testified as an expert witness before the Interstate Commerce Commission that the railroads could save $1 million per day by using the methods and philosophy of scientific management.

Emerson's ideas are embodied in a set of principles that define the manner in which the efficient use of the resources is to be accomplished. His principles encompass the basic elements of the scientific management approach. In summary, they state that a manager should (1) use scientific, objective, and factual analyses; (2) define the aims of undertaking; (3) relate each part of the whole; (4) provide standardized procedures and methods; and (5) reward individuals for successful execution of the task.

Emerson's contributions go beyond his principles of efficiency. He also recognized the positive lessons to be learned from the military's use of the formalized staff and advisory positions. In his capacity as one of the first management consultants, he proposed the creation of an organization whose activities would be defined by clear statements of goals and purposes.

The significant and lasting contribution of scientific management, however, has been the identification of management's responsibilities for managing work. According to the classical approach, management has the following responsibilities:

* *Planning* the work by predetermining the expected quantity and quality of output for each job.
* *Organizing* the work by specifying the appropriate way and means to perform each task.
* *Leading and influencing* others to engage in work behavior to achieve the results desired.
* *Controlling* the work by (a) selecting and training qualified individuals, (b) overseeing the actual job performance, and (c) verifying that the actual quantity and quality of output meet expectations.

At the work level, the responsibilities of management were defined in functions: planning, organizing, leading, and controlling.

Discussion and Review Questions:

1. What is scientific management? Please explain the value of scientific management.

2. What early evidence of management practices can you describe?

3. Please describe the important contributions made by classical management theorists.

4. What are the responsibilities of management? How do you understand each responsibility?

5. What are Taylor's four principles of scientific management? What do you learn from this?

Unit 2

The Scope of Management

Text

Management is needed in every type of organization. An auto plant, a city government, a baseball team, an army, and a school all require management. Every organization has **goals**. Management **entails** planning, organizing, coordinating, leading, and controlling resources (land, labor, capital and information) to efficiently reach these goals. The challenges of management include maintaining an organizational structure, developing both long- and short-term plans, motivating employees, and maintaining quality—a measure of how closely goods and services **conform** to predetermined standards and customer expectations. To meet these challenges, managers must possess certain skills that enable them to fulfill specific roles. As Bill Gates has demonstrated, when managers possess the right combination of **vision**, skill, experience, and determination, they can lead an organization to success.

Managerial Goals

Why do organizations like Microsoft, Intel, Ford, and General Electric exist? Like most organizations, they were formed in order to realize a vision, a realistic, credible, and attractive view of the future that grows out of and improves upon the present. Henry Ford **envisioned** making **affordable** transportation available to every person. Bill Gates envisioned making the computer a useful household and business tool. Without such visionary managers, who knows how the world would be different? In today's innovative and competitive business environment, companies that **strive** to envision and define the future often have an advantage over those that simply react to the present.

Of course, having a vision is no guarantee of success. In order to transform vision to reality, managers must define specific goals and **objectives**. A starting point is to write a **mission statement** that defines why the organization exists and what it seeks to accomplish. A mission statement often focuses on the market and customers that the company serves. A statement may also describe the company's products and services as well as its value and culture (including ethics and social responsibility). Regardless, it should be both focused enough to be attainable and broad enough to allow the company to evolve. It should also inspire and guide management and employees alike. As the company grows, management can refer to the mission statement as a means of evaluating whether proposed actions are in line with the company's stated purpose and values. Consider Edge Learning Institute, an employee-training firm based in Tempe, Arizona. Edge executives were considering mass-marketing their training videos through television "**informercials**". However, they realized that this was contrary to the company's mission of using "the human touch when providing individuals and organizations with information". So they decided instead to expand Edge's reach by developing a network of **franchises** that follow the company's training methods. Edge now has four franchises and eight more in the works.

As managers at Edge Learning Institute know, a company's mission is realized by establishing goals and objectives. Although these terms are often used interchangeably, a goal is a broad, long-range target of the organization, and an objective is a specific, short-range target. For Edge, a goal might be to become the West Coast leader in employee training, and an objective might be to open ten franchises in its year of expansion. The best organizational goals are specific, measurable, relevant, challenging, attainable, and time-limited. Moreover, goals are often designed to give the company a competitive edge through at least one of three methods:

* **Differentiation.** A company using differentiation develops a level of service, a product image, unique product features (including quality), or new technologies that distinguish its product from competitors' products.
* **Cost leadership**. With cost leadership, the organization seeks to produce products more efficiently than competitors, thereby offering lower prices or increasing profits.
* **Focus**. When using a focus strategy, companies concentrate on a specific regional market or consumer group, for example, northeast part of China or economy car drivers. This type of strategy enables organizations to develop a better understanding of their customers and to tailor their products specifically to customer needs.

Setting appropriate goals increases employee motivation, establishes standards for measuring individual and group performance, guides employee activity, and clarifies management's expectations.

Managerial Structure

In order to distinguish among the various types of goals that managers set, you must first understand how management is structured. In all but the smallest organizations, more than one manager is necessary to guide the organization's activities. That's why most companies form a **management pyramid** with top, middle, and bottom management levels. More managers are at the bottom level than at the top. However, in many of today's leaner companies, fewer levels separate managers at the top and bottom. Computer Associates is a software company with over 10,000 employees and a reputation for being a tough competitor. The company has just four management layers between the lowest-level employees and the top brass. To put this into perspective, even the notoriously lean Toyota had seven layers of management until it recently reorganized.

Top managers are the upper-level managers who have the most power and who take overall responsibility for the organization. An example is the chief executive officer (CEO). Top managers set **strategic goals**, which focus on broad issues, apply to the company as a whole, and aim to enhance the company's performance. These goals encompass eight major areas of concern: market standing, innovation, human resources, financial resources, physical resources, productivity, social responsibility and financial performance. Top managers also make long-range plans, establish major policies, and represent the company to the outside world at official functions and fund-raisers.

Middle managers report to the top level managers. They develop plans for implementing the broad goals set by top managers, and they coordinate the work of **first-line managers**. To accomplish this, middle managers set **tactical objectives**, which focus on **departmental** issues and define the results necessary to achieve the organization's strategic goals. At the middle level are plant managers, division managers, branch managers, and other similar positions.

At the bottom of the management pyramid are **first-line managers** (or supervisory managers). These managers oversee the work of operating employees. And they put into action the plans developed at higher levels. First-line managers set operational objectives, which focus on short-term issues and define the results necessary to achieve both the tactic objectives and the strategic goals. Positions at this level include supervisor, department head, and office manager.

Managerial Roles

Managers perform a number of duties as they coordinate the organization's work. They also build a network of relationships with bosses, **peers**, and employees. These duties and relationships can be described as roles, or behavioral patterns, and they fall into three categories:

* ★ **Interpersonal roles**. Managers perform ceremonial obligations, provide leadership to employees, and act as liaison to groups and individuals both inside and outside the company (such as suppliers, competitors, government agencies, consumers, special-interest groups, and interrelated work groups).
* ★ **Informational roles**. Managers spend a fair amount of time gathering information by questioning people both inside and outside the organization. They also distribute information to employees, other managers and outsiders.
* ★ **Decisional roles**. Managers use the information they gather to encourage innovation, to solve unexpected problems that threaten organizational goals (such as reacting to an economic crisis), and to decide how organizational resources will be used to meet planned objectives. They also negotiate with many individuals and groups, including suppliers, employees, and unions.

Certain managerial roles may be emphasized more than others, depending on a manager's organizational level. However, being able to move easily between these roles is a skill that serves managers well throughout their career.

Managerial Skills

In addition to setting goals and assuming various roles, managers also employ skills that fall into three basic categories: **interpersonal**, technical, and conceptual skills. As managers rise through the hierarchy, they may need to strengthen their abilities in one or more of these skills; fortunately, managerial skills can usually be learned.

Interpersonal Skills

All the skills required to communicate with other people, work effectively with them, motivate them, and lead them are interpersonal skills. Because they mainly get things done through people, managers at all levels of the organization use interpersonal skills in countless situations. Encouraging employees to work together toward common goals, interacting with employees and other managers, negotiating with partners and suppliers, developing employee trust and loyalty, and **fostering** innovation—all these activities require interpersonal skills.

Communication, or exchanging information, is the most important and **pervasive** interpersonal skill that managers use. Your ability to communicate increases your own productivity as well as the organization's. It shapes the impressions you make on your colleagues, employees, supervisors, investors, and customers. Communication allows you to perceive the needs of these **stakeholders** (your first step toward satisfying them), and it helps you respond to those needs. All businesses are built on relationships, as Microsoft's early alliance with IBM illustrates, and all relationships **flourish** with good communication.

Technical Skills

A person who knows how to operate a machine, prepare a financial statement, program a computer, or pass a football has technical skills; that is, he or she has the knowledge and ability to perform the mechanics of a particular job. Technical skills are more important at lower organization levels. First-line managers need particularly strong technical skills because they work directly with the tools and techniques of a particular specialty, such as **automotive** assembly or computer programming, and because they manage other technical employees. However, managers at all levels use administrative skills, which are the technical skills necessary to manage an organization. Administrative skills include the ability to make schedules, gather information, analyze data, plan, and organize. Managers often develop such skills through education and then improve them by working in one or more functional areas of an organization, such as accounting or marketing.

Conceptual Skills

Managers need conceptual skills to see the organization as a whole, in the context of its environment, and to understand how the various parts interrelate. Conceptual skills are especially important to top managers. These managers are the strategists who develop the plans that guide the organization toward its goals. Managers like Microsoft's Bill Gates use their conceptual skills to acquire and analyze information, identify both problems and opportunities, understand the competitive environment in which their companies operate, develop strategies, and make decisions.

A key managerial activity requiring conceptual skills is decision making, which has five distinct steps: recognizing the need for a decision, analyzing and defining the problem or opportunity, developing alternatives, selecting and implementing the chosen alternative, and evaluating the results. Managers monitor the results of decisions overtime and to see whether the chosen alternative works, whether any new problem or opportunity arises because of the decision, and whether a new decision must be made.

There are two types of management decisions. *Programmed decisions* are routine, recurring decisions made according to a predetermined system of decision rules. In contrast, *nonprogrammed decisions* are unique and **nonroutine**. As a result, they generally cannot be made according to any set procedures or rules, although **analogues**, similar past experiences, or common sense may offer some guidance. Managers make both types of decisions based on varying amounts of information, which means their decisions have varying degrees of possible success or failure. Generally speaking, nonprogrammed decisions are riskier than programmed decisions because they carry a stronger element of the unknown. The less information a manager has, the larger the risk. However, great organizations like Microsoft are built by managers who aren't afraid to take calculated risks. After all, between the current situation and a vision of the future are a lot of unknown factors.

Glossary

entail   *v.*   to have, impose, or require as a necessary accompaniment or consequence 伴随

conform   *v.*   to act or be in accord or agreement; comply 使和谐一致

envision   *v.*   to picture in the mind; imagine 想象

affordable   *a.*   that can be afforded 买得起的

strive   *v.*   to exert much effort or energy; to endeavor 努力

mission   *n.*   a special assignment given to a person or group 任务

informercial   *n.*   a commercial television program or relatively long commercial segment offering consumer information, such as educational or instructional material, related to the sponsor's product or service 商业信息片

franchise   *n.*   authorization granted to someone to sell or distribute a company's goods or services in a certain area 特许经营权

tactical   *a.*   of, relating to, or using tactics 战术的

departmental   *a.*   relating to a department 部门的

peer   *n.*   a person who has equal standing with another or others, as in rank, class, or age 同等的人, 与他人在如爵位、阶级或年龄上相当的人

interpersonal   *a.*   relating to, occurring among, or involving several people 人与人之间的

foster   *v.*   to promote the growth and development of; cultivate 促进

pervasive   *a.*   having the quality or tendency to pervade or permeate 渗透性的

stakeholder   *n.*   one who has a share or an interest, as in an enterprise 股东

flourish   *v.*   to be in a period of highest productivity, excellence, or influence 活跃

automotive   *a.*   moving by itself; self-propelling or self-propelled 自动的

nonroutine   *a.*   special or unusual, rather than part of what usually happens 非常规程序的

analogue   *n.*   something that bears an analogy to something else 类似情况

Key Terms and Concepts

Goal：A broad long-range target or aim.（长期）目标
Vision：A viable view of the future that is rooted in but improves on the present. 愿景，洞察力，远见
Objective：A specific，short-range target or aim.（短期）目标
Mission statement：A statement of the organization's purpose. 任务表述，使命表述
Management pyramid：Organizational structure comprising top，middle，and lower management. 管理结构，科层式组织结构
Top managers：Those at the highest level of the organization's management hierarchy；they are responsible for setting strategic goals，and they have the most power and responsibility in the organization. 高层管理者
Strategic goals：Goals that focus on broad organizational issues and aim to improve performance. 战略目标
Middle managers：Those in the middle of the management hierarchy；they develop plans to implement the goals of top managers and coordinate the work of first-line managers. 中层管理者
First-line managers：Those at the lowest management hierarchy，who supervise the operating employees and implement the plans set at the higher management levels；also called supervisory managers. 一线管理者
Tactical objectives：Objectives that focus on departmental issues and describe the results necessary to achieve organization's strategic goals. 战术目标

Exercises

I. Discussion and Review Questions.

1. What is a mission statement of a business firm? Please give an example.
2. How do you define the strategic goals and tactic objectives of a firm according to the text?
3. What are the three levels of management?
4. What are the three basic categories of managerial skills that are needed in managing an enterprise? And can these managerial skills be learned?
5. What kinds of managerial roles are mentioned in the text?
6. Why are interpersonal skills important to managers at all levels?
7. What are the two categories of managerial decisions and how do they differ?
8. Is it true to say that top managers communicate often with their employees?

II. *Vocabulary Review: Without referring to the text, fill in the blanks in the following sentences with the correct words from this list. You may change the tense, number, or form of the words to fit the context. Use each word only once; not all of the words on the list will be used.*

entail	foster	automotive	pervasive	peer
strive	tactical	analogue	affordable	nonroutine
differentiation	stakeholder	edge	conform	

1. In today's innovative and competitive business environment, companies that _____ to envision and define the future often have an advantage over those that simply react to the present.

2. Communication, or exchanging information, is the most important and _____ interpersonal skill that managers use.

3. Management _____ planning, organizing, coordinating, leading, and controlling resources (land, labor, capital and information) to efficiently reach these goals.

4. First-line managers need particularly strong technical skills because they work directly with the tools and techniques of a particular specialty, such as _____ assembly or computer programming, and because they manage other technical employees.

5. To accomplish this, middle managers set _____ objectives, which focus on departmental issues and define the results necessary to achieve the organization's strategic goals.

6. Henry Ford envisioned making _____ transportation available to every person.

7. Encouraging employees to work together toward common goals, interacting with employees and other managers, negotiating with partners and suppliers, developing employee trust and loyalty, and _____ innovation—all these activities require interpersonal skills.

8. They also build a network of relationships with bosses, _____, and employees.

9. The challenges of management include maintaining an organizational structure, developing both long- and short-term plans, motivating employees, and maintaining quality—a measure of how closely goods and services _____ to predetermined standards and customer expectations.

10. As a result, they generally can not be made according to any set procedures or rules, although _____, similar past experiences, or common sense may offer some guidance.

1. tactical	a. a margin of superiority; an advantage
2. franchise	b. moving by itself; self-propelling or self-propelled
3. peer	c. a special assignment given to a person or group; an agent on a secret mission
4. flourish	d. to promote the growth and development of; cultivate
5. mission	e. a person who has equal standing with another or others, as in rank, class, or age
6. automotive	f. authorization granted to someone to sell or distribute a company's goods or services in a certain area
7. edge	g. of, relating to, or using tactics
8. foster	h. to be in a period of highest productivity, excellence, or influence

1. Management is needed in every type of organization. (   )

2. To meet challenges of management, managers don't need to possess any specific skills that enable them to fulfill specific roles. (   )

3. In order to transform vision to reality, managers must define specific goals and objectives. (   )

4. As the company grows, management can refer to the mission statement as a means of evaluating whether proposed actions are in line with the company's stated purpose and values. (   )

5. To define goals and objectives of an organization, a starting point is to write a mission statement that defines how the organization exists and what it seeks to accomplish. (   )

6. Technical skills are more important at higher organization levels. (   )

Management Functions and Process

In the early part of the twentieth century, a French industrialist by the name of Henri Fayol proposed that all managers perform five management functions: planning, organizing, commanding, coordinating, and controlling. In the mid-1950s, a management textbook first used the functions of planning, organizing, staffing, directing, and controlling as a framework. Most management text books (and this one is no exception) still continue to be organized around the management functions, although they have been condensed down to four basic and very important functions: planning, organizing, leading, and controlling. Let's briefly define what each of these management functions encompasses.

If you have no particular destination in mind, then you can take any road. However, if you have some place in particular you want to go, then you've got to plan the best way to get there. Because organizations exist to achieve some particular purpose, someone must clearly define that purpose and the means for its achievement. Management is that someone. The **planning** function involves the process of defining goals, establishing strategies for achieving those goals, and developing plans to integrate and coordinate activities.

Managers are also responsible for arranging work to accomplish the organization's goals. We call this function **organizing**. It involves the process of determining what tasks are to be done, who is to do them, how the tasks are to be grouped, who reports to whom, and where decisions are to be made.

Every organization includes people, and management's job is to work with and through people to accomplish organizational goals. This is the **leading** function. When managers motivate subordinates, influence individuals or teams as they work, select the most effective communication channel, or deal in any way with employee behavior issues, they are leading.

The final management function managers perform is **controlling**. After the goals are set and the plans are formulated (planning), the structural arrangements determined (organizing), and the people hired, trained, and motivated (leading), there has to be some evaluation of whether things are going as planned. To ensure that work is going as it should, managers must monitor and evaluate performance. Actual performance must be compared with the previously set goals. If there are any significant deviations, it's management's job to get work performance back on track. This process of monitoring, comparing, and correcting is what we mean by the controlling function.

The reality of managing isn't quite as simplistic as these descriptions of the management functions might lead you to believe. There are no simple, cut-and-dried beginning or ending points as managers plan, organize, lead, and control. As managers do their jobs, they often find themselves doing some planning, some organizing, some leading, and some controlling, and maybe not even in that sequential order. It's probably more realistic to describe the functions managers perform from the perspective of a process. The **management process** is the set of ongoing decisions and work activities in which managers engage as they plan, organize, lead, and control. What this means is that as managers manage, their work activities are usually done in a continuous manner—that is, in a process. The continued popularity of the functional and process approaches to describe what managers do is a tribute to their clarity and simplicity—managers plan, organize, lead, and control.

VI. Translate the following into English.

1. 当然，拥有愿景并不是成功的保证。

2. 通常，一份任务报告书的目标总是聚焦于该企业所服务的市场和顾客群。

3. 这些管理人员都是能制定计划并引导企业朝目标前进的战略家。

4. 与其他人沟通、和他们一起高效率地工作、激励他们、领导他们，所有这些活动所需的能力，都是人际交往能力。

5. 为了把愿景变为现实,管理人员必须制定出明确的目的和目标。

6. 最好的企业目标应是明确的、可测量的、有关联性的、有挑战性的、可以实现的以及有时间限制的。

Supplemental Reading Material

The Process of Management

A managerial structure, specific goals and skilled managers are key ingredients in any successful organization. However, these factors are not all that is required. Achieving a vision also depends on policies and processes that allow managers to make the most of both their talents and resources available to them within the organization. In this way, they can perform the four basic functions necessary for the organizations success: (1) planning, (2) organizing, (3) leading, and (4) controlling. One way that managers are able to perform these four functions efficiently is through total quality management (TQM). Let us first take a close look at some of the fundamentals of TQM, and then discuss each of the management functions in detail and examine how TQM influences the managers performing each function.

Total Quality Management (TQM) is both a management philosophy and a strategic management process that focuses on delivering the optimal level of quality to customers by building quality into every organizational activities. Although it has only recently been adopted by some of the companies even in the U.S., TQM has been popular in Japan since the 1950s, when Japanese businesses turned to the quality teachings of W. Edwards Deming and J. M. Juran to rebuild their industrial strength. TQM redirects management to focus on four key elements: employee involvement, customer focus, benchmarking, and continuous improvement.

Employee Involvement   TQM involves every employee in quality assurance. Workers are trained in quality methods, and they are empowered to stop a work process if they feel that products or services are not meeting quality standards. It also means that managers encourage employees to speak up when employees think of better ways of doing things. At Landis, a machine-tool manufacturer, every employee undergoes at least 25 hours of quality training. In addition, Landis management has changed its rigidly hierarchical management structure in order to empower employees. Landis general manager C. L. Hartle encourages employees to run their own departments, and he strives to give workers on the plant floor greater decision-making power. At the same time, Landis' managers share all of the information they can with all employees and supervisors. Landis' new approach to managing the company exemplifies a participative management style. This sharing of information at all levels of the organization is also known as *open-book management*.

Customer Focus   Focusing on the customer simply means finding out what customers really want and then providing with it. This requires casting aside assumptions about customers and relying instead on accurate research. At Honeywell, CEO Micheach Bonsignore looks to customers for input about how Honeywell can improve its products and services. Customer-feedback systems encourage an ongoing dialogue between the company and its customers. "Our customer-feedback mechanisms not only tell us whether they are satisfied but also why they are satisfied or dissatisfied and what we can do differently." Says Bonsignore. Customer feedback has even led to new products and processes at Ames Rubber Corporation. Vice president of sales and marketing Robert G. Dondero says that dialogue with customers "solved some key technology problems" and enables the company to reduce costs, cycle time (the steps required to complete a process), and scrap (waste).

Benchmarking　　Benchmarking is comparing your company's processes and products to the standards of the world's best companies and working to match or exceed those standards. This means rating the manufacturing process, product development, distribution and other key functions against those of acknowledged leaders; analyzing how these role models achieve their outstanding results; and then applying that knowledge to make quality improvements. Among the world-class organizations frequently cited as benchmarks for production are Toyota, IBM, and Hewlett-Packard; for distribution are L. L. Bean and FedEx; and for customer service are American Express and Nordstrom. Xerox is frequently cited for the benchmarking programs themselves.

Continuous Improvement　　Total quality management can work only when companies are committed to continuously improving their goods, services, and processes. This requires an ongoing effort to reduce defects, cut costs, slash production and delivery times, and offer customers innovative products. Improvements are often small, incremental changes that add up to greater competitiveness over the long run. Responsibility for such improvements often falls on employees, so management must provide incentives for them in order to make continuous improvement. Geon, a manufacturer of polyvinyl chloride (PVC) resins, motivates its employees through two programs. The first links employees' bonuses to improvements in productivity, quality, and manufacturing. In recent years, employees have received an average bonus of 11 percent of their annual salaries through the program. The second program is a success-sharing plan tied to sales gains and stock price. This plan pays out millions of dollars in stock each year. Both incentives have helped Geon produce 20 percent more PVC resin with 25 percent less manufacturing capacity, putting the company in a much better financial position.

Discussion and Review Questions:
1. What is Total Quality Management? How do you understand Total Quality Management?
2. What are the four elements of Total Quality Management?
3. How does Total Quality Management achieve organizational goals?
4. How do you understand benchmarking? Give a concrete example of this approach in reality.
5. What is the relationship between TQM and the management function?

The Increasing Importance of Strategic Management

Text

Changes in the global and domestic business environments during the twentieth century gave rise to the need for new management techniques. The dual tasks of efficiently running a large, often multinational firm and guiding its course became too difficult for any one leader to handle alone. New organizational forms emerged, with new divisions of managerial labor and new managerial techniques. Also, while the large organizations that formed during the early part of the century were internally focused on efficiency (a management science approach combined with basic financial planning), they soon learned that effective management in a rapidly changing business environment required more of an outward orientation.

Business schools responded to changing top management needs by offering a course on business policy. The business policy course applied general administrative principles to a variety of business situations through cases, which described real-world businesses and the challenges they faced.

The process influencing the environment to make it less hostile and more **conducive** to organizational success is called **enactment.** Organizations that have reached phase 4 in their planning efforts engage in significant amounts of both adaptation and enactment, as opposed to organizations in earlier phases that focus primarily on adaptation.

The strategic management process begins with (1) analysis of the broad and **operating environments** of the organization and (2) the organization itself, followed by the (3) establishment of strategic direction, reflected in missions, visions, and/or long-term goals, (4) formulation of specific strategies, (5) implementation of those strategies, and (6) development of control systems to ensure that they are both successfully carried out and still appropriate for the firm in its current environment. Finally, strategic **restructuring** may occur as a firm makes major changes to its strategic direction, strategies, and/or the way those strategies are implemented, usually in response to inconsistencies between expected and actual performance.

Start-up firms seldom exhibit the **sophisticated** planning processes associated with phase 4 planning. Start-ups often begin with an entrepreneur who has an idea for a product or service that he or she believes will lead to market success. Venture capital is raised through a variety of public or private sources and a new business is born. The entrepreneur may establish an informal sense of direction and a few goals, but the rest of the formal strategy process may be overlooked. If the organization is successful, it will typically expand in both sales and personnel until it reaches a critical point at which the original **entrepreneur** feels a loss of control. At this point the entrepreneur may attempt to formalize various aspects of strategic planning, either by hiring outside consultants, by creating planning positions within the firm, or by involving other managers in planning activities. This same process is typical of nonprofit start-ups as well, except that the nature of the cause (i. e., **humanitarian**, educational) may place tighter constraints on the way the firm is financed and organized.

Nevertheless, the progression of activities—from analysis to plan to action control—provides a logical way to study strategic management. Furthermore, the activities relate equally well to for-profit, nonprofit, manufacturing, and service organizations, although some of the differences in the way these organizations approaching strategic management are described throughout the text.

Environmental and Organizational Analysis

This book utilizes a stakeholder approach to strategic management. Just as the chief aim of an organization is the satisfaction of its key stakeholders, these stakeholders form the basis for analysis of the environment and the organization. For the purposes of this book, an organization's environment includes groups, individuals, and forces outside of the traditional boundaries of the organization that are significantly influenced by or have a major impact on the organization. The **organization** includes all of the stakeholders, resources, and processes that exist within the boundaries of the firm.

Examples of key stakeholders within the organization are managers, employees, and owners. Organizational analysis also includes a broader evaluation of all of the organization's resources and capabilities. External stakeholders, which are a part of an organization's **operating environment**, include competitors, customers, suppliers, financial intermediaries, local communities, unions, activist groups, and government agencies and administrators. The **broad environment** forms the context in which the organization and its operating environment exist, and includes sociocultural forces, global economic forces, technological change, and global political and legal forces. One organization, acting independently, can have very little influence on the forces in the broad environment; however, the forces in this environment can have a tremendous impact on the organization.

All of the stakeholders inside and outside of the organization should be analyzed at both domestic and international levels. In all of the countries in which a company operates, managers must interact with government agencies, employees, competitors, and activist groups. In addition, the global perspective certainly applies to sociocultural, political, economic, and technological forces.

Analyzing the environment and the organization assists the organization in all of the other tasks of strategic management. For example, an organization's managers should formulate strategies based on organizational strengths and weaknesses and in the context of the opportunities and threats found in its environment. In addition, strategic direction is an outcome of melding the desires of key organizational stakeholders with environmental realities.

Strategic Direction

Strategic direction pertains to the longer term goals and objectives of the organization. At a more fundamental level, strategic direction defines the purposes for which an organization exists and operates. This direction is often contained in **mission and vision statements**. Unlike shorter term goals and strategies, a mission is an enduring part of planning processes within the organization. Often missions also describe the areas or industries in which an organization operates.

A vision statement expresses what the organization wants to be in the future, which may involve a fundamental change in its business. For example, a start-up firm may have a mission to provide software design and support for its clients, but its long-range vision may be to become a fully integrated Internet provider. Although the mission directs the business for now, the mission will gradually change as the organization moves over time toward fulfillment of its vision. A well-established strategic direction provides guidance to the stakeholders inside the organization who are largely responsible for carrying it out. A well-defined direction also provides external stakeholders with a greater understanding of the organization and its activities. The next logical step in the strategic management process is strategy formulation.

Strategy Formulation

A strategy can be thought of in two ways: (1) as a pattern that emerges in a sequence of decisions over time and (2) as an organizational plan of action that is intended to move an organization toward the achievement of its fundamental purposes. In some organizations, particularly small businesses and those experiencing rapid environmental changes, strategies are not "planned" in the formal sense of the word. Instead, managers seize opportunities as they come up, but within guidelines or boundaries defined by the firm's strategic direction or mission. In those cases, the strategy reflects the insight and intuition of the strategist or business owner and becomes clear over time as a pattern in a stream of decisions.

Strategies as "plans" are common in most organizations, however. Strategy formulation—the process of planning strategies—is often divided into three levels: corporate, business, and functional.

Corporate-level strategy formulation refers primarily to domain definition, or the selection of business areas in which the organization will compete. Although some firms, such as McDonald's, are involved in one basic business, diversified organizations are involved in several different businesses and serve a variety of customer groups. **Business-level strategy formulation**, on the other hand, pertains to domain direction and navigation, or how businesses compete in the areas they have selected. **Functional-level strategy formulation** contains the details of how the functional areas such as marketing, operations, finance, and research should work together to achieve the business-level strategy. Thus, functional-level strategy is most closely associated with strategy implementation.

Another way to distinguish among the three levels is to determine the level at which decisions are made. Corporate-level decisions are typically made at the highest levels of the organization by the chief executive officer (CEO) and/or board of directors, although these individuals may receive input from managers at other levels. If an organization is only involved in one area of business, then business-level decisions tend to be made by the same people. However, in organizations that have diversified into many areas, which are represented by different operating divisions or lines of business, business-level decisions are made by functional managers, who represent organizational areas such as operations, finance, personnel, accounting, research and development, or information systems.

Strategy Implementation and Control

Strategy formulation, as described in the last section, results in a plan of action for the organization and its various levels. **Strategy implementation**, on the other hand, represents a pattern of decisions and the actions needed to carry out the plan. Strategy implementation involves creating the functional strategies, systems, structures, and processes needed by the organization to achieve strategic ends. Functional strategies outline the specific actions that each function must undertake to convert business- and corporate-level strategies into actions. Organizational systems are developed to gather, analyze, and convey information. Structures reflect the way people and work are organized, which includes reporting relationships and formation into work groups, teams, and departments. Processes, such as standard operating procedures, are developed to create uniformity across the organization and promote efficiency.

Good control is also critical to organizational success. **Strategic control** refers to the processes that lead to adjustments in strategic direction, strategies, or the implementation plan, when necessary. Thus, managers may collect information that leads them to believe that the organizational mission is no longer appropriate or that its strategies are not leading to the desired outcomes. On the other hand, the strategic control system may tell managers that the mission and strategies are appropriate, but they have not been well executed. In such cases, adjustments should be made to the implementation process.

Strategic Restructuring

At some point in the life of almost every organization, growth will slow and some stakeholders will begin to feel dissatisfied. Wal-Mart is an excellent example of this phenomenon. After two decades of incredible growth in sales, earnings, and stock value, Wal-Mart has begun to level-off. In fact, Wal-Mart stock recently has been listed as a poor investment by some major financial advisors. Some assert that Sam Walton's death **triggered** the decline. Others argue that Wal-Mart is suffering from market saturation.

Regardless of the reasons, many organizations eventually feel the need to reevaluate, in a major way, their strategies and how they are executing them.

Restructuring typically involves a renewed emphasis on the things an organization does well, combined with a variety of tactics to **revitalize** the organization and strengthen its competitive position. Current popular restructuring tactics include refocusing on a more limited set of activities by divesting parts of the business retrenchment (scaling back of growth efforts), reorganization, leveraged buyouts, and changes to the organizational structure.

Now that the strategic management process has been described and the outline of the book presented, we will establish a foundation on which the rest of the book will rest. We first describe the various theoretical perspectives that underlie the field of strategic management. Then we briefly outline stakeholder analysis and the ethics associated with working with stakeholders. Finally, we turn out attention to the trends that are accelerating organizational movement toward a global playing field.

Alternative Perspectives on Strategy Development

The traditional process for developing strategy consists of analyzing the internal and external environments of the organization to arrive at organizational strengths, weaknesses, opportunities, and threats (SWOT). The results from this **situation analysis**, as this process is sometimes called, are the basis for developing missions, goals, and strategies. In general, an organization should select strategies that (1) take advantage of organizational strengths and environmental opportunities or (2) neutralize or overcome organizational weaknesses and environmental threats.

The traditional approach to strategy development is conceptually related to **environmental determinism**. According to this view, good management is associated with determining which strategy will best fit environmental, technical, and human forces at a particular point in time, then working to accomplish that strategy. From this perspective, the most successful organization will be the one that best adapts to existing forces. In other words, the environment is the primary determinant of strategy.

The principle of enactment, which we discussed earlier, assumes that organizations do not have to submit to existing forces in the environment—they can, in part, create their environments through strategic alliances with stakeholders, investments in leading technologies, advertising, political lobbying, and a variety of other abilities. Of course, smaller, independent organizations are somewhat limited in their ability to influence some components of their environments, such as national government agencies and administrators; however, they typically have more influence on forces in their local operating environments.

Glossary

conducive *a.*   tending to bring about; being partly responsible for 有助于……的

enactment *n.*   the passing of a law by a legislative body (法律的)制定,颁布;法律,法规;扮演

sophisticated *a.*   having or appealing to those having worldly knowledge and refinement and savior-faire 老练的,精密的

entrepreneur *n.*   someone who organizes a business venture and assumes the risk for it 企业家;承包人

humanitarian *a.*   marked by humanistic values and devotion to human welfare 人道主义的

              n.   someone devoted to the promotion of human welfare and to social reforms 人道主义者

trigger *v.*   to cause something to start 触发

revitalize *v.*   to restore strength; to give new life or vigor to 使恢复元气

Key Terms and Concepts

Operating environment: An organization's external stakeholders: competitors, customers, suppliers, financial intermediaries, local communities, unions, activist groups, and government agencies and administrators. 运营环境

Restructuring: Streamlining and reorienting an organization's current format of operations to place it in a position in which it is better able to compete; often involves reducing the scope of the business at the corporate level combined with refocusing efforts on the things the organization does well. 流程再造

Broad environment: Sociocultural forces, global economic forces, technological change, and global political legal forces. 宏观环境,外部环境

Mission statement: Statement expressing the organization's overall purpose, broad goals, and the scope of its operations. 使命

Vision statement: Statement expressing management's view of what the organization can or should become in the future. 愿景

Corporate-level strategy formulation: Selection of business areas in which the organization will compete. 公司层面战略制定

Business-level strategy formulation: How organizations will compete in the areas they have selected. 业务层面战略制定

Functional-level strategy formulation: How an organization's functional areas should work together to achieve the business-level strategy. 职能层面战略制定

Strategy implementation: Creating the functional strategies, systems, structures, and processes needed by the organization to achieve strategic goals. 战略执行

Strategic control: Ongoing evaluation and appropriate adjustments of the mission, goals, strategies, or implementation plan. 战略控制

Situation analysis: Analyzing the internal and external environments of the organization to arrive at organizational strengths, weaknesses, opportunities, and threats (SWOT). 环境分析

Environmental determinism: The view that good management is associated with determining which strategy will best fit environmental, technical, and human forces at a particular point in time and then working to carry it out. 环境决定论

Exercises

I. Discussion and Review Questions.

1. Discuss the strategic management process.
2. What does organization's environment include?

3. What do mission and vision statements mean?
4. What are the three levels of strategy formulation?
5. Discuss the process of strategic control.
6. What do you do when you want to restructure?

II. Vocabulary Review: Without referring to the text, fill in the the following sentences with the correct words from the may change the tense, number, or form of the words to context. Use each word only once.

business-level strategy formulation	operating environment
strategy implementation	environmental determinism
corporate-level strategy formulation	functional-level strategy formulation
situation analysis	

1. External stakeholders, which are a part of an organization's _____ _____, include competitors, customers, suppliers, financial intermediaries, local communities, unions, activist groups, and government agencies and administrators.

2. _____ refers primarily to domain definition, or the selection of business areas in which the organization will compete.

3. _____, on the other hand, pertains to domain direction and navigation, or how businesses compete in the areas they have selected.

4. _____ contains the details of how the functional areas such as marketing, operations, finance, and research should work together to achieve the business-level strategy.

5. _____, on the other hand, represents a pattern of decisions and the actions needed to carry out the plan.

6. The results from this _____, as this process is sometimes called, are the basis for developing missions, goals, and strategies.

7. The traditional approach to strategy development is conceptually related to _____.

III. Match the terms and expressions on the left with the explanations on the right.

1. broad environment   a. an organization's external stakeholders: competitors, customers, suppliers, financial intermediaries, local communities, unions, activist groups, and government agencies and administrators

2. mission statement   b. statement expressing the organization's overall purpose, broad goals, and the scope of its operations

3. vision statement   c. how organizations will compete in the areas they have selected

4. corporate-level strategy formulation
d. sociocultural forces, global economic forces, technological change, and global political legal forces

5. business-level strategy formulation
e. selection of business areas in which the organization will compete

6. functional-level strategy formulation
f. how an organization's functional areas should work together to achieve the business-level strategy

7. enactment
g. statement expressing management's view of what the organization can or should become in the future

8. operating environment
h. the passing of a law by a legislative body

IV. True and False statements.

1. The organization includes all of the stakeholders, resources, and processes that exist within the boundaries of the firm. (   )

2. External stakeholders, which are not a part of an organization's operating environment, include competitors, customers, suppliers, financial intermediaries, local communities, unions, activist groups, and government agencies and administrators. (   )

3. One organization, acting independently, can have much influence on the forces in the broad environment; however, the forces in this environment can have a tremendous impact on the organization. (   )

4. A vision statement expresses what the organization wants to be right now, which may involve a fundamental change in its business. (   )

5. A strategy can be thought of in two ways: (1) as a pattern that emerges in a sequence of decisions over time and (2) as an organizational plan of action that is intended to move an organization toward the achievement of its fundamental purposes. (   )

6. Strategies as "plans" are common in most organizations, however. Strategy formulation—the process of planning strategies—is often divided into three levels: corporate, business, and functional. (   )

V. Translate the following into Chinese.

Strategy formulation, as described in the last section, results in a plan of action for the organization and its various levels. Strategy implementation, on the other hand, represents a pattern of decisions and the actions needed to carry out the plan. Strategy implementation involves creating the functional strategies, systems, structures, and processes needed by the organization to achieve strategic ends. Functional strategies outline the specific actions that each function must undertake to convert business- and corporate-level strategies into actions. Organizational systems are developed to gather, analyze, and convey information. Structures reflect the way people and work are organized, which includes reporting relationships and formation into work groups, teams, and departments. Processes, such as standard operating procedures, are developed to create uniformity across the organization and promote efficiency. Strategy implementation may require changes to any of these factors as the organization pursues new strategies over time.

1. 二战以后，由于技术优势，以及其他国家的基础设施在战争中遭受严重破坏，美国的企业主导了全球的经济。

2. 外部环境构成了组织及其运营环境存在的大背景，包括社会文化环境、全球经济环境、技术变革和全球政治法律环境。

3. 一个战略可以从两个方面理解：一是作为一种模式，随着时间推移，体现在一系列的决策中；二是作为组织行动的计划，使组织在其重要目标的方向上更进一步。

4. 战略控制是指在必要的时候调整战略方向、战略或实施计划的过程。

5. 流程再造通常指重新强调组织擅长之事，加上各种策略，重振组织并强化组织的竞争力。

Supplemental Reading Material

The Evaluation of Employee on Enterprise Restructuring

1. Introduction

The reform and restructuring of the state-owned or collective enterprises in the 1990s is the most important economic phenomenon in China in the past two decades. At present, the restructuring for the local small and medium-sized state-owned enterprises (SOEs) has been completed. Basically this has happened under the guidance of large enterprises who have adopted more flexible polices towards small companies during privatization. However, the restructuring of the large and medium-sized state enterprises is still at a crucial stage. Recently, the report "China 2030: Building a Modern, Harmonious, and Creative High Income Society" has been published by the World Bank and China State Council Development Research Center.

The recommendation about enhancing the reform for state enterprises in this book has attracted a great deal of controversy. With the reform of state enterprises, some group conflicts have attracted public concern. Hence the conflicts arising during the reform for state-owned enterprises have been listed as the key issues closely related to people's livelihood and social construction in China national "12th Five-Year Plan".

Enterprise restructuring brings great changes in the structures and organizational forms. Whether the employee is involved in the whole process and is respected as the stakeholder, whether their active participation has some significant impact on enterprise performance and whether the changes of work and benefits for the employee affect the employees' evaluation for the restructuring are the focus of this paper. These questions will be answered in this article to provide a useful reference for the enterprise reform. The paper is based on the relevant literature review. It takes the employee's perspective and other relevant factors into consideration, measuring their evaluation of the reform performance and recognition. Data from the micro survey on the reform of state-owned or collective enterprises were used.

2. Literature Review

Organization theory treats the organization as a whole unit and focuses on its constituent department and members (mainly the middle and senior management group), as well as the differences among the structures and actions. The complexity theory which brings a new perspective to study the organization (especially the business organization) puts the organization in an open, dynamic complex system, focusing on the interaction, adaption and co-evolution between organizations as well as on the organization and environment.

The organization (especially a large one) should regard the process as a complex adaptive system. The speed with which the organization adapts to the environment is mostly dependent on the internal communication. So for the organization to reform or redesign, it must consider not only the structure, but also the social, cultural, technical, political, economic and other relevant conditions. The New Institutionalism argues that the organizational structure can be determined by institutional environment to some extent.

The interaction between enterprise and environment is reflected not only on the factors such as technology and raw material, but also on the concept of corporate culture, symbol and belief. Therefore, the cognition on legitimacy from the organization member plays a key role. For the organization, whether it is to establish the self-leadership team or the organic management process and system, or the participatory culture, the efforts of sharing rights through the whole organization have been widely attempted during the process. Empowerment, i.e. to access the employee to rights, freedom and information, so as to make decisions and have full participation, is not only an indispensable strategic measure to improve the products and services, but also the imitation of the others. Meanwhile, it's the basis to build a learning organization with outstanding performance ability, making the enterprises maintain sustainable competitive advantages. The reform and restructuring of SOEs in China serves as a typical experience for organizational change. According to the new organization theory, the restructuring and reconstruction of the enterprises should adapt to the environmental changes as well as make wise use of the working environment, and pay enough attention to the employee's participation and assessment, in order to improve the reform performance. Many scholars study the restructuring performance of the reform of state-owned and collective enterprises from the macro and micro economic perspectives.

Lu and Liu employ micro data to analyze the relationship between the reform mode and the firm performance. The finding shows that privatized firms have higher efficiency than those of public firms. Different types of privatization and their resulting ownership structures are important determining factors in the firms' performance. Specifically, the equity structure of operators holding majority of stocks is the most efficient, while equal division among the insider workers is the least. Liu and Li conducted a survey on the impacts of reform on enterprise performance in China on the basis of the 451 sample firms in competitive industries, the result of which indicates that the state ownership has significant negative impacts on enterprise performance while the non-state ownership has the significant positive relations on performance, and the private ownership plays most significant roles of promoting enterprise performance. The research completed by Song and Yao proves that restructuring has a significantly positive impact on corporate profit but it has a weak or non-significant impact on unit cost and labor productivity. Jefferson and Su find that the conversion of SOEs to shareholding enterprises contributes to overall increases in both current productivity and innovative effort. Bai et al. combine the economic benefit of the firm with its social effect, and it is found that the ownership reform improves firm performance mainly through reducing managerial expenses, and that the social costs of ownership reform are limited compared to international experiences. Liu studies the business performance of state-holding listed companies after the ownership reform, and the research shows that in addition to profitability, all performance indicators improve significantly when the stockholdings are purchased by the internal manager (including the staff). On the other hand, when the stock-holdings are purchased by private enterprises, most of the performance indicators improve significantly—this improvement is partly due to the transformation of main businesses and downsizing. Deng et al. argue how different reorganization modes affect controlling share-holder's embezzlement of listed company's funds after their post-IPO. The result reveals that, compared to those restructured companies, controlling shareholder group of incomplete reorganization has higher tendency to have embezzlement problem, resulting in significantly worse performance. Yang et al. employ the data from nationwide collective enterprises to analyze the impact of the government control on the enterprise performance, employee welfare and tax. It is confirmed that the government control within the collective enterprises can reduce the production cost while bringing higher management and financial costs. It is also proved that through re-structuring and withdrawing the government control from the enterprise, the performance of the companies would be improved significantly.

Researches on the restructuring of state-owned enterprises conducted by the scholars mainly focus on the influence of the reform on enterprise performance and ignore the employees' situation. Although some studies involve the selection of restructuring mode and the impact of reform on the labor market, factors such as the environment as well as the employee participation are ignored. Therefore, this article employs the theory of new organization to study the enterprise restructuring from the perspective of employees.

Discussion and Review Questions:

1. How to define the organization complexity theory? Give a concrete example of this theory in reality.

2. What factors must be considered if an organization is to be reformed or redesigned?

3. What does the complexity theory focus on?

4. What influence(s) the interaction between enterprise and environment?

5. What determine(s) the organizational structure according to the new institutionalism?

Unit 4

What Is Organizational Behavior?

Text

Course work in human behavior and people skills received minimal attention relative to the technical aspects of management. Over the past decade, however, business faculty have come to realize the importance that an understanding of human behavior plays in determining a manager's effectiveness, and required courses on people skills have been widely added to the **curriculum**.

We have come to understand that **technical skills** are necessary, but insufficient, for succeeding in management. Today, in increasingly competitive and demanding workplace, managers can't succeed on their technical skills alone. They also have to have good people skills. This book has been written to managers and potential managers to develop those people skills.

What Managers Do

Let's begin by briefly defining the terms manager and the place where managers work—the organization. Then let's find out: What do managers do?

Managers get things done through other people. They make decisions, allocate resources, and direct the activities of others to attain goals. Managers do their work in an **organization**. This is a consciously coordinated social unit, composed of two or more people, that functions on a relatively continuous basis to achieve a common goal or set of goals.

Management Functions

In the early part of the twentieth century, a French industrialist by the name of Henri Fayol wrote that all managers perform five management functions: They plan, organize, command, coordinate, and control. Today, we have condensed those down to four: planning, organizing, leading, and controlling.

The **planning** function encompasses defining an organization's goals, establishing an overall strategy for achieving those goals, and developing a comprehensive **hierarchy** of plans to integrate and coordinate activities.

Managers are also responsible for designing an organization's structure. We call this function **organizing**. It includes the determination of what tasks are to be done, who is to do them, how the tasks are to be grouped, who reports to whom, and where decisions are to be made.

Every organization contains people, and it is management's job to direct and coordinate those people. This is the **leading** function. When managers motivate employees, direct the activities of others, select the most effective communication channels, or resolve conflicts among members, they are engaging in leading.

The final function managers perform is **controlling**. To ensure that things are going as they should, management must monitor the organization's performance. Actual performance must be compared with the previously set goals. If there are any significant **deviations**, it's management's job to get the organization back on track. This monitoring, comparing, and potential correcting is what is meant by the controlling function.

Management Roles

In the late 1960s, a graduate student at MIT, Henry Mintzberg, undertook a careful study of five executives to determine what these managers did on their jobs. On the basis of his observations of these managers, Mintzberg concluded that managers perform 10 different, highly interrelated roles, or sets of behaviors attributable to their jobs. These 10 roles can be grouped as being primarily concerned with interpersonal relationships, the transfer of information, and decision making.

Interpersonal Roles

All managers are required to perform duties that are ceremonial and symbolic in nature. When the president of a college hands out diplomas at commencement or a factory supervisor gives a group of high school students a tour of the plant, he or she is acting in a *figurehead* role. All managers also have a *leadership* role. The third role within the grouping is the *liaison* role. Mintzberg described this activity as contacting others who provide the manager with information. These may be individuals or groups inside or outside the organization.

Information Roles

All managers, to some degree, collect information from organizations and institutions outside their own. Typically, they get information by reading magazines and talking with other people, to learn of changes in the public's tastes, what competitors may be planning, and the like. Mintzberg called this the *monitor* role. Managers also act as a **conduit** to transmit information to organizational members. This is the *disseminator* role. Managers additionally perform a *spokesperson* role when they represent the organization to outsiders.

Decisional Roles

Finally, Mintzberg identified four roles that revolve around the making of choices. In the *entrepreneur* role, managers initiate and oversee new projects that will improve their organization's performance. As *disturbance handlers*, managers take corrective action in response to unforeseen problems. As *resource allocators*, managers are responsible for allocating human, physical, and monetary resources. Last, managers perform a *negotiator* role, in which they discuss issues and bargain with other units to gain advantages for their own unit.

Management Skills

Still another way of considering what managers do is to look at the skills or competencies they need to successfully achieve their goals. Robert Katz has identified three essential management skills: technical, human, and conceptual.

Technical Skills

Technical skills encompass the ability to apply specialized knowledge or expertise. Through extensive formal education, they have learned the special knowledge and practices of their field. Of course, professionals don't have a monopoly on technical skills, and not all technical skills have to be learned in schools or formal training programs.

Human Skills

The ability to work with, understand, and motivate other people, both individually and in groups, describes **human skills**. Since managers get things done through other people, they must have good human skills to communicate, motivate, and delegate.

Conceptual Skills

Managers must have the mental ability to analyze and diagnose complex situations. These tasks require **conceptual skills**. Managers can be technically and interpersonally competent yet still fail because of an inability to rationally process and interpret information.

Effectives vs. Successful Managerial Activities

Fred Luthans and his associates looked at the issue of what managers do from a somewhat different perspective. They asked the question: Do managers who move up most quickly in an organization do the same emphasis as managers who do the best job?

Luthans and his associates studied more than 450 managers. What they found was that these managers all engaged in four managerial activities:

1. *Traditional management*. Decision making, planning, and controlling.
2. *Communication*. Exchanging routine information and processing paperwork.
3. *Human resource management*. Motivating, disciplining, managing conflict, staffing, and training.
4. *Networking*. Socializing, politicking, and interacting with outsiders.

A Review of the Manager's Job

One common **thread** runs through the functions, roles, skills, and activities approaches to management: Each recognizes the **paramount** importance of managing people. Regardless of whether it's called "the leading function", "interpersonal roles", "human skills", or "human resource management, communication, and networking activities", it's clear that managers need to develop their people skills if they're going to be effective and successful.

Enter Organizational Behavior

Organizational behavior (often abbreviated as OB) is a field of study that investigates the impact that individuals, groups, and structure have on behavior within organizations for the purpose of applying such knowledge toward improving an organization's effectiveness.

Political Science

Although frequently overlooked, the contributions of political scientists are significant to the understanding of behavior in organizations. **Political science** studies the behavior of individuals and groups within a political environment. Specific topics of concern here include structuring of conflict, allocation of power, and how people manipulate power for individual self-interest.

There Are Few Absolutes in OB

There are few, if any, simple and universal principles that explain organizational behavior. As one noted behavioral researcher **aptly** concluded, "God gave all the easy problems to the physicists". Human beings are complex. Because they are not alike, our ability to make simple, accurate, and sweeping generalizations is limited.

That doesn't mean, of course, that we can't offer reasonably accurate explanations of human behavior or make valid predictions. It does mean, however, that OB concepts must reflect situational, or **contingency**, conditions. We can say that x leads to y, but only under conditions specified in z (the **contingency variables**). The science of OB has developed by using general concepts and then altering their application to the particular situation.

Challenges and Opportunities for OB

Understanding organizational behavior has never been more important for managers. There are a lot of challenges and opportunities today for managers to use OB concepts. In this section, we review some of the more critical issues confronting managers for which OB offers solutions.

Responding to Globalization

Globalization affects a manager's people skills in at least two ways. First, if you're a manager, you're increasingly likely to find yourself in a foreign assignment. You may be transferred to your employer's operating division or subsidiary in another country. Once there, you'll have to manage a workforce that is likely to be very different in needs, aspirations, and attitudes from the ones you were used to back home. Second, even in your own country, you're going to find yourself working with bosses, peers, and other employees who were born and raised in different cultures. What motivates you may not motivate them. To work effectively with these people, you'll need to understand their culture, how it has shaped them, and how to adapt your management style to their differences.

Managing Workforce Diversity

Workforce diversity means that organizations are becoming more **heterogeneous** in terms of gender, race, and **ethnicity**. But the term encompasses anyone who varies from the so-called norm. In addition to the more obvious groups—women, African Americans, Hispanic Americans, Asian Americans—it also includes the physically disabled, gays and lesbians, and the elderly.

Workforce diversity has important implications for management practice. Managers will need to shift their philosophy from treating everyone alike to recognizing differences and responding to those differences in ways that will ensure employee retention and greater productivity while, at the same time, not discriminating.

Improving Quality and Productivity

More and more managers are confronting the challenges that improve quality and productivity. Toward the goal of improving quality and productivity, they are implementing programs such as total quality management and reengineering.

Total quality management (**TQM**) is also a philosophy of management that is driven by the constant attainment of customer satisfaction through the continuous improvement of all organizational processes. TQM has implications for OB because it requires employees to rethink what they do and become more involved in workplace decisions.

In times of rapid and dramatic change, it's sometimes necessary to approach improving quality and productivity from the perspective of "How would we do things around here if we were starting over from scratch?". That, in essence, is the approach of **reengineering**. It asks managers to reconsider how work would be done and their organization structured if they were starting over.

Empowering People

In many organizations, employees are now called associates. And there's a blurring between the roles of managers and workers. Decision making is being pushed down to the operating level, where workers are being given the freedom to make choices about schedules and procedures and to solve work-related problems. An increasing number of organizations are using self-managed teams, where workers operate largely without bosses.

What's going on is that managers are **empowering employees**. They are putting employees in charge of what they do. And in so doing, managers are having to learn how to give up control, and employees are having to learn how to take responsibility for their work and make appropriate decisions.

Coping with "Temporariness"

In the past, managing could be characterized by long periods of stability, interrupted occasionally by short periods of change. Managing today would be more accurately described as long periods of ongoing change, interrupted occasionally by short periods of stability! The world that most managers and employees face today is one of permanent temporariness.

Today's managers and employees must learn to cope with temporariness. They have to learn to live with flexibility, **spontaneity**, and unpredictability. The study of OB can provide important insights into helping them better understand a work world of continual change, how to overcome resistance to change, and how best to create an organizational culture that thrives on change.

Stimulating Innovation and Change

An organization's employees can be the **impetus** for innovation and change or they can be a major stumbling block. The challenge for managers is to stimulate employee creativity and tolerance for change. The field of OB provides a wealth of ideas and techniques to aid in realizing these goals.

Improving Ethical Behavior

In an organizational world characterized by cutbacks, expectations of increasing worker productivity, and tough competition in the marketplace, it's not altogether surprising that many employees, feel pressured to cut corners, break rules, and engage in other forms of questionable practices.

Members of organizations are increasingly finding themselves facing **ethical dilemmas**, situations in which they are required to define right and wrong conduct.

Glossary

curriculum   *n.*   an integrated course of academic studies 总课程

manager   *n.*   someone who controls resources and expenditures 管理者；监督者；支配者；经理

organization   *n.*   a group of people who work together 组织；机构；体制；团体

planning   *n.*   an act of formulating a program for a definite course of action 计划编制；规划；计划的实行部署；设计；策划

hierarchy   *n.*   a group of persons or things organized into ranks or grades with each level subordinate to the one above 层级；等级制度

organize   *v.*   to cause to be structured or ordered or operating according to some principle or idea 组织；安排；整理；使系统化

lead   *v.*   to guide or direct 领导；指挥

control   *v.*   to check, limit, or regulate 控制

deviation   *n.*   a variation that deviates from the standard or norm 偏差；误差；背离

conduit   *n.*   a passage (a pipe or tunnel) through which water or electric wires can pass（水、电线的）导管

thread   *n.*   the way that something develops, one part connecting another 思路

paramount   *a.*   having superior power and influence 最重要的，主要的；至高无上的

aptly   *ad.*   in a competent capable manner 适宜地；适当地

contingency   *n.*   a possible event or occurrence or result 可能发生的事；不测事件

heterogeneous   *a.*   consisting of elements that are not of the same kind or nature 混杂的，由不同成分形成的

ethnicity   *n.*   an ethnic quality or affiliation resulting from racial or cultural ties 种族渊源，种族特点

reengineering   *n.*   the restructuring of a company or part of its operations, esp. by utilizing information 企业再造；再造工程；重建

spontaneity   *n.*   the quality of being spontaneous and coming from natural feelings without constraint 自发性；自然发生

impetus   *n.*   a force that moves something along 动力；促进；冲力

Key Terms and Concepts

Technical skills：The ability to apply specialized knowledge or expertise. 技术技能
Human skills：The ability to work with, understand, and motivate other people, both

individually and in groups. 人际技能

Conceptual skills：The metal ability to analyze and diagnose complex situations. 概念性技能

Organizational behavior（**OB**）：A field of study that investigates the impact that individuals，groups，and structure have on behavior within organizations，for the purpose of applying such knowledge toward improving an organization's effectiveness. 组织行为学

Contingency variables：Situational factors；variables that moderate the relationship between two or more other variables and improve the correlation. 权变变量

Workforce diversity：The increasing heterogeneity of organizations with the inclusion of different groups. 劳动力多元化

Total quality management（**TQM**）：A philosophy of management that is driven by the constant attainment of customer satisfaction through the continuous improvement of all organizational processes. 全面质量管理

Empowering employees：Putting employees in charge of what they do. 授权员工

Ethical dilemma：Situation in which an individual is required to define right and wrong conduct. 道德困境

Exercises

I. Discussion and Review Questions.

1. Explain the value of the systematic study of OB.
2. List the major challenges and opportunities for managers to use OB concepts.
3. Describe why managers require a knowledge of OB.
4. Explain the need for a contingency approach to the study of OB.
5. Identify the three levels of analysis in this book's OB model.

II. Vocabulary Review: Without referring to the text, fill in the blanks in the following sentences with the correct words from this list. You may change the tense, number, or form of the words to fit the context. Use each word only once.

managers	planning	human skill	organizational behavior
total quality management	leading	organization	conceptual skills
political science	reengineering	workforce diversity	

1. _____ get things done through other people. They make decisions，allocate resources，and direct the activities of others to attain goals.

2. _____ is a consciously coordinated social unit，composed of two or

more people, which functions on a relatively continuous basis to achieve a common goal or set of goals.

3. The _____ function encompasses defining an organization's goals, establishing an overall strategy for achieving those goals, and developing a comprehensive hierarchy of plans to integrate and coordinate activities.

4. When managers motivate employees, direct the activities of others, select the most effective communication channels, or resolve conflicts among members, they are engaging in _____ .

5. The ability to work with, understand, and motivate other people, both individually and in groups, describes _____ .

6. Managers must have the mental ability to analyze and diagnose complex situations. These tasks require _____ .

7. _____ is a field of study that investigates the impact that individuals, groups, and structure have on behavior within organizations for the purpose of applying such knowledge toward improving an organization's effectiveness.

8. _____ studies the behavior of individuals and groups within a political environment.

9. _____ means that organizations are becoming more heterogeneous in terms of gender, race, and ethnicity.

10. _____ is also a philosophy of management that is driven by the constant attainment of customer satisfaction through the continuous improvement of all organizational processes.

11. _____ asks managers to reconsider how work would be done and their organization structured if they were starting over.

III. Match the terms and expressions on the left with the explanations on the right.

1. impetus
2. ethnicity
3. deviation
4. curriculum
5. hierarchy
6. paramount
7. contingency

a. a variation that deviates from the standard or norm
b. the organization of people or things at different ranks in a group
c. an integrated course of academic studies
d. a possible event or occurrence or result
e. having superior power and influence
f. a force that moves something along
g. an ethnic quality or affiliation resulting from racial or cultural ties

IV. True and False statements.

1. Organizational behavior is concerned with the study of what people do in an organization and how that behavior affects the performance of the organization. (   )

2. An organization's employees can be the impetus for innovation and change or they can be a major stumbling block. (   )

3. Today's managers and employees do not have to learn to cope with temporariness. （　　）

4. Now，managing could be characterized by long periods of stability，interrupted occasionally by short periods of change. （　　）

5. Managers are having to learn how to give up control，and employees are having to learn how to take responsibility for their work and make appropriate decisions. （　　）

6. We now recognize that employees set aside their cultural values and lifestyle preferences when they come to work. （　　）

V. Translate the following into Chinese.

Organizational behavior （often abbreviated as OB） is a field of study that investigates the impact that individuals，groups，and structure have on behavior within organizations for the purpose of applying such knowledge toward improving an organization's effectiveness. That's a lot of words，so let's break it down.

Organizational behavior is a field of study. That statement means that it is a distinct area of expertise with a common body of knowledge. What does it study? It studies three determinants of behavior in organizations：individuals，groups，and structure. In addition，OB applies the knowledge gained about individuals，groups，and the effect of structure on behavior in order to make organizations work more effectively.

To sum up our definition，OB is concerned with the study of what people do in an organization and how that behavior affects the performance of the organization. And because OB is specifically concerned with employment-related situations，emphasizes behavior as related to jobs，work，absenteeism，employment turnover，productivity，human performance and management.

VI. Translate the following into English.

1. 重视培养管理者的人际关系技能与组织吸收和留住高效率员工的需求息息相关。

2. 在组织中监督其他人的活动并负责完成目标的人就是管理者。

3. 计划职能包括定义组织的目标,建立一个全面战略以达成目标的,并规划综合的、层次分明的一整套计划以协调、整合活动。

4. 当管理者激励员工、指导他们的工作、选择最有效率的沟通渠道,或者解决成员之间的冲突时,他们就是在发挥领导职能。

5. 一个普遍的思维贯穿管理的职能、角色、技能和活动:每个管理者都认识到了管理人是至关重要的。

6. 管理者需要转换管理哲学,从用同样的方法管理所有人到认识到每个人的不同,根据每个人的不同,选择不同的方法确保员工能够留任并有更高的生产率,同时又不要有歧视。

Supplemental Reading Material

Construction Model of Safe Community Based on Science of Organizational Behavior

1. Introduction

Creating a good residing environment has already become an inevitable trend of city development in the 21st century. Safe community construction will become an important content of city development in the future. As the basic organization system of city habitation environment, the safe community construction is important to realize city public safety and gradually becomes a basic content of city work safety. But, independent community development of China still contains many obstacles. The safe community construction of China is still in underway stage. Although some achievements were made in the safe community construction, there still are some problems. The reformation and development of city intensively require policy makers to strengthen community construction and transfer city work to community in time. Due to new situation and challenge, developing the activities of safe community construction and tamping substrate foundation work are imperative.

As an important branch of knowledge of behavior science, which is applied in management area, the science of organizational behavior synthetically uses various knowledge on human behaviors, and researches the regulation of human mentality and behavior in a certain organization. It mainly researches the behavior regulation of individual, group, organization and their relationships in organization system in order to improve governor's abilities to predict, induct and control human behavior and raise the operation efficiency of organization. The science of organizational behavior values person's factor and values the research that scoops out potential and motive of person, and emphasizes the humanism and humanities spirit of "people foremost". This enlightens and guides the safe community construction. It has important research and practice value to survey the safe community construction from angle of organizational behavior. Therefore, in the light of the basic standards of the designated safe community by WHO, this paper studies the model of safe community construction based on the theory of organizational behavior science.

2. Development Situation and Standards of Safe Community Both at Home and Abroad

The concept of safe community comes from the safe community declaration which was established in the first accident and injury prevention conference of the World Health Organization (WHO) in 1989. Since then, generalizing the concept of safe community has become an important work that WHO does in expanding the health and safe work.

Since the First Accident and Injury Prevention Conference approved the safe Community Declaration, the safe community has developed rapidly in the whole world. Currently, there are 99 WHO-designated Safe Communities in the world and mostly are distributed in Euro-American regions, but the first safe community in Asia is Suwon in Korea. On the 12th safe community annual convention held in Hong Kong SAR, China in March, 2003, Tunmen area and Kuiqing area in Hong Kong, China were formally designated as safe communities by the WHO, and became the first two WHO-designated safe communities in China. In 2006 eight communities were scheduled for WHO designation and another 61 communities were preparing to seek designation. As a result, the WHO Safe Community network could increase by 93%. On March 1, 2006, the WHO Collaborating Centre on Community Safety Promotion formally designated the Youth Park Community in Jinan City, Shandong Province as a safe community. It is the first safe community in the Chinese mainland. Other regions of China, such as Beijing, Shanghai, Guangdong, etc., also carry on or brew the plan for seeking designation.

Designation as a WHO safe community is based on capacity to meet six indicators.

(1) a cross-sectional infrastructure, based on partnership and collaborations, which is responsible for injury prevention and takes charge of safety promotion in their community;

(2) long-term and sustainable programs, covering both genders and all ages, environments, and situations;

(3) programs that target high-risk groups and environments, and promote safety for vulnerable groups;

(4) ongoing documentation of frequency and causes of injuries;

(5) regular evaluation to assess the programs, processes, and the effects of change;

(6) participation of program staff in national and international safe communities networks.

In recent years, on the basis of summarizing the experience of safe community construction and development, the WHO Collaborating Centre on Community Safety Promotion constituted nine work aspects of safe community based on the above six standards, including: traffic safety, safety in the workplace, safety in public place, water safety, school safety, the elderly safety, children safety, residence safety, athletics safety, etc. Each aspect has seven concrete indexes severally and adds up to 63 indexes.

3. Science of Organizational Behavior

As an applied science, the science of organizational behavior was built up on the foundation of several behavior sciences and the main study areas are psychology, sociology, social psychology, anthropology, etc. The science of organizational behavior was established in the United States in the 1960s. From then on, it not only developed rapidly in the United States, but also became widespread in Europe, Japan and China. It made good achievement in management fulfillment. In the 1980s, the science of organizational behavior concentrated on two main directions: microcosmic study and macroscopical study. The microcosmic study pays attention to the regulations and control methods of individual, group and leadership behaviors in organization; the macroscopical study pays attention to discussing the theories and methods of organization behavior study, human resource management study, organization theory study and organizational development study. The organization behavior study mainly researches individual, group and leadership behavior; the human resource management study emphasizes individual evaluation and development in the organization, the theory and method of motivation; the organization theory study mainly researches and evaluates the characteristic, principle and gist of various traditional and modern organization theories; the organization development study mainly researches the principles of organization development and change, the methods of organization structure reform and institutional reform.

The behavior content of the science of organizational behavior generally divides into three parts, namely, individual behavior, group behavior and organizational behavior.

Some human behaviors in organizations mainly take individual behavior as the main body, for example: what influence individual mental process, mental personality, etc. have on individual behavior; how individual behavior changes under the condition of research, aggrandizement and pressure, etc; how to encourage individual enthusiasm and so on. This kind of problem belongs to the microcosmic study of organizational behavior science and is generally called individual behavior. Group behavior mainly occurs in groups, for example: why there is conformity behavior in groups; why conflict occurs between groups; how to communicate in or between groups; how group cohesiveness produces and exerts functions; how the group makes decisions; how to create the effective leadership to groups and so on. This kind of problem belongs to the medium view study. But human behavior is more relevant with the overall organization, such as: what influence the structure design and job plan of organization have on the behavior of organization member, how to evaluate organization performance, how organization culture forms and exerts function, how to realize the change and development of organization and so on. This kind of problem belongs to the macroscopical study of organizational behavior science and is generally called organizational behavior.

4. Construction of Safe Community Model

A community has four basic factors, namely, population, region, administrative apparatus and collective morality and practices. The basic characteristics of community are: substantiality, namely that it is composed of a group of active people; regionality, namely that a group of people possess collective residential area; intercommunity, namely that they have collective common life style, language and custom; foundation, namely that some communities constitute society. Therefore, according to the science of organizational behavior theories, a safe community can be constructed from three aspects: individual behavior, group behavior and organizational system. The concept of organizational behavior comes from the discussion on individual behavior. The purpose of appending the organizational restriction in discussing individual behavior and group behavior is to finally attain the level of organizational behavior.

According to the basic analysis related to the construction model of framework of the community organizational behavior science, the author thinks a safe community should be carried out from the following six aspects.

4.1 Optimizing the system of disaster prevention and calamity reduction

The community is the basic social mass organization which composes the modern city. When a city suffers from disaster, the community residents are not only the direct acceptors of the disaster but also the main body who stands against the disaster.

Although the factor which threats the community safety comes from three aspects, namely the social layer, the technical layer and environmental layer, each community can't blindly pursue the capability of emergency adapting and the emergency proceeding on the safety layout of disaster prevention and mitigation. The community should change the normal construction of disaster prevention and mitigation. A wise community governor, after each disaster comes and quenches, not only has to profoundly analyze the previous disaster. What is more important is to predict new disaster conditions, so a view of comprehensive disaster prevention and mitigation should be set up.

The pre-disaster-planning of community is the most important link of the city's whole disaster system, but the former programming exactly lacks this content, so at the present time, the primary problem of safe community construction is how to construct and optimize the behavior mechanism of comprehensive disaster prevention and mitigation. As the basic constitution unit of society, the community is referred to economical prosperity and social stability, so the comprehensive disaster prevention and mitigation of community must work well, the constructions of the accident preplanning, early-warning mechanism and emergency rescue system should be accelerated, the system of disaster prevention and mitigation should be optimized, the safety quality of the community crew should be improved, and the forces in all directions and institutions of the community should be agglomerated in order to reduce accidents and decrease injuries.

4.2　Establishing multi-center governing model

The safe community construction is a complicated social system and needs to build up a perfect organizational management system and work system. In the safe community construction, no matter the government management department or autonomic management organization in community, even the resident individual of community is all indispensable.

The chief characteristic of safe community construction is that the government guidance and community autonomy are combined and change management to governing—not only bring into play the function advantage of the government, but also sufficiently mobilize the enthusiasm of vast community crowds. The concrete methods are: 1) take community autonomy as the main carrier, with government departments or comprehensive treatment committees of community responsible for macro strategy guidance and technique support and put the emphasis on promoting the community autonomy and launching crowd's autonomic participation and so on; 2) give full play to the function of community autonomic organization which takes the committee of community residents as the core and the function of the organization of mass prevention and mass treatment; 3) develop security guarding of the community and other comprehensive treatments mainly dependent on the crowds and furthest establish safe community construction on the foundation of the vastest crowds; 4) integrate the whole existing safety strength inside the community and build a self-contained safety work system in order to make all kinds of safe defense and precaution resources work in harmony. At the same time, the government must strengthen macro lead and support to ensure the system run normally and orderly.

4.3　Setting up safe precautionary system of community and family

The resident individual is the premise and foundation of community construction. The components and diathesis of community members relate to the safety construction of a community. With the rapid development of social economy, residents' life and generalized safety conditions such as medical treatment and sanitation conditions, human's health condition, etc., are all greatly improved, but the intrinsic safety of community still faces a huge challenge.

The direct living space of community residents is their own family and the strongest demand of them is the family safe precaution. The family safe precaution is the foundation and premise to realize community safe precaution. Therefore, in the safe community construction, the following requirements should be realized: it should stick to "people foremost", actively set up the support system unit of family disaster prevention and mitigation; initiate the residential safety and carry on family safety education, psychological consultation, knowledge of family first aid and popularize common disease knowledge; carry on the work of "anti-domestic violence" and improve the anti-domestic violence network which is composed of community sanitation service center, psychological counseling clinic, community police affairs and safeguard, right volunteer service station, etc., to actively intervene and mediate the family violence. Additionally, it should actively consummate the community support system of neighborhood rescue and vigorously develop the nongovernmental community organization to support individual disaster prevention system.

4.4　Generalizing safety culture in full power

The negative effect brought by the modern civilization is that people lack vigilance to paroxysmal accidents. The "situation of a disaster" which is not big originally usually results in expanding, so it is very essential to bring in safety culture mechanism. In the construction framework of safety culture, not only will humanity get further development but also self-protection and rescue or even volunteer behavior will become a kind of self-discipline. It is just the key strength where the safety culture is different from safety management, which can make a difference to human society and keep safety situation permanent.

In construction of a community's safety culture, it should generalize safety culture and safety training in full power, and improve safety culture level of community residents. The concrete methods are: 1) rely on community schools, citizens' evening schools and training spots, etc., take full advantage of the safety management personnel with high quality and give play to the function of public participation such as safety education lecturing groups; 2) aim at different crowds such as the community residents, hobbledehoys, workers to carry on abundant popularization activities of safety culture education concerning families, roadway, fire-fighting, environment, health and sanitation, etc.; 3) improve the safe precautionary consciousness of community members; foster community safety culture, strengthen community belongingness and responsibility and make a community form its own unique guiding ideology, manage ideas and tenets, and have specific values, moral codes, culture tradition and life faith; 4) form the common target, direction and mission in the whole residents and improve community residents' safe precaution consciousness and thereby resolve safety problems at the root.

4.5　Doing well in stability work of community

A community is an important living space in which kids grow up and is also the extension and supplement of school and family, so it is receiving more and more concern and attention. Especially in recent years, with continuous rising of teenager's crime rate, there have been important topics of community legal popularization: how to bring into play the advantage of community special region and build up a trinity education network of society, family and school, and how to form an education model with school as the center, community as the extracurricular activity site in order to strengthen legal education to the teenager.

Therefore, in the construction model of safe community, it should build and improve mass prevention and mass treatment network and strengthen contacts with the administrative-legal departments through popularizing knowledge of law; periodically check the unstable factors; do assisting work well, educate and arrange the disimprisoned criminals and prevent the crime of young people and floating population; improve and consummate the system of minimal living security and realize the insurance and the utmost insurance under the dynamics management, seriously get done with the work of rescuing the exceeding hard groups, dissolve various contradiction and disputes that may cause bodily injury in the budding state, and effectively safeguard community personal safety and social stability.

4.6   Strengthening experience intercourse with international safe communities

The quality of community staff decides the community construction level, but currently, the whole knowledge level of community staff in China is at a low level and the age structure is not reasonable, let alone the shortage of full time safety management professionals. Although there is safety management department in colleges and universities, these talented persons don't get into communities. It is urgent to resolve problem of scarcity on community safety management professionals, and therefore the following measures should be taken: innovate the mechanism of increasing human resource development; hire a mass of young and professional safety management talents who have strong organization and coordination capability, good interpersonal communication capability and enthusiasm for the community construction; enrich management staff teams and improve the structure of staff teams and increase their whole quality.

In China, the safe community construction is just in the underway phase and urgently needs related international organizations and government institutions, science and technology fields, community erectors and governors to participate, improve and consummate the course together. Therefore, it should actively understand and track the domestic and international information of community, study the advanced experience of community construction and disaster prevention and take mitigation countermeasures both domestically and overseas, introduce and absorb foreign advanced theories and techniques of safe community construction, actively join in the international safe community network, and organize and participate in communication activities about safe community construction and injury prevention both domestically and overseas.

Discussion and Review Questions:

1. What does organizational behavior science focus on?
2. How to define a WHO Safe Community? How many indicators does it have to meet and what are they?
3. Which subject is the organizational behavior science based on?
4. What are the main directions of organizational behavior science?
5. How to construct a community's safety culture and what are the concrete methods?

Production and Operations Management

Text

As the preceding articles suggest, production and operations management is emerging as an important discipline in the struggle to make corporations competitive with manufacturers from other nations of the world.

Of the many functions in business, there are three primary functions: production, marketing, and finance. This unit is about production and operations management.

Production and operations management (**POM**) is the management of an organization's production system, which converts inputs into the organization's products and services.

A production system takes inputs—raw materials, personnel, machines, buildings, technology, cash, and other resources—and converts them into outputs—products and services. This conversion process is the heart of what is called **production** and is the predominant activity of a production system. Because managers in POM, whom we shall simply call **operations managers**, manage the production system, their primary concern is with the activities of the conversion process or production.

Managers in the marketing function are responsible for creating a demand for an organization's products and services. Managers in the finance function are responsible for achieving the financial objectives of the firm. Businesses cannot succeed without production, marketing, or finance. Without production, no products or services could be produced; without marketing, no products or services could be sold; and without finance, financial failure would surely result. Whereas production, marketing, and finance act independently to achieve their individual functional goals, they act together to achieve the organization's goals. Achievement of the organizational goals of profitability, survival, and growth in a dynamic business climate requires cooperative teamwork among these primary business functions. While managers in production, marketing, and finance have much in common, the decisions that they make can be distinctly different. In this study of POM, we shall pay particular attention to the decisions that operations managers make and how they make them.

Career opportunities abound in the field of production and operations management. Exhibit 5. 1 illustrates some of the entry-level jobs available today. These entry-level positions can lead to mid-career jobs such as manufacturing manager, operations manager, plant manager, factory manager, production control manager, inventory manager, manager of production analysis, and quality control manager and eventually to executive positions such as vice-president of manufacturing, vice-president for materials management, vice-president of operations, and even president or chief operating officer. Large corporations such as Wal-Mart, Motorola, Eastman Kodak, General Foods, NationsBank, Johnson & Johnson, Texaco, Trane, Ford, General Electric, Procter & Gamble and many smaller companies are beating paths to the doors of colleges and universities to hire creative persons to enter career paths in manufacturing and service operations.

Exhibit 5. 1   Some Entry-Level Jobs in Production and Operations Management

Job Title	Line/Staff	Job Descriptions/Duties
Production supervisor	Line	Supervises employees as products or services are produced. Responsible for cost, quality, and schedule performance.
Purchasing buyer	Staff	Buys products or services to support production. Responsible for supplier performance.
Inventory analyst	Staff	Oversees all aspects of inventories. Responsible for inventory levels, audits, record accuracy, authorizing orders, and expediting.
Production controller	Staff	Authorizes production of orders, develops production schedules and plans, and expedites orders. Responsible for meeting customer due dates and efficient shop loading.
Production analyst	Staff	Analyzes production problems, develops forecasts, plans for new products, and other special projects.
Quality specialist	Staff	Oversees acceptance sampling, process control, and quality management. Responsible for product quality from suppliers and from production.

Why would you want to consider a career in operations management? I have asked many operations managers what they liked about their jobs, and their answers were interesting. One operations manager's answer from Motorola was particularly graphic:

In my job, I'm doing the main job of business—making products for customers. Being involved in the process of producing products and services is something tangible that I can grab on to and understand. Every day is interesting because there is such a variety of things that I do, from solving problems related to quality to installing a new robotic machine. And there are plenty of opportunities for dealing with people, from suppliers, to our personnel, to customers. After being here, I don't think that I could handle a job that deals only in intangibles like debits and credits.

Interesting and challenging work, opportunities for advancement and high salaries are the key reasons given by operations managers for liking their work.

How does one qualify for a career in production and operations management? Understanding the concepts in this course is a first step. A college degree in production and operations management or another business discipline can qualify you for the company training programs that lead to entry-level positions, and then you're on your way. Is a challenging and interesting career in production and operations management in your future? A good source of information about jobs in small and large companies is the *College Edition of the National Business Employment Weekly: Managing Your Career*, which is published each fall by *The Wall Street Journal*, Dow Jones & Company.

POM has evolved to its present form by adapting to the challenges of each new era. Exhibit 5.2 illustrates that POM today is an interesting blend of time-tested practices from the past and a search for new ways to manage production systems. This introductory study of POM will explore both the historical developments in POM and today's challenges in POM.

Exhibit 5.2   The Evolution of POM

Industrial Revolution / Scientific Management / Operations Research / Today's Developments

Reality of Global Competition
U.S. Quality, Customer Service and Cost Challenges
Rapid Expansion of Advanced Production Technology
Continued Growth of the U.S. Service Sector
Scarcity of Production Resources
Social-Responsibility Issues

Continual Evolution of POM   Tomorrow

Post-Civil War Period / Human Relations and Behavioralism / Service Revolution

Historical Milestones in POM

For an examination of their impact on POM, we shall study six historical developments: the **industrial revolution**, the post-Civil War period, scientific management, human relations and behavioralism, operations research, and the service revolution.

The Industrial Revolution

There have always been production systems. The Egyptian pyramids, the Greek Parthenon, the Great Wall of China, and the aqueducts and roads of the Roman

Empire attest to the industry of the peoples of ancient times. But the ways that these ancient peoples produced products were quite different from the production methods of today. Production systems prior to the 1700s are often referred to as the **cottage system**, because the production of products took place in homes or cottages where craftsmen directed apprentices in performing handwork on products.

In England in the 1700s, a development occurred that we refer to as the industrial revolution. This advancement involved two principal elements: the widespread substitution of **machine power** for human and water power and the establishment of the factory system. The steam engine, radically improved by James Watt in 1765, provided machine power for factories and stimulated other inventions of the time. The availability of the steam engine and production machines made practical the gathering of workers into factories away from rivers. The large number of workers congregated into factories created the need for organizing them in logical ways to produce products. The publication of Adam Smith's *The Wealth of Nations* in 1776 touted the economic benefits of the **division of labor**, also referred to as the **specialization of labor**, which broke the production of products into small, specialized tasks that were assigned to workers along production lines. Thus the factories of the late 1700s had developed not only production machinery but also ways of planning and controlling the work of production workers.

The industrial revolution spread from England to other European countries and to the United States. In 1790 Eli Whitney, the American inventor, developed the concept of **interchangeable parts**. Whitney designed rifles to be manufactured for the U. S. government on an assembly line, such that parts were produced to tolerances, allowing every part to fit right the first time. This method of production displaced the old method of either sorting through parts to find one that fit or modifying a part so that it would fit.

The first great industry in the United States was the textile industry. By the War of 1812, there were almost 200 textile mills in New England. The industrial revolution was advanced further with the development of the gasoline engine and electricity in the 1800s. Other industries emerged, and the need for products to support the Civil War stimulated the establishment of more factories. By the middle 1800s, the old cottage system of producing products had been replaced, by the factory system, but vast improvements to factories were yet to come.

Post-Civil War Period

A new industrial era for the United States was ushered in with the coming of the twentieth century. The post-Civil War period set the stage for the great expansion of production capacity in the new century. The abolition of slave labor, the exodus of farm laborers to the cities, and the massive influx of immigrants in the 1865 – 1900 period provided a large work force for the rapidly developing urban industrial centers.

The end of the Civil War witnessed the beginning of modern forms of capital through the establishment of joint stock companies. This development led to the separation of the capitalist from the employer, with managers becoming salaried employees of the financiers who owned the capital. During the post-Civil War period, J. P. Morgan, Jay Gould, Cornelius Vanderbilt, and others built industrial empires. These entrepreneurs and the vast accumulation of capital in this period created a great

U. S. production capacity that was to mushroom at the turn of the century.

The rapid exploration and settlement of the West created the need for numerous products and a means to deliver them to the product-hungry settlers. The post-Civil War period produced the large railroads, the second great U. S. industry. Rail lines were extended; new territories were developed; and with the coming of the twentieth century, an effective and economical transportation system, national in scope, was in operation.

By 1900 all of these developments—increased capital and production capacity, the expanded urban workforce, new Western markets, and an effective national transportation system—set the stage for the great production explosion of the early twentieth century.

Glossary

production *n.* manufacturing or mining or growing something (usually in large quantities) for sale 生产

operations manager a person in charge of the planning and execution of the routine functions and activities of an organization 业务经理;营运经理;操作经理

industrial revolution the transformation from an agricultural to an industrial nation 工业革命

cottage system a system of production where goods and services are produced at home in small amounts 村舍制;家庭形态

division of labor the separation of a work process into a number of tasks, with each task performed by a separate person or group of persons 劳动力的分工

specialization of labor an alternative term for "division of labor" 劳动专业化

interchangeable parts parts made to specifications that ensure that they are so nearly identical that they will fit into any assembly of the same type 通用件;互换部件

Key Terms and Concepts

POM: Production and operations management, is the management of an organization's production system, which converts inputs into the organization's products and services. 生产与作业管理

Exercises

I. Discussion and Review Questions

1. What is POM?
2. What is a manager in the marketing function responsible for?
3. Why are production systems prior to the 1700s often called the "cottage

system"?

    4. What are the two principle elements of the industrial revolution?

    5. What is the first great industry in the U. S. ?

    6. Who developed the concept of interchangeable parts?

    7. What created the need for numerous products and a means to deliver them to the product-hungry settlers?

II. Vocabulary Review: Without referring to the text, fill in the blanks in the following sentences with the correct words from this list. You may change the tense, number, or form of the words to fit the context. Use each word only once; not all of the words on the list will be used.

| operation managers | production | inputs | outputs | marketing function |
| finance functions | cooperative teamwork | financial objectives | marketing | finance |

    1. A production system takes _____ — raw materials, personnel, machines, buildings, technology, cash, and other resources — and converts them into _____ — products and services.

    2. This conversion process is the heart of what is called _____ and is the predominant activity of a production system.

    3. Without _____, no products or services could be sold.

    4. Without _____, financial failure would surely result.

    5. Achievement of the organizational goals of profitability, survival, and growth in a dynamic business climate requires _____ among these primary business functions.

    6. Managers in the finance function are responsible for achieving the _____ _____ of the firm.

III. Match the terms and expressions on the left with the explanations on the right.

    1. production   a. parts that are so nearly identical that they will fit into any assembly of the same type

    2. industrial revolution   b. the management of an organization production system, which converts inputs into the organization's products and services

    3. interchangeable parts   c. the transformation from an agricultural to an industrial nation

    4. POM   d. manufacturing or mining or growing something for sale

IV. True and False statements.

1. Managers in the marketing function are responsible for creating a demand for an organization's products and services. （　　）
2. Without finance，no products or services could be produced；without marketing，no products or services could be sold；and without production，financial failure would surely result. （　　）
3. Whereas production，marketing，and finance act independently to achieve their individual functional goals，they act together to achieve the organization's goals. （　　）
4. Interesting and challenging work，opportunities for advancement and high salaries are the key reasons given by operations managers for liking their work. （　　）
5. The availability of the steam engine and production machines made unpractical the gathering of workers into factories away from rivers. （　　）
6. The post-Civil War period produced the large railroads，the second great U.S. industry. （　　）

V. Translate the following into Chinese.

A production system takes inputs—raw materials，personnel，machines，buildings，technology，cash，and other resources—and converts them into outputs—products and services. This conversion process is the heart of what is called production and is the predominant activity of a production system. Because managers in POM，whom we shall simply call operations managers，manage the production system，their primary concern is with the activities of the conversion process or production.

Whereas production，marketing，and finance act independently to achieve their individual functional goals，they act together to achieve the organization's goals. Achievement of the organizational goals of profitability，survival，and growth in a dynamic business climate requires cooperative teamwork among these primary business functions. While managers in production，marketing，and finance have much in common，the decisions that they make can be distinctly different.

The rapid exploration and settlement of the West created the need for numerous products and a means to deliver them to the product-hungry settlers. The post-Civil War period produced the large railroads，the second great U.S. industry. Rail lines were extended；new territories were developed；and with the coming of the twentieth century，an effective and economical transportation system，national in scope，was in operation.

VI. Translate the following into English.

1. 生产运营管理经理（我们简称为业务经理）负责生产系统，因此他们主要关注的是与转化过程或生产相关的活动。

2. 尽管生产、营销、财务在达成各自的职能目标时是各自独立作用的，但在实现组织目标时是相互结合、共同作用的。

3. 尽管生产经理、营销经理、财务经理有许多共同之处,但他们所做出的决策可能截然不同。

4. 西部的快速开发和居民定居创造了人们对诸多产品的需求以及将产品转移到匮乏地区的手段。

Supplemental Reading Material

Scientific Management

The economic and social environments of the new country formed the crucible in which scientific management was formulated. The one missing link was management—the ability to develop this great production machine to satisfy the massive markets of the day. A nucleus of engineers, business executives, consultants, educators, and researchers developed the methods and philosophy called scientific management. Exhibit 5.3 presents the main characters of the scientific management era.

Exhibit 5.3   Scientific Management: The Players and Their Parts

Contributor	Lifespan	Contributions
Frederick Winslow Taylor	1856 – 1915	Scientific management principles, exception principle, time study, methods analysis, standards, planning, control
Frank B. Gilbreth	1868 – 1934	Motion study, methods, therbligs, construction contracting, consulting
Lillian M. Gilbreth	1878 – 1973	Fatigue studies, human factor in work, employee selection and training
Henry L. Gantt	1861 – 1919	Gantt charts, incentive pay systems, humanistic approach to labor, training
Carl G. Barth	1860 – 1939	Mathematical analysis, slide rule, feeds and speeds studies, consulting to automobile industry
Harrington Emerson	1885 – 1931	Principles of efficiency, million-dollars-a-day savings in railroads, methods of control
Morris L. Cooke	1872 – 1960	Scientific management application to education and government

Frederick Winslow Taylor is known as the father of scientific management. He studied the factory problems of his day scientifically and popularized the notion of efficiency—getting the desired result with the least waste of time, effort, or materials.

Taylor was born in 1856 in Pennsylvania, the son of a prosperous attorney. With a plan to follow in his father's professional footsteps, he attended preparatory school and applied such energy in his studies that he gradually impaired his eyesight. Although he passed the entrance exams to Harvard Law School with honors, his poor health prevented him from continuing in the legal profession. He turned instead to a four-year apprentice program for pattern makers and machinists. It was here in industry that Taylor found outlets for his interests — scientific investigation, experimentation, and improving and reforming things on the basis of fact. Taylor found industrial conditions that he could not tolerate — worker soldiering (loafing), poor management, and lack of harmony between workers and managers.

Although jobs were scarce in 1878, Taylor found work as a laborer at the Midvale Steel Company in Philadelphia. In six years he rose from laborer to clerk, to machinist, to gang boss of machinists, to foreman, to master mechanic of maintenance, and finally to chief engineer of the works. While advancing through these positions, he attended Stevens Institute of Technology and received a degree in mechanical engineering. Taylor owed his rapid advancement at Midvale Steel in large part to his scientific investigations into improvements in worker efficiency that resulted in great labor cost savings.

Taylor's shop system, a systematic approach to improving worker efficiency, employed the following steps:

1. Skill, strength, and learning ability were determined for each worker so that individuals could be placed in jobs for which they were best suited.

2. Stopwatch studies were used to precisely set standard output per worker on each task. The expected output on each job was used for planning and scheduling work and for comparing different methods of performing tasks.

3. Instruction cards, routing sequences, and materials specifications were used to coordinate and organize the shop so that work methods and work flow could be standardized and labor output standards could be met.

4. Supervision was improved through careful selection and training. Taylor frequently indicated that management was negligent in performing its functions. He believed that management had to accept planning, organizing, controlling, and methods determination responsibilities, rather than leave these important functions to the workers.

5. Incentive pay systems were initiated to increase efficiency and to relieve foremen of their traditional responsibility of driving the workers.

In 1893 Taylor left Midvale to form a private consulting practice in order to apply his system to a broader range of situations. Those analysts who followed Taylor were known as efficiency experts, efficiency engineers, and, finally, industrial engineers. In addition to the title of father of scientific management, Taylor is known as the father of industrial engineering.

Taylor spent a total of 12 hours over a 4-day period in the witness chair before a 1911 congressional investigating committee responding to labor, congressmen, and newsmen on charges that scientific management treated labor unfairly. It is interesting to note that while Taylor has been much maligned in his day and ours with charges of treating workers unfairly, there is no evidence that any company with which Taylor was associated ever experienced a strike over his methods. The great publicity from his testimony at these congressional hearings, together with Louis Brandeis's call for the use of scientific management in the railroad industry to avoid railroad rate increases in 1910, gave scientific management the public attention it needed to gain widespread acceptance in a broad range of industrial settings in the United States and abroad.

The other scientific management pioneers listed in Exhibit 5.3 rallied to spread the gospel of efficiency. Each of these individuals contributed valuable techniques and approaches that eventually shaped scientific management into a powerful force to facilitate mass production. This force was so successfully applied during the U.S. buildup of output for World War I that after the war European countries imported scientific management methods to develop their factories.

Scientific management has dramatically affected today's management practices. Scientific management's struggle to find the one best way to operate factories leads logically to a questioning attitude on the part of managers in every phase of production systems. This questioning attitude encourages managers to attempt to build factories that operate with clockwork efficiency.

The high-water mark of scientific management occurred at the Ford Motor Company early in the twentieth century. Henry Ford (1863 – 1947) designed the "Model T" Ford automobile to be built on assembly lines. In Ford's assembly lines were embodied the chief elements of scientific management—standardized product designs, mass production, low manufacturing costs, mechanized assembly lines, specialization of labor, and interchangeable parts. Although Ford did not invent many of the production methods that he used, he did, perhaps more than any other industrial leader of his time, incorporate into his factories the best of that period's efficient production methods. In fact, he was responsible in large measure for popularizing assembly lines as the way to produce large volumes of low-cost products. Later this popularity spread to other industries in the United States and abroad.

The technology of assembly lines, refined to an art at Ford's massive Rouge plant in the 1920s the Rouge, expanded and grew throughout the buildup of production capacity during World War II. And Ford not only was concerned with mass production, he also was concerned for his workers. He paid his workers more than the going wage of the day so that they could afford to buy his cars, and he established "sociological departments" that were forerunners of today's personnel departments.

Scientific management's thrust was at the lower level of the organization's hierarchy—the shop floor, workers, foremen, superintendents, and lower middle management. Taylor and his associates concentrated on the shop level because it was here that most management problems of the day were found. What was needed was mass production and efficiency while focusing on the details of operations. Scientific management methods met that challenge.

Discussion and Review Questions:
1. Please list the main characters of the scientific management era.
2. What steps did the Taylor's shop system take to improve worker efficiency?
3. What are the contributions of Frederick Winslow Taylor to scientific management?
4. Please list the differences of contributions between Taylor and Cooke.
5. What is the high-water mark of scientific management?

Developing Quality and Competitive Advantage

Text

The managers at Harley-Davidson faced the same situation that managers around the world are facing today. The extremely competitive nature of the global business environment requires companies to produce high-quality goods in the most efficient way possible or else be shredded by the competition. In almost every industry you can name, this global challenge has caused companies to reexamine their definition of quality. High efficiency, few defects, fast production, low costs, excellent customer service, broad market reach, **innovative** products and processes, less waste, and high flexibility are all objectives that improve quality by adding value to the goods or service being produced. Companies pursue these objectives in order to maintain competitive advantage. And as Harley-Davidson's managers learned, the level of quality that a company aspires to is a strategic decision that affects the production process.

Production is the transformation of resources into goods or services that people need or want. At the core of production is the conversion process, the sequence of events that convert resources into products. The conversion process can be diagrammed simply:

Input —→ Transformation —→ Output

This formula applies to both intangible services and tangible goods. For example, for a taxi cab company to serve its customers, tangible and intangible resources—the cab, the driver's skill, the fuel, and a passenger—are transformed into the intangible service of transporting the customer to the destination. For a shirt maker to produce a shirt, the resources that are converted—cloth, thread, and buttons—are tangible and so is the output—the shirt.

Conversion is of two basic types. An analytic system breaks raw materials into one or more distinct products, which may or may not resemble the original material in form and function. In meatpacking, for example, a steer is divided into hide, bone, steaks, and so on. A synthetic system combines two or more materials to form a single product. For example, in steel manufacturing, iron is combined with small quantities of other minerals at high temperatures to make steel.

Production and operations management (POM) is the coordination of an organization's resources for manufacturing goods or producing services. Like other types of management, POM involves the basic function of planning, organizing, leading, and controlling. It also requires careful consideration of the company's goals, the strategies for attaining those goals, and the standards against which results will be measured.

POM is growing as one of the business world's most dynamic areas of specialization. For one thing, it is becoming the focus of many companies' efforts to improve quality and competitiveness. The field is challenging because (1) it is undergoing rapid changes; (2) it involves many activities, from interpreting market research (determining what kinds of goods and services should be produced) to production planning and control of the production process; and (3) it applies to all kinds of companies, regardless of size or product. As a result, POM is enjoying a surge in popularity as a business career track.

Understanding the Evolution of Production

Throughout most of human history, people have sought ways of improving production efficiency—lowering costs by **optimizing** output from each resource used in the production process. Consider the feudal system, the political and economic system of **medieval** Europe in which lords rented land and gave protection to their **tenant** farmers in exchange for a portion of their output. Production under the feudal system provided a more efficient division of labor than nomadic life or small tribal settlements.

Later, a series of technological advances in eighteenth-century England brought about even more efficient production and **ushered** in a period known as the Industrial Revolution. The first of these technological advances was mechanization, the use of machines to do work previously done by people. Adding to mechanization's efficiency was standardization, or the production of uniform, interchangeable parts. This development eliminated the need to craft products one at a time, and it reduced the level of skill that workers needed to produce many goods.

In the early twentieth century, Henry Ford was a big fan of standardization. He once commented that customers could have any color car they wanted as long as it was black. Ford also introduced the technological advance with the most wide-ranging influence, the assembly line, which involves putting a product together as it progresses past a number of workstations where each employee performs a specific task.

As manufacturers became more adept at integrating mechanization, standardization, and the assembly line into the production process, they turned their attention toward eliminating as much costly manual labor as possible through automation, the process of performing a mechanical operation with the absolute minimum of human intervention. In automated production, people put the machines into operation, monitor or regulate them, and inspect their output. Beyond that, the machines do the work. These four advances in production efficiency allowed for the development of mass production—manufacturing uniform goods in great quantities. Mass production reduces production costs and makes products available to more people. Some service companies also use mass production techniques. For example, fast-food chains, hotels, accounting firms, car-rental agencies, and even some real estate firms mass-produce their services through standardized and automated procedures.

Even though mass production has several advantages, the competitive pressures of the global economy often require production techniques that are more flexible, customer-focused, and quality-oriented. Sometimes these techniques replace traditional mass production, and sometimes they simply improve on it. Consider Andersen Windows. Throughout its long history, Andersen made a range of standard windows in large batches. However, in the early 1990s customer demands and an increasing error rate caused Andersen to rethink the way it built windows. To better meet customer needs, the company developed an interactive computer catalog that allows customers to add, change, and remove features of Andersen's standard windows until they've designed the windows they want. The computer then automatically generates a price quote and sends the order to the factory, where standardized parts are tailored to customer specifications. The company now offers close to 200,000 different products and is virtually error free. Andersen's new production system is known as **mass customization**—using mass production techniques to produce customized goods. The company's next goal is to use batch-of-one manufacturing, in which every product is made to order from scratch and virtually no standard inventory is kept on hand. Andersen is already achieving this in one factory that makes customized replacement windows.

Improving Production Through Technology

Managers at Andersen Windows strive for quality production. They are able to achieve their goals for flexibility and customer service partly as a result of recent advances in production technology. In fact, together with innovative management, technology is making production a strategic weapon in gaining a competitive advantage.

Today more and more U. S. companies are refitting and reorganizing their factories to improve efficiency and productivity. The most visible advances in production technology are computers and robots—programmable machines that work with tools and materials to perform various tasks. Although industrial robots may seem **exotic**, like some science fiction creation, they are quite common and are really nothing more than smart tools. Industrial robots can easily perform precision functions as well as repetitive, **strenuous**, or **hazardous** tasks. For instance, Toyota uses robots to handle jobs that are dirty and noisy (such as sanding car bodies) as well as delicate tasks (such as aligning car hoods with engine compartments). In fact, more than any other industry, car companies use robots for painting, welding, and moving objects from one specific place to another nearby (known as pick and place functions). Other uses for robots include testing electronics and even assisting with surgery.

Another type of robot is the automated guided vehicle (AGV)—a driverless, computer-controlled vehicle that moves materials from any location of the factory floor to any other location. Although an AGV's movements must be preprogrammed, some robots are being given limited **artificial intelligence** that enables them to make certain decisions. AGVs will probably lead to robots with **navigational** capabilities, which will enable them to move under their own power of direction. Hospitals, security companies, hazardous-material-disposal companies, and the military are all currently using mobile-robot technology.

Computer-Aided Design and Engineering

The starting point for all production is product design. Widely used today is **computer-aided design** (CAD), the application of computer graphics and mathematical modeling in the design of products. A related process is **computer-aided engineering** (CAE), the use of computer-generated three-dimensional images and computerized calculations that allow engineers to test products. With CAE, engineers can subject proposed products to changing temperatures, various stresses, and even simulated accidents, without ever building preliminary models. Moreover, the virtual reality capability of today's computers even allows designers to see and feel how finished products will look and operate before physical **prototypes** are built.

Using computers to aid design and engineering saves time and money because revising computer designs is much faster than revising hand-drafted designs and building physical models. In addition, designs can be adapted more easily to other products. All of this leads to better overall product quality. For example, when Boeing engineers designed the new 777 airplane, they corrected problems and tried out new ideas entirely on their computer screens. Digitally pre-assembling the 3 million parts of the 777 allowed Boeing to exceed its goals for reducing errors, changes, and rework. Thanks to computers and other technology a product can now be perfected— or a bad idea abandoned—before production even begins.

Computer-Aided Manufacturing

The use of computers to control production equipment is called **computer-aided manufacturing** (CAM). In a CAD/CAM system, computer-aided design data are converted automatically into processing instructions for production equipment to manufacture the part. This integration of design and production can increase the output, speed, and precision of assembly lines, as well as making customized production much easier. In addition, the latest CAD/CAM software allows company departments to share designs and data over intranets and the Internet, enabling geographically dispersed departments to work together on complex projects.

Computer-aided systems are improving the quality of production in all sorts of companies. For example, Ford uses a CAD/CAM/CAE system called C3P to develop new vehicle **prototypes**. It used to take 2 to 3 months to build, assemble, and test a car **chassis** prototype, but C3P enables the company to complete the entire process in less than 2 weeks. Although the program is still quite new, Ford expects it to improve engineering efficiency by 35 percent and reduce prototype costs by up to 40 percent.

Computer-Integrated Manufacturing

The highest level of computerization in operations management is **computer-integrated manufacturing** (CIM), in which all the elements of design, engineering, testing, production, inspection, and materials handling are integrated by computer networks linked across departments. CIM is not a specific technology, but rather a strategy that uses technology for organizing and controlling a factory. Its role is to link the people, machines, databases, and decisions involved in each step of producing a good.

Flexible Manufacturing System

Advances in design technology have been accompanied by changes in the way the production process is organized. Traditional automated manufacturing equipment is fixed or hard-wired, meaning it is capable of handling only one specific task. Although fixed automation is efficient when one type or model of goods is mass produced, a change in product design requires extensive equipment changes. Such adjustments may involve high setup costs, the expenses incurred each time a manufacturer begins a production run of a different type or item. In addition, the initial investment for fixed automation equipment is high because specialized equipment is required for each of the operations involved in making a single item. Only after much production on a massive scale can a company recoup the cost of that specialized equipment. For example, Harley-Davidson invested $4.8 million in fixed manufacturing to make a particular motorcycle—only to dismantle the operation when demand for that product faded.

An alternative is a **flexible manufacturing system** (**FMS**), which links numerous programmable machine tools by an automated material handling system of conveyors or AGVs. The system is controlled by a central computer network. With flexible manufacturing, changing from one product design to another requires only a few signals from the computer. Each machine changes tools automatically, making appropriate selections from built-in storage **carousels** that can hold more than 100 tools. In addition, the sequence of events involved in building an item can be completely rearranged. This flexibility saves both time and setup costs. Moreover, producers can **outmaneuver** less agile competitors by moving swiftly into **profitable** new fields. Flexible manufacturing also allows producers to adapt their products quickly to changing customer needs.

As a $10 million manufacturer of precision metal parts, Cook Specialty is one small company that is able to compete with larger manufacturers through flexible manufacturing. Cook used to make only certain products, such as basketball hoops and display racks. However, the company has transformed its production facilities so that it is now capable of manufacturing custom-engineered medical instruments and precision parts for high-tech equipment. Technical innovations for these devices advance rapidly, but Cook is able to adapt its production facilities to keep up with the changes. In fact, almost one-third of the products Cook manufactures each year are new. Multifunctional teams of people and arrangements of equipment are quickly reconfigured as needed. The company works with its customers to custom design new products that meet customers' precise standards. "We don't really have a product line," says president Tom Panzarella. "What we have is expertise in engineering and manufacturing."

Flexible manufacturing systems are particularly desirable for job shops, which make dissimilar items or produce at so irregular a rate that repetitive operations won't help. Most small machine shops are examples. Many job shops are becoming even more flexible by partnering with other shops to share ideas, resources, and suppliers. For example, in Pennsylvania a group of 19 small companies that represent a wide range of functional areas have come together in what they call the Agile Web. When a customer firm wants to outsource the design and manufacture of a complex component, it calls the Web's **CEO**, Ted Nickel. Nickel then notifies Web members who have expertise in designing or building the component the customer needs. A team can be assembled in 24 hour to meet with the customer, come up with a plan, and provide price quotes. By working together in a virtual organization, the Web companies are able to do more in less time. And by focusing on customization and quick response, they are able to serve customer needs better than many large companies can.

Glossary

innovative　*a.*　marked by or given to innovations 革新的，创新的

optimize　*v.*　to make as perfect or effective as possible 使最优化，使尽可能地完善或有效

medieval　*a.*　relating or belonging to the Middle Ages 中世纪的

tenant　*n.*　one that pays rent to use or occupy land, a building, or other property owned by another 佃户

usher　*v.*　to precede and introduce; inaugurate 宣告，展示介绍；开始，开创

exotic　*a.*　intriguingly unusual or different; excitingly strange 异乎寻常的；奇异的

strenuous　*a.*　requiring great effort, energy, or exertion 艰巨的，需要巨大努力、能量或投入的

hazardous　*a.*　marked by danger; perilous 带有危险性的；危险的

artificial intelligence　the ability of a machine to perform those activities that are normally thought to require intelligence 人工智能

navigational　*a.*　relating to the navigation of a ship, etc. or to the act of finding your way from one place to another 导航的

prototype　*n.*　an original type, form, or instance that serves as a model on which later stages are based or judged 原型

chassis　*n.*　the rectangular steel frame, supported on springs and attached to the axles, that holds the body and motor of an automotive vehicle 底盘

carousel　*n.*　a circular conveyor on which objects are displayed or rotated 旋转式传送带

outmaneuver　*v.*　to overcome (an opponent) by artful, clever maneuvering 智胜，在机智、谋略上胜过（对手）

profitable　*a.*　yielding profit; advantageous or lucrative 有利可图的

CEO　Chief Executive Officer 执行总裁

Key Terms and Concepts

Mass customization: Using mass production techniques to produce customized goods. It refers to batch-of-one manufacturing, in which every product is made to order from scratch and virtually no standard inventory is kept on hand. 大规模定制（生产）

Computer-Aided Design (CAD) and Engineering: It refers to the application of computer graphics and mathematical modeling in the design of products. A related process is Computer-Aided Engineering (CAE) which is the use of computer-generated three-dimensional images and computerized calculations that allow engineers to test products. 计算机辅助设计和施工

Computer-Aided Manufacturing (CAM): The use of computers to control production equipment is called computer-aided manufacturing (CAM). In a CAD/CAM system, computer-aided design data are converted automatically into processing instructions for production equipment to manufacture the part. This integration of design and production can increase the output, speed, and precision of assembly lines, as well as making customized production much easier. In addition, the latest CAD/CAM software allows company departments to share designs and data over intranets and the Internet, enabling geographically dispersed departments to work together on complex projects. 计算机辅助制造

Flexible Manufacturing System（FMS）： FMS is a manufacturing system which links numerous programmable machine tools by an automated material handling system of conveyors or AGVs. The system is controlled by a central computer network. With flexible manufacturing, changing from one product design to another requires only a few signals from the computer. Each machine changes tools automatically, making appropriate selections from built-in storage carousels that can hold more than 100 tools. In addition, the sequence of events involved in building an item can be completely rearranged. 灵活制造系统

Exercises

I. Discussion and Review Questions

1. What does production mean in this context? And what does POM stand for?
2. When and where did the Industrial Revolution take place?
3. What are the differences between mechanization and automation?
4. What is mass production and what is mass customization?
5. Explain a CAD/CAM system in your own words.
6. What does CAE stand for in engineering?
7. Look up the words "carousel", "chassis" and "prototype" in an acceptable dictionary.
8. What is the highest level of computerization in operations management according to our text?
9. What is Flexible Manufacturing System?
10. Why can using computers to aid design and engineering save time and money?

II. Vocabulary Review: Without referring to the text, fill in the blanks the following sentences with the correct words from this list. may change the tense, number, or form of the words to context. Use each word only once; not all of the words will be used.

synthetic	exotic	navigation	carousel	outmaneuver	analytic	medieval
hazardous	optimize	mechanization	innovate	standardization	prototypes	

1. In fact, together with _____ management, technology is making production a strategic weapon in gaining a competitive advantage.

2. The first of these technological advances was _____ , the use of machines to do work previously done by people. Adding to mechanization's efficiency was _____ , or the production of uniform, interchangeable parts.

3. Conversion is of two basic types. A(n) _____ system breaks raw materials into one or more distinct products, which may or may not resemble the original material in form and function.

4. Throughout most of human history, people have sought ways of improving production efficiency—lowering costs by _____ output from each resource used in the production process.

5. AGVs will probably lead to robots with _____ capabilities, which will enable them to move under their own power of direction.

6. Each machine changes tools automatically, making appropriate selections from built-in storage _____ that can hold more than 100 tools.

7. This flexibility saves both time and setup costs. Moreover, producers can _____ less agile competitors by moving swiftly into profitable new fields.

8. Industrial robots can easily perform precision functions as well as repetitive, strenuous, or _____ tasks.

9. Although industrial robots may seem _____ , like some science fiction creation, they are quite common and are really nothing more than smart tools.

10. Consider the feudal system, the political and economic system of _____ Europe in which lords rented land and gave protection to their tenant farmers in exchange for a portion of their output.

III. Match the terms and expressions on the left with the explanations on the right.

1. usher
2. profitable
3. exotic
4. hazardous

5. outmaneuver
6. customization
7. automation
8. optimize

a. to make as perfect or effective as possible
b. the process of designing a data-processing installation or network to meet the requirements of particular users
c. to precede and introduce; inaugurate
d. the automatic operation or control of equipment, a process, or a system
e. marked by danger; perilous
f. intriguingly unusual or different; excitingly strange
g. to overcome (an opponent) by artful, clever maneuvering
h. yielding profit; advantageous or lucrative

IV. True and False statements.

1. Throughout most of human history, people have sought ways of improving production efficiency—lowering costs by optimizing input from each resource used in the production process. (   )

2. Computer-aided engineering is the use of computer-generated three-dimensional images and computerized calculations that allow engineers to test products. (   )

3. AGVs will probably lead to robots with navigational capabilities, which will

disable them to move under their own power of direction.(   )

4. This integration of design and production can increase the output, speed, and precision of assembly lines, as well as making customized production much easier. (   )

5. For a fixed manufacturing system, equipment changes may involve low setup costs, the expenses incurred each time a manufacturer begins a production run of a different type or item.(   )

V. Translate the following into Chinese

Smart Factories and the Revival of U.S. Manufacturing

The force behind this industrial renaissance is the microprocessor, the computer-on-a-chip device that controls just about everything from toasters to automobile engines. In factories such as Motorola's, microprocessors route customer orders, direct robots, and control the flow along assembly lines. However, this isn't the hands-off, robotic automation often associated with flexible manufacturing systems (FMS). Humans play the central role here, making split-second decisions and performing precision assembly work that robots stumble over.

Motorola's plant and others like it are built around teams of highly trained employees and agile computer systems. The idea is not to produce thousands of identical products one after another, but to customize products as much as possible for every customer. Because information flow is so vital when you're building in small batches or even individual units, software has become more important than machinery in these factories.

An IBM manufacturing manager calls the microprocessor "America's secret weapon" in the global marketplace. In fact, some of Japan's massive automated factories that inspired awe and even fear just a few years ago are now starting to look like a disadvantage. Not only does their complexity create all kinds of operating problems, but also they have trouble responding to the growing demand for customized products. The best sign of how well U.S. manufacturers are doing these days is the number of overseas visitors trooping through U.S. factories to see what this secret weapon is all about.

VI. Translate the following into English

1. 生产就是把资源转化成人们所需求的商品和服务。

2. 企业追求这些目标是为了维持竞争优势。

3. 虽然工业机器人看起来像科幻小说中所创造出来的奇特的东西,但它们确实很普通,不过是聪明的工具而已。

4. 生产者可以通过迅速转入可赢利的新领域来轻易地战胜反应稍慢的竞争者。

5. 使用计算机来辅助设计和施工节省了时间和金钱,因为修改计算机的设计比修改手绘的设计和建造物理模型要快得多。

Supplemental Reading Material

Electronic Information Systems

Of course, none of the production technologies mentioned above will increase profits unless the company designs products to customer expectations. Today, many companies recognized for their quality link themselves with their customers through information systems. These systems enable companies to respond immediately to customer issues, support rapid changes in customer needs, and offer "made to order" products. Moreover, information technology allows customers to track their products and obtain status reports throughout the production cycle. It can also promote better communication within the company, thereby increasing the efficiency of employees and machines alike. In fact, many companies now rely on information systems to help establish a competitive advantage. For example, Siemens, a global producer of goods and services in industries ranging from communications to health care, cites its use of information technology as the key to its rapid growth in productivity.

One important type of information technology is **electronic data interchange** (**EDI**). EDI systems transmit specially formatted documents (such as invoices and purchase orders) from one company's computers to another's. This can greatly reduce the time, paperwork, and cost associated with placing and processing orders, thereby making it easier and more profitable for a customer to do business with the company.

Wise Use of Technology

Even though robots, automation, and information systems can greatly improve the way a company designs, manufactures, and delivers goods, one of the worst mistakes the company can make is to automate a series of tasks without first examining the underlying process. If the basic process creates the wrong products or involves needless steps, nothing is gained by automating it without first cleaning it up. Otherwise you run the risk of simply doing the wrong things faster. Problems can also result from using production technology without properly preparing the work force to implement and use the technology.

TRW is a global manufacturing and service company that targets the automotive, space, and defense industries. TRW regularly and carefully checks its automated production systems to make sure it's improving the production process without wasting capital. One employee focuses full-time on auditing machines for output mistakes, developing strategies for error reduction, and training other employees. Rather than automating for speed, the company focuses its efforts on designing "mistake-proofing" technology into its equipment, ensuring that it uses technology to work smarter as well as faster.

Discussion and Review Questions:

1. How do companies rely on information systems to build competitive advantage (竞争优势)? Give a concrete example of this approach in reality.

2. What is the EDI? How does it work?

3. What are some of the common mistakes in automating?

4. How do TRW's automated production systems work?

5. What is the impact of electronic information systems on the development of management?

Unit 7

Materials and Process: Management of a Company

Text

In order to reduce the total costs and increase the competitiveness of the firms, many forward-thinking companies have realized that maintaining a competitive advantage requires continuously seeking ways to reduce costs, increase manufacturing efficiency, and improve customer value. They know how wasteful it is to tie up large sums of money in **inventory**—the goods and materials kept in stock for production or sale. On the other hand, not having an adequate supply of inventory can delay production and result in unhappy customers. That's why more and more companies are changing the way they purchase and handle the materials they use to produce goods and services.

In the past a company designed a product and all the parts needed to build it. The company gave the parts specifications to suppliers, each supplier **submitted** a bid to produce the necessary parts for the product, the lowest **bidder** received the contract, the company bought a large enough inventory to make sure it would not run out during peak production times, and new parts were ordered when inventory levels dropped to a predetermined level. Many companies continue to operate this way, which does offer certain benefits. For example, companies typically get a better price when they buy inventory in bulk, and having a large supply on hand enables them to meet customer demand quickly. Unfortunately, carrying a large inventory also ties up the company's money and increases the risk of products becoming **obsolete**. Moreover, maintaining distant relationships with suppliers can lead to poor-quality components and delayed deliveries.

So many companies today are seeking new ways of managing inventory. One of their goals is to shorten and stabilize the **lead time**—the period that elapses between placing the supply order and receiving the materials. Another goal is to **establish** a system of **inventory control**—some way of (1) determining the right quantities of supplies and products to have on hand and (2) tracking where those items are. Two methods that companies use to control inventory and manage the production process are **materials requirement planning** and **manufacturing resource planning**.

Material requirements planning (**MRP**) is an inventory-control technique that helps a manufacturer get the correct materials where they are needed, when they are needed, and without unnecessary **stockpiling**. Managers use computer programs to **calculate** when certain materials are needed, when they should be ordered, and when they should be delivered so that they won't cost too much to store. MRP systems are so effective at reducing inventory levels that they are used almost universally in both large and small manufacturing firms.

MRP systems are especially powerful when combined with electronic data **interchange** technology. Take one company called XEL Communications, which makes electronic products for the **telecommunications** industry, for example. The company transmits its **MRP** information to key suppliers via a computer network, thereby giving suppliers advanced information about what the company will need in the future. XEL's production team says that the system has reduced lead and cycle times and has decreased the number of purchase orders and other paperwork necessary to manage materials efficiently.

A more automated form of materials requirement planning is the **perpetual inventory** system in which computers monitor inventory levels and automatically generate purchase orders when supplies fall below a certain point. The price scanners found at the checkout counters of many stores are part of perpetual inventory systems. Every time a product is purchased, the scanner deletes that particular item from the computer system's inventory data. When inventory of the product reaches a predetermined level, the system generates an order for more. Often the store's system is linked to the supplier's own computer system, which enables the order to be placed with virtually no human involvement.

Manufacturing Resource Planning   The MRP systems on the market today are made up of various modules, including inventory control, purchasing, customer order entry, production planning, shop-floor control, accounting, and others. With the addition of more and more modules that focus on capacity planning, marketing, and finance, the MRP system evolves into a **manufacturing resource planning** (**MRP II**) system.

Because it draws together all departments, an MRP II system produces a company-wide game plan that allows everyone to work with the same numbers. People on the factory floor can even draw on data once reserved for top **executives**, such as inventory levels, back orders, and unpaid bills. Moreover, the system can track each step of production, allowing managers throughout the company to consult other managers' inventories, schedules, and plans. In addition, MRP II systems are capable of running **simulations** (models of possible operations systems) that enable managers to plan and test alternative strategies. And thanks to the Internet and some highly complex software, even geographically distant facilities can now be integrated into the planning system as though they were all under one roof.

Just-in-Time System   An increasingly popular method of managing operations, including inventory control and production planning, is the **just-in-time** (**JIT**)

system. Like MRP, the just-in-time system aims to have only the right amounts of materials arrive at precisely the times they are needed. A manufacturer produces only enough to fill orders when they are due, thus eliminating finished-goods inventory. Workers on the production line take only those parts or materials from the previous station that they can process immediately, thus pulling the work through the system rather than pushing it through the way mass production does. And the manufacturer orders supplies to arrive just as they are needed, and no sooner, thus eliminating raw materials inventories. As a result, waste is reduced and quality is improved.

JIT evolved in Japan during the 1950s when demand for Japanese automobiles was so low that no manufacturer was able to apply the **principles** of mass production. Japanese firms were also short of capital and storage space following World War II. Therefore, they strove to reduce inventory, which soaks up both capital and storage space. Eiji Toyota of Toyota told his employees to **eliminate** all waste, which he defined as anything more than the minimum amount of equipment, materials, parts, space, and time absolutely necessary to add value to the product. The result of Toyota's directives was the JIT production system, which is characterized by **multifunctional** teamwork, **flexible** manufacturing, small-batch production, strict production control, quick setups, consistent production levels, preventive maintenance, and reliable supplier networks. When all of these factors work together in sync, the manufacturer achieves *lean production*—that is, it can do more with less.

A JIT system requires careful planning, which has some indirect benefits. For instance, reducing stocks of parts to practically nothing ("zero inventory") encourages factories to keep production flowing smoothly, from beginning to end, without any **holdups**. And a constant flow requires good teamwork. On the other hand, JIT exposes a company to greater risks, as a disruption process. JIT also places a heavy burden on suppliers, such as the steel companies that supply a car factory, because they must be able to meet the production schedules of their customers. However, the conversion of a major customer to a JIT system can provide an **incentive** for suppliers to adopt the system as well.

Because of the inability of manufacturers and suppliers to **coordinate** their schedules, JIT doesn't always work. For example, Dell Computer's ability to quickly assemble made-to-order computers is sometimes constrained by suppliers' long lead times. Additional factors can also affect JIT: whether a product is seasonal or promotional or perishable; whether it has unusual handling characteristics; its size; its weight; and the sales cycle.

Glossary

inventory　*n.*　the quantity of goods and materials on hand; stock 库存

submit　*v.*　to commit (something) to the consideration or judgment of another 使……听从

bidder　*n.*　one who attempts to win a contract by bidding 投标人

obsolete　*a.*　outmoded in design, style, or construction 过时的

establish　*v.*　to set up; found 建立

resource *n.* the total means available to a company for increasing production or profit, including plant, labor, and raw material; assets 储备力量

stockpile *v.* to accumulate and maintain a supply of something for future use 储存

calculate *v.* to make an estimate of; evaluate 计算

interchange *v.* to give and receive mutually; exchange 交换

telecommunication *n.* the electronic systems used in transmitting messages, as by telegraph, cable, telephone, radio, or television 电信

executive *n.* a person or group having administrative or managerial authority in an organization 经营管理人员

simulation *n.* representation of the operation or features of one process or system through the use of another 模拟

principle *n.* a fixed or predetermined policy or mode of action 准则

eliminate *v.* to get rid of; remove 消除

multifunctional *a.* 多功能的

flexible *a.* responsive to change; adaptable 可变通的;灵活的

holdup *n.* an interruption or a delay 停顿

incentive *n.* something, such as the fear of punishment or the expectation of reward, that induces action or motivates effort 诱因;动机

coordinate *v.* to harmonize in a common action or effort; to work together harmoniously 调整

Key Terms and Concepts

Lead time: Period that elapses between the ordering of materials and their arrival from the suppliers. 订货至交货时间

Inventory control: System for determining the right quantity of various items to have on hand and keeping track of their location, use, and condition. 库存控制

Material requirements planning (MRP): Method of getting the correct materials where they are needed, on time, and without carrying unnecessary inventory. 物资需求计划

Manufacturing resource planning (MRP II): Computer-based system that integrates data from all departments to manage inventory and production planning and control. 制造资源规划

Perpetual inventory: System that uses computers to monitor inventory levels and automatically generate purchasing orders when supplies are needed. 永续盘存

Just-in-time (JIT) system: Continuous system that pulls materials through the production process, making sure that all materials arrive just when they are needed with minimal or no inventory or waste. 准时系统

Exercises

I. Discussion and Review Questions

1. What is an inventory control system and why is an effective system of inventory control important to every company?
2. What is material requirements planning (MRP)?

3. What is perpetual inventory system and how does it work?

4. What is manufacturing resource planning (MRP II)?

5. How does material requirements planning (MRP) differ from manufacturing resource planning (MRP II)?

6. How can manufacturing resource planning (MRP II) help a company establish a comparative advantage?

7. When and where was the just-in-time (JIT) system introduced in the manufacturing process?

8. Explain how JIT systems go beyond simply controlling inventory.

II. Vocabulary Review: Without referring to the text, fill in the blanks in the following sentences with the correct words from this list. You may change the tense, number, or form of the words to fit the context. Use each word only once; not all of the words on the list will be used.

inventory	obsolete	submit	bidder	establish	resource
stockpile	interchange	telecommunicate	executive	simulation	eliminate
principle	volatility	coordinate	incentive	calculate	multifunctional
flexible	holdup	exclude	holdback		

1. Because of the inability of manufacturers and suppliers to _____ their schedules, JIT doesn't always work.

2. However, the conversion of a major customer to a JIT system can provide a(n) _____ for suppliers to adopt the system as well.

3. Eiji Toyota of Toyota told his employees to _____ all waste, which he defined as anything more than the minimum amount of equipment, materials, parts, space, and time absolutely necessary to add value to the product.

4. In addition, MRP II systems are capable of running _____ (models of possible operations systems) that enable managers to plan and test alternative strategies.

5. A more automated form of materials requirement planning is the perpetual _____ system in which computers monitor inventory levels and automatically generate purchase orders when supplies fall below a certain point.

6. MRP systems are especially powerful when combined with electronic data _____ technology.

7. Another goal is to _____ a system of inventory control—some way of (1) determining the right quantities of supplies and products to have on hand and (2) tracking where those items are.

8. People on the factory floor can even draw on data once reserved for top _____ , such as inventory levels, back orders, and unpaid bills.

9. JIT evolved in Japan during the 1950s when demand for Japanese automobiles was so low that no manufacturer was able to apply the _____ of mass production.

10. For instance, reducing stocks of parts to practically nothing ("zero

inventory") encourages factories to keep production flowing smoothly, from beginning to end, without any _____ .

11. Unfortunately, carrying a large inventory also ties up the company's money and increases the risk of products becoming _____ .

III. Match the terms and expressions on the left with the explanations on the right.

1. inventory   a. to set up; found
2. obsolete   b. to give and receive mutually; exchange
3. submit   c. responsive to change; adaptable
4. establish   d. the quantity of goods and materials on hand; stock
5. stockpile   e. to commit (something) to the consideration or judgment of another
6. incentive   f. to accumulate and maintain a supply of something for future use
7. flexible   g. outmoded in design, style, or construction
8. interchange   h. something, such as the fear of punishment or the expectation of reward, that induces action or motivates effort

IV. True and False statements.

1. On the other hand, not having an adequate supply of inventory can delay production and result in unhappy customers. (   )

2. Unfortunately, carrying a large inventory also ties up the company's money and increases the risk of products becoming obsolete. (   )

3. One of their goals is to lengthen and stabilize the lead time—the period that elapses between placing the supply order and receiving the materials. (   )

4. MRP systems are so effective at reducing inventory levels that they are used almost universally in both large and small manufacturing firms. (   )

5. Because it draws together all departments, an MRP II system produces a company-wide game plan that prevents everyone from working with the same numbers. (   )

6. On the other hand, JIT exposes a company to greater risks, as a disruption process. (   )

V. Translate the following into Chinese.

Just-in-Time System

An increasingly popular method of managing operations, including inventory control and production planning, is the just-in-time (JIT) system. Like MRP, the just-in-time system aims to have only the right amounts of materials arrive at precisely the times they are needed. A manufacturer produces only enough to fill orders when they are due, thus eliminating finished-goods inventory. Workers on the production line take only those parts or materials from the previous station that they can process immediately, thus pulling the work through the system rather than pushing it through the way mass production does. And the manufacturer orders supplies to arrive just as they are needed, and no sooner, thus eliminating raw materials inventories. As a result, waste is reduced and quality is improved.

JIT evolved in Japan during the 1950s when demand for Japanese automobiles was so low that no manufacturer was able to apply the principles of mass production. Japanese firms were also short of capital and storage space following World War II. Therefore, they strove to reduce inventory, which soaks up both capital and storage space. Eiji Toyota of Toyota told his employees to eliminate all waste, which he defined as anything more than the minimum amount of equipment, materials, parts, space, and time absolutely necessary to add value to the product. The result of Toyota's directives was the JIT production system, which is characterized by multifunctional teamwork, flexible manufacturing, small-batch production, strict production control, quick setups, consistent production levels, preventive maintenance, and reliable supplier networks. When all of these factors work together in sync, the manufacturer achieves *lean production*—that is, it can do more with less.

VI. Translate the following into English.

1. 如果没有足够的库存供应,会导致生产的延迟和顾客的不满。

2. 如今,许多企业都在寻求新的库存管理方法。

3. 管理人员使用电脑程序来计算何时需要原料、何时订货以及何时装运,这样他们就不会在储存上花费太多。

4. 设立在许多商店收银台处的价格扫描器,就是永续盘存系统的组成部分之一。

5. 每当一件商品售出时,扫描器就会从电脑系统的库存数据中删除相应的项目。

6. 这就是为什么越来越多的企业,正在改变他们为了生产和服务而购买和使用原料的方法的原因。

Supplemental Reading Material

Quality Assurance

As we have seen so far, companies today are more focused on quality than ever before. Like Harley-Davidson, many U. S. companies have been forced to examine the quality of their goods, services, and processes largely as a result of tough foreign competition. And just as Harley-Davidson was able to reestablish itself as the worldwide quality leader, today many U. S. companies are setting new standards for quality.

The traditional means of maintaining quality is called **quality control**—measuring quality against established standards after the goods or service has been produced and weeding out any defects. A more comprehensive approach is **quality assurance**, a system of company wide policies, practices, and procedures to ensure that every product meets preset quality standards. Quality assurance includes quality control as well as doing the job right the first time by designing tools and machinery properly, demanding quality parts from suppliers, encouraging customer feedback, training employees better, empowering employees, and encouraging them to take pride in their work. A pioneer of the quality movement, Armand Feigenbaum says that the goal of quality assurance is to reduce the costs of failing to do things right. By eliminating only one inefficiency, such as a defect or an excessively complex process, you reduce total product costs because less money is spent on inspection, complaints, and product service. In addition, as you reduce failure costs, which Feigenbaum estimates average 25 percent of gross sales in most large U.S. firms, by definition you improve customer satisfaction.

Companies approach quality assurance in various ways. As a builder of sheet-metal components and electromechanical assemblies, Trident Precision Manufacturing empowers workers to make decisions on the shop floor, and it spends 4.7 percent of payroll on employee training. High-end computer maker Sequent Computer Systems has a "customer process engineering manager" whose primary responsibility is to continually communicate with customers and identify any recurring problems. Throughout the day, MBNA America Bank posts customer service performance measurements on scoreboards set up in its offices, keeping employees tuned into quality goals. In service organizations like MBNA where no tangible product is manufactured, taking regular measurements of customer satisfaction is especially important to maintaining quality standards.

Statistical Quality Control   Quality assurance also includes the now widely used concept of **statistical process control (SPC)**, in which all aspects of the production process are monitored so that managers can see whether the process is operating as it should. The primary tool of SQC is called **statistical quality control (SQC)**, which involves taking samples from the process periodically and plotting observations of the samples on a *control chart*. A sample provides a reasonable estimate of the entire process. By observing the random fluctuations in the process that are graphed on the chart, managers and workers can identify whether such changes are normal or whether they indicate that some corrective action is required. In this way SPC can prevent poor quality before it occurs.

As one of the fundamental teachings of quality guru W. Edwards Deming, statistical quality control is not limited to goods-producing industries. For example, financial services provider G. E. Capital uses statistical control methods to make sure the bills it sends to customers are correct. This lowers the cost of making adjustments while improving customer satisfaction.

Continuous Improvement   In addition to using statistical quality control, companies can empower each employee to continuously improve the quality of goods production or service delivery. The Japanese word for continuous improvement is *kaizen*. Japanese manufacturers learned long before many U.S. manufacturers did that continuous improvement is not something that can be delegated to one or a few people. Instead it requires the full participation of every employee. This means encouraging all workers to spot quality problems, halt production when necessary, generate ideas for improvement, and adjust work routines as needed.

Global Quality Standards and Awards Companies that do business in Europe have to leap an extra quality hurdle. Many manufacturers and service providers in Europe require their suppliers to comply with **ISO 9000**, a set of international quality standards that establishes a minimum level of acceptable quality. Set by the International Organization for Standardization, a non-government entity based in Geneva, Switzerland, ISO 9000 focuses on internal production and process issues that affect quality, but it doesn't measure quality in terms of customer satisfaction or business results. Usually the standards are applied to products that have health- and safety-related features. However, even companies that manufacture products not covered by ISO 9000 standards are being forced to gain accreditation by customers seeking quality assurance. The standards are now recognized in over 100 countries, and one-fourth of all of the world's corporations insist that all their suppliers be ISO 9000 certified. Even the U.S. Navy requires its suppliers to meet ISO 9000 standards.

ISO 9000 helps companies develop *world-class manufacturing*, a term used to describe the level of quality and operational effectiveness that puts a company among the top performers in the world. Companies seeking world-class quality can use as benchmarks those companies that are globally recognized quality leaders. They can also follow the guidelines of various national or state quality awards. The European Quality Award, for example, honors outstanding performance in quality leadership, customer satisfaction, and business results. In Japan, the Deming Prize is a highly regarded industrial quality award. The Canada Awards for Business Excellence looks at total quality management as well as entrepreneurship and innovation. In the United States, the Malcolm Baldrige National Quality Award honors the quality achievement of U.S. companies. And Delaware, Florida, Maine, New York, and Wyoming are just some of the states that have instituted quality awards to encourage higher quality levels.

Custom Research of Minneapolis recently became only the second service company to win the Baldrige award for small businesses. For one thing, Custom Research interviewed customers to find out how to better serve them, which enabled the company to significantly increase customer satisfaction. "We're really proud that we're able to apply Baldrige criteria to a service company and measure things that have not been measured before," says co-owner Judy Carson. Of course, even if an organization doesn't want to actually apply for an award, quality can be improved by measuring performance against the award's standards and working to overcome any problems uncovered by this process.

Production Forecasting and Control

In order to oversee creation of the product, production and operations managers must be able to estimate future demand, foresee possible product changes, and gather the resources needed to respond to customer or competitor shifts. To do so, they start with **production forecasting**, which deals specifically with the question of how much to produce in a certain time span. Using customer feedback, market research, past sales figures, industry analyses, and educated guesses about the future behavior of the economy and competitors, managers estimate future demand for the company's products. These estimates are used to plan, budget, and schedule the use of resources.

However, remember that forecasts are never 100 percent accurate. Many factors cause variances between the estimates and actual demand. And the more a company uses JIT production methods, the more it can base production on customer orders rather than on forecasts.

To oversee the actual process of production, POM managers use **production control**—a set of steps leaking to the efficient production of a high-quality product. The manufacture of complex goods is not simply a matter of adding part A to part B to part C and so forth until a product emerges ready to ship. For example, the new Mercedes M-Class sport-utility vehicle is assembled from subunits built by 65 major suppliers and many other smaller ones. Making sure that all the pieces are put together in the proper sequence and at the proper time requires large-scale planning and scheduling. The same is true for the production of complex services.

Production-control procedures vary from company to company. However, most manufacturing processes have five steps: planning, routing, scheduling, dispatching, and following up. To get a feel for the complexities involved, follow the five steps taken by an imaginary small company as it makes a simple product—wooden tables. The company has just received a rush order for 500 white and 500 unpainted tables.

Step 1: Production Planning From industrial and design teams, the production manager receives lists of all the labor, machinery, and materials needed to make the 1,000 tables that have been ordered. A **bill of materials** lists all the required parts and materials and specifies whether they are to be made or purchased:

Make	Purchase
1,000 tabletops 4,000 table legs	4,000 dowels (one to fasten each leg) 50 gallons of white paint

The production manager must determine the quantity of these materials already on hand. A report from the MRP system reveals that the company has enough wood and paint but only 2,000 dowels. So an additional 2,000 dowels are ordered via EDI from a trusted supplier who can deliver on time.

Step 2: Routing Routing is the task of specifying the sequence of operations and the path through the facility that the work will take. The way production is routed depends on the type of product and the layout of the plant.

The table-manufacturing company uses a process layout because it has three departments, each handling a different phase of the table's manufacture and each equipped with specialized tools, machines, and employees. Department 1 cuts wood into tabletops and legs. These pieces are then sent to department 2, where holes are drilled and rough finishing is done. Finally, the individual pieces are routed to department 3, where the tables are assembled and painted. The dowels and paint are routed directly to department 3 from inventory.

Step 3: Scheduling　In any production process, managers must use **scheduling**—determining how long each operation takes and setting a starting and ending time for each. This is not easy, even in a business as simple as our hypothetical table company. Here is what the table manufacturer's production manager has to consider in order to construct a schedule: If department 2 can drill 4,000 dowel holes in a day, then all 4,000 legs and all 1,000 tabletops should arrive in department 2 on the same day. If department 1 can make 1,000 tabletops and 1,000 legs a week, it should start on the legs weeks before it starts to cut the tops, or not all of the parts will be ready for departments 2 and 3 at the same time. If the entire order is to be shipped at the same time and as soon as possible, department 3 should paint the first 500 tables as they are assembled and finished so that the paint will be dry by the time the last 500 are completed. The schedule must also show how much time will elapse before the job reaches department 3—that is, how much time department 3 has available to work on other jobs before this one arrives.

When a job has relatively few activities and relationships, like our table example, many production managers keep the process on schedule with a **Gantt chart**. Developed by Henry L. Gantt earlier this century, the Gantt chart is a bar chart showing the amount of time required to accomplish each part of a manufacturing process. It allows managers to see at a glance whether the process is in line with the schedule they had planned.

For more complex jobs, the **program evaluation and review technique (PERT)** is helpful. PERT is a planning tool that helps managers identify the optimal sequencing of activities, the expected time for project completion, and the best use of resources within a complex project. It was originally developed in 1957, when the U. S. Navy was grappling with the enormous task of coordinating the thousands of suppliers and activities needed to build the Polaris submarine fleet. Today it is used by businesses to schedule production tasks.

To use PERT, the manager must (1) identify the activities to be performed, (2) determine the sequence of activities, (3) establish the time needed to complete each activity, (4) diagram the network of activities, (5) calculate the longest path through the network that leads to project completion, and (6) refine the network's timing or use of resources as activities are completed. The longest path through the network is known as the **critical path** because it represents the minimum amount of time needed to complete the project.

In place of a single time projection for each task, PERT uses four figures: an *optimistic* estimate (if things go well), a *pessimistic* estimate (if they don't go well), a *most likely* estimate (how long the task usually takes), and an *expected* time estimate, an average of the other three estimates. The expected time is used to diagram the network of activities and determine the length of the critical path.

Step 4: Dispatching　Dispatching is issuing work orders to department supervisors. These orders specify the work to be done and the schedule for its completion. In the case of the table manufacturer, the production manager would dispatch orders to the storeroom, requesting delivery of the needed materials (wood, dowels, paint) to the appropriate departments and machines before the scheduled starting time (although if the company were utilizing a JIT system, these items would come directly from suppliers). The work orders also inform department supervisors of their operational priorities and the schedule they must maintain.

Step 5: Following Up   Once the schedule has been set and the orders dispatched, a production manager cannot just sit back and assume that the work will get done correctly and on time. Even the best scheduler may misjudge the time needed to complete an operation, and production may be delayed by accidents, mechanical breakdowns, or supplier problems. Therefore, the production manager needs a system for handling delays and preventing a minor disruption from growing into chaos. A successful system is based on good communication between the employees and the production manager.

Suppose a machine breakdown causes department 2 of the table company to lose half a day of drilling time. If the schedule is not altered to direct other work to department 3, the employees and equipment in department 3 will sit idle for some time. However, if department 2 informs the production manager of its machine problem right away, the production manager can immediately reschedule some fill-in work for department 3.

In addition to such a follow-up system, production managers must make sure products meet quality standards. As discussed earlier in this chapter, managers may use a variety of quality assurance measures. However, it is most important to give all employees responsibility for maintaining the quality of their work, to empower them to stop the production process if quality is suffering, and to motivate them to continuously improve the quality of the company's products and services.

Discussion and Review Questions:

1. What is quality assurance? Give a concrete example of this approach in reality.

2. How do you understand statistical quality control and ISO 9000?

3. What is the role of production forecasting and control?

4. Please explain the process of production control.

5. Discuss some contemporary quality control issues.

Introduction to Financial Management

Unit 8

Text

Introduction

Today, external factors have an increasing impact on the financial manager. Heightened corporate competition, technological change, **volatility** in inflation and interest rates, worldwide economic uncertainty, fluctuating exchange rates, tax law changes, and ethical concerns over certain financial dealings must be dealt with almost daily. Since the 1990s, finance has played an ever more vital strategic role within the corporation. The chief financial officer (CFO) has emerged as a team player in the overall effort of a company to create value. The "old ways of doing things" simply are not good enough in a world where old ways quickly become obsolete. Thus, today's financial manager must have the flexibility to adapt to the changing external environment if his or her firm is to survive.

What Is Financial Management?

Financial management is concerned with the acquisition, financing, and management of assets with some overall goal in mind. Thus, the decision function of financial management can be broken down into three major areas: the investment, financing, and asset management decisions.

Investment Decision

The investment decision is the most important of the firm's three major decisions. It begins with a determination of the total amount of assets needed to be held by the firm. Picture the firm's balance sheet in your mind for a moment. Imagine liabilities and owners' equity being listed on the right side of the firm's balance sheet and its assets on the left. The financial manager needs to determine the dollar amount that appears above the double lines on the left-hand side of the balance sheet—that is, the size of the firm. Even when this number is known, the composition of the assets must still be decided. For example, how much of the firm's total assets should be devoted to cash or to inventory? Also, the flip side of investment—disinvestment— must not be ignored. Assets that can no longer be economically justified may need to be reduced, eliminated, or replaced.

Financing Decision

The second major decision of the firm is the financing decision. Here the financial manager is concerned with the makeup of the right-hand side of the balance sheet. If you look at the mix of financing for firms across industries, you will see marked differences. Some firms have relatively large amounts of debt, while others are almost debt free. Does the type of financing employed make a difference? If so, why? And, in some sense, can a certain mix of financing be thought of as best?

In addition, dividend policy must be viewed as an integral part of the firm's financing decision. The dividend-payout ratio determines the amount of earnings that can be retained in the firm. Retaining a greater amount of current earnings in the firm means that fewer dollars will be available for current dividend payments. The value of the dividends paid to stockholders must therefore be balanced against the opportunity cost of retained earnings lost as a means of **equity** financing.

Asset Management Decision

The third important decision of the firm is the asset management decision. Once assets have been acquired and appropriate financing provided, these assets must still be managed efficiently. The financial manager is charged with varying degrees of operating responsibility over existing assets. These responsibilities require that the financial manager be more concerned with the management of current assets than with that of fixed assets. A large share of the responsibility for the management of fixed assets would reside with the operating managers who employ these assets.

The Goal of the Firm

Efficient financial management requires the existence of some objective or goal because judgment as to whether or not a financial decision is efficient must be made in light of some standard. Although various objectives are possible, we assume in this book that the goal of the firm is to maximize the wealth of the firm's present owners.

Shares of common stock give evidence of ownership in a corporation. Shareholder wealth is represented by the market price per share of the firm's common stock, which, in turn, is a reflection of the firm's investment, financing, and asset management decisions. The idea is that the success of a business decision should be judged by the effect that it ultimately has on share price.

Profit Maximization vs. Value Creation

Frequently, **profit maximization** is offered as the proper objective of the firm. However, under this goal a manager could continue to show profit increases by merely issuing stock and using the proceeds to invest in Treasury bills. For most firms, this would result in a decrease in each owner's share of profits—that is, **earnings per share** would fall. Maximizing earnings per share, therefore, is often advocated as an improved version of profit maximization. However, maximization of earnings per share is not a fully appropriate goal because it does not specify the timing or duration of expected returns.

Is the investment project that will produce a $100,000 return five years from now more valuable than the project that will produce annual returns of $15,000 in each of the next five years? An answer to this question depends on the time value of money to the firm and to investors at the margin. Few existing stockholders would think favorably of a project that promised its first return in 100 years, no matter how large this return. Therefore, our analysis must take into account the time pattern of returns.

Finally, this objective does not allow for the effect of dividend policy on the market price of the stock. If the only objective were to maximize earnings per share, the firm would never pay a dividend. It could always improve earnings per share by retaining earnings and investing them at any position rate of return, however small. To the extent that the payment of dividends can affect the value of the stock, the maximization of earnings per share will not be a satisfactory objective by itself.

For the reasons just given, an objective of maximizing earnings per share may not be the same as maximizing market price per share. The market price of a firm's stock represents the focal judgment of all market participants as to the value of the particular firm. It takes into account present and prospective future earnings per share; the timing, duration, and risk of these earnings; the dividend policy of the firm; and other factors that bear upon the market price of the stock. The market price serves as a **barometer** for business performance; it indicates how well management is doing on behalf of its shareholders.

Management is under continuous review. Shareholders who are dissatisfied with management performance may sell their share and invest in another company. This action, if taken by other dissatisfied shareholders, will put downward pressure on market price per share. Thus, management must focus on creating value for shareholders. This requires management to judge alternative investment, financing, and asset management strategies in terms of their effect on shareholder value (share price). In addition, management should pursue product-market strategies, such as building market share or increasing customer satisfaction, only if they too will increase shareholder value.

Management vs. Shareholders

It has long been recognized that the separation of ownership and control in the modern corporation results in potential conflicts between owners and managers. In particular, the objectives of management may differ from those of the firm's shareholders. In a large corporation, stock may be so widely held that shareholders cannot even make known their objectives, much less control or influence management. Thus, this separation of ownership from management creates a situation in which management may act in its own best interests rather than those of the shareholders.

We may think of management as the **agents** of the owners. Shareholders, hoping that the agents will act in the shareholders' best interests, delegate decision-making authority to them. Jensen and Meckling were the first to develop a comprehensive theory of the firm under **agency** arrangements. According to the agency theory, the principals, in our case the shareholders, can assure themselves that the agents will make optimal decisions only if appropriate incentives are given and only if the agents are monitored. **Incentives** include stock options, bonuses, and **perquisites** ("perks", such as company automobiles and expensive offices), and these must be directly related to how close management decisions come to the interests of the shareholders. Monitoring is done by bonding the agent, systematically reviewing management perquisites, auditing financial statements, and limiting management decisions. These monitoring activities necessarily involve costs, an inevitable result of the separation of ownership and control of a corporation. The less the ownership percentage of the managers, the less the likelihood that they will behave in a manner consistent with maximizing shareholder wealth, and the greater the need for outside shareholders to monitor their activities.

Some people suggest that the primary monitoring of managers comes not from the owners but from the managerial labor market. They argue that efficient capital markets provide signals about the value of a company's securities and, thus about the performance of its managers. Managers with good performance records should have an easier time finding other employment, if they need to, than managers with poor performance records. Thus, if the managerial labor market is competitive both within and outside the firm, it will tend to discipline managers. In that situation, the signals given by changes in the total market value of the firm's securities become very important.

Social Responsibility

Maximizing shareholder wealth does not imply that management should ignore social responsibility such as protecting the consumer, paying fair wages to employees, maintaining fair hiring practices and safe working conditions, supporting education, and becoming involved in environmental issues such as clean air and water. Many people feel that a firm has no choice but to act in socially responsible ways. They argue that shareholder wealth and, perhaps, the corporation's very existence, depend on its being social responsible. Because the criteria for social responsibility are not clearly defined, however, it is difficult to formulate consistent policies. When society, acting through Congress and other representative bodies, establishes the rules governing the trade-off between social goals and economic efficiency, the task for the corporation is clearer. The company can then be viewed as producing both private and social goods, and the maximization of shareholder wealth remains a viable corporate objective.

Organization of the Financial Management Function

Whether your business career takes you in the direction of manufacturing, marketing, finance, or accounting, it is important for you to understand the role that financial management plays in the operations of the firm. As the head of one of the three major functional areas of the firm, the vice president of finance, or chief financial officer (CFO), generally reports directly to the president, or chief executive officer (CEO). In large firms, the financial operations overseen by the CFO will be split into two branches, with one headed by treasurer and the other by a controller.

The controller's responsibilities are primarily accounting in nature. Cost accounting, as well as budgets and forecasts, concerns internal consumption. External financial reporting is provided to the IRS, to the Securities and Exchange Commission (SEC), and to stockholders.

The treasurer's responsibilities fall into the decision areas most commonly associated with financial management: investment (capital budgeting, pension management), financing (commercial banking and investment banking relationships, investor relations, dividend **disbursement**), and asset management (cash management, credit management). The organization chart may give you the false impression that a clear split exists between treasurer and controller responsibilities. In a well-functioning firm, information will flow easily back and forth between both branches. In small firms the treasurer and controller functions may be combined into one position with a resulting commingling of activities.

Summary

We began this chapter by offering the warning that today's financial manager must have the flexibility to adapt to the changing external environment if his or her firm is to survive. The recent past has witnessed the production of sophisticated new technology-driven techniques for raising and investing money that offer only a hint of things to come. But, take heart. While the techniques of financial management change, the principles do not.

As we introduce you to the most current techniques of financial management, our focus will be on the underlying principles or fundamentals. In this way, we feel that we can best prepare you to adapt to change over your entire business career.

Glossary

volatility *n.* the quality or state of being likely to change suddenly, esp. by becoming worse 易变;反复无常

equity *n.* the difference between the market value of a property and the claims held against it 公平,公正;衡平法;普通股;抵押资产的净值

barometer *n.* anything that shows change or impending change 晴雨表;显示变化的事物

incentive *n.* an additional payment (or other remuneration) to employees as a means of increasing output 动机;刺激

perquisite *n.* an incidental benefit awarded for certain types of employment (especially if it is regarded as a right) 额外补贴;临时津贴;特权

disbursement *n.* amounts paid for goods and services that may be currently tax deductible (as opposed to capital expenditures) 支出,支付

Key Terms and Concepts

Financial management：The acquisition，financing，and management of assets with some overall goal in a business or an organization. 财务管理；金融管理

Profit maximization：Maximizing a firm's earnings after taxes（EAT）. 利润最大化；最高利润

Earnings per share（**EPS**）：Earnings after taxes（EAT）divided by the number of common shares outstanding. 每股收益

Agent（**s**）：Individual（s）authorized by another person，called the principal，to act in the latter's behalf. 代理

Agency（**theory**）：A branch of economics relating to the behavior of principals（such as owners）and their agents（such as managers）. 代理（理论）

Exercises

I. Discussion and Review Questions

1. What is financial management?
2. Discuss a firm's three major decisions.
3. What is the goal of a firm's financial management?
4. Please explain how to settle the conflict between the owners and managers.
5. What are the firm's social responsibilities?

II. Vocabulary Review: Without referring to the text, fill in the blanks in the following sentences with the correct words from this list. You may change the tense, number, or form of the words to fit the context. Use each word only once.

equity	barometer	volatility	perquisites	incentives

1. Heightened corporate competition，technological change，_____ in inflation and interest rates，worldwide economic uncertainty，fluctuating exchange rates，tax law changes，and ethical concerns over certain financial dealings must be dealt with almost daily.
2. The value of the dividends paid to stockholders must therefore be balanced against

the opportunity cost of retained earnings lost as a means of _____ financing.

3. The market price serves as a(n) _____ for business performance; it indicates how well management is doing on behalf of its shareholders.

4. _____ include stock options, bonuses, and perquisites ("perks", such as company automobiles and expensive offices), and these must be directly related to how close management decisions come to the interests of the shareholders.

5. Monitoring is done by bonding the agent, systematically reviewing management _____, auditing financial statements, and limiting management decisions.

III. Match the terms and expressions on the left with the explanations on the right.

1. volatility	a. the difference between the market value of a property and the claims held against it
2. equity	b. an incidental benefit awarded for certain types of employment
3. barometer	c. maximizing a firm's earnings after taxes
4. incentive	d. an additional payment to employees as a means of increasing output
5. perquisite	e. anything that shows change or impending change
6. disbursement	f. the quality or state of being likely to change suddenly, esp. by becoming worse
7. profit maximization	g. earnings after taxes divided by the number of common shares outstanding
8. earnings per share	h. amounts paid for goods and services that may be currently tax deductible

IV. True and False statements.

1. Today's financial manager no longer needs to have the flexibility to adapt to the changing external environment if his or her firm is to survive. (   )

2. The decision function of financial management can be broken down into three major areas: the investment, financing, and asset management decisions. (   )

3. However, maximization of earnings per share is a fully appropriate goal because it specifies the timing or duration of expected returns. (   )

4. Shareholders, hoping that the agents will act in the shareholders' best interests, delegate decision-making authority to them. (   )

5. If the managerial labor market is competitive both within and outside the firm, it will tend to discipline managers. (   )

V. Translate the following into Chinese.

The second major decision of the firm is the financing decision. Here the financial manager is concerned with the makeup of the right-hand side of the balance sheet. If you look at the mix of financing for firms across industries, you will see marked differences. Some firms have relatively large amounts of debt, while others are almost debt free. Does the type of financing employed make a difference? If so, why? And, in some sense, can a certain mix of financing be thought of as best?

In addition, dividend policy must be viewed as an integral part of the firm's financing decision. The dividend-payout ratio determines the amount of earnings that can be retained in the firm. Retaining a greater amount of current earnings in the firm means that fewer dollars will be available for current dividend payments. The value of the dividends paid to stockholders must therefore be balanced against the opportunity cost of retained earnings lost as a means of equity financing.

Once the mix of financing has been decided, the financial manager must still determine how best to physically acquire the needed funds. The mechanics of getting a short-term loan, entering into a long-term lease arrangement, or negotiating a sale of bonds or stock must be understood.

VI. Translate the following into English.

1. 财务经理在现代公司发展中起到了能动作用。

2. 在一个经济体中,有效的资源分配对最优经济增长至关重要;对确保满足个体最高层次的个人需求也十分重要。

3. 财务管理的决策职能可以分成三个主要的部分:投资决策、融资决策和资产管理决策。

4. 两个公司可能有相同的每股收益期望,但是如果其中一个的收益流量比另一个风险大,那么该公司的股票的每股市场价格可能会较小。

5. 不论你的职业生涯是否会朝着制造业、营销、金融或会计的方向发展,对你而言,明白财务管理在公司运作中的重要性都是十分必要的。

6. 当经济需求没有得到满足时,这种资金的不当分配可能会有损于社会。

7. 股息分配政策是公司融资决策的不可分割的一部分。

8. 而且,一个公司的风险情况取决于其资本结构中负债额与资产净值的比例关系。

9. 一旦确定混合融资的方式,财务经理必须决定如何用最优的方式获取所需资金。

10. 通常,利润最大化被视为公司的最优目标。

Supplemental Reading Material

Exploration on Curriculum Rationality of Financial Management Offered in Undergraduate Major of Applied Financial Management

The Financial Management being listed into the Undergraduate Specialty

Catalogue as a third-level discipline by the Chinese Ministry of Education in 1999 becomes a very popular major in the institutions of higher learning and the society. And its curriculum system is gradually stabilized.

1. Curriculum Settings of Financial Management and Other Courses Offered in Undergraduate Major of Applied Financial Management

Many universities have not clearly identified themselves as application-oriented institutions of higher learning. In addition, it is widely recognized that those included in the 211 and 985 projects are comprehensive universities. Thus we select the finance-focused universities as the samples of our research. With the help of five young teachers newly recruited in 2012 and their alumni and friends, we identify ten universities which operate the undergraduate major—Finance Management, learning their curriculum settings of this major. The ten universities are as follows: Dongbei University of Finance and Economics, Lanzhou Commercial College, Capital University of Economics and Business, Beijing Technology and Business University, Shanghai Institute of Foreign Trade, Jilin Business and Technology College, Nanjing University of Finance and Economics, Zhejiang University of Finance and Economics, Tianjin University of Commerce, Tianjin University of Finance and Economics.

All ten universities offer the courses of Financial Management and Management Accounting; eight offer Financial Analysis; six offer Securities Investment Theories, Advanced Financial Management and Financial Accounting.

2. Fundamental Contents of Financial Management

We have difficulty in investigating the basic contents of the course of Financial Management, because there are few financial management textbooks clearly marked as application-oriented. In addition, many application-oriented universities do not necessarily choose textbooks clearly marked as for "application-oriented" undergraduate education. Therefore, we pick three textbooks for the course of Financial Management which are recently published by well-known publishing houses which have launched many textbooks about finance and economics, so we can summarize the basic contents of this course. The three books are as follows: *Financial Management* written by Shangguan Jingzhi, published in July, 2010; *Financial Management* edited by Cheng Wenli, published in August, 2010; *Financial Management* edited by Liu Jinhui, published in October, 2010.

After analyzing the contents of those three books, we argue that the contents of the course include following blocs:

(1) Basic bloc

We compare and summarize the three textbooks, finding that pandect and values of financial management are covered in all of them. In terms of pandect of financial management, they differ in the scheduling order and space: the two versions of *Financial Management* published by Higher Education Press and Shanghai University of Finance and Economics Press bring the overview, objectives, principles and environment of financial management into the contents of the pandect, while the one published by Lixin Accounting Publishing House regards environment of financial management as a single chapter. However, regarding to the contents of the three versions, we can summarize the contents of the pandect into four aspects of financial management such as overview, objectives, principles and environment. As for the values of financial management, each version has introduced the time value of capital and risks and rewards.

(2) Financing management bloc

We incorporate several aspects of knowledge into this bloc, including the overview of various financing methods, calculation of capital cost, lever principle and capital structure decisions. The version published by Higher Education Press spends three chapters in explaining this bloc of knowledge; the version published by Lixin Accounting Publishing House spends two; the version published by Shanghai University of Finance and Economics Press spends only one. In addition, we find that "Prediction of Capital Requirements" does not exist in the last two versions. But we thought it should be included in the financing management. Therefore, we put this into the knowledge bloc of financing management in later analysis. We conclude that this bloc should include five aspects, i. e. various long-term and short-term financing methods, prediction of capital requirements, calculation of capital cost, lever principle, and capital structure decisions.

(3) Investment management bloc

All three versions mainly tell us basic theories of investment, project investment and securities investment. The two versions of Higher Education Press and Shanghai University of Finance and Economics Press use two chapters to cover these knowledge areas, while the third version only uses one chapter to cover it. The basic theories cover the following: the significance, types and principles of investment, the analysis of investment environment and the prediction of investment amount. Project investment focuses on the evaluation of cash flow, the calculation and application of decision index and the evaluation criteria. Securities investment includes the decision analysis of risks and returns of the investment of stock, bond and fund.

(4) Operating funds management bloc

The operating funds management focuses on current assets management in the three versions. Current assets include cash management, accounts receivable management and inventory management. The version produced by Higher Education Press adopts two chapters to cover this bloc, while the other two versions adopt just one chapter to cover this bloc.

(5) Operating funds management bloc

All versions use one chapter to cover this bloc including the overview of profit distribution and dividend policies.

(6) Other knowledge blocs

Besides, financial analysis, financial budget, and corporate mergers, acquisitions and reorganizations are mentioned in the two versions published by Higher Education Press and Shanghai University of Finance and Economics Press. For the sake of comparison, we place these contents into the same bloc. Financial analysis focuses on corporate debt solvency, operating capability, profitability, development ability and comprehensive financial analysis. Financial budget emphasizes the making methods of financial budget and the financial budget making. Corporate mergers, acquisitions and reorganizations lay weight on the merging, purchasing and restructuring of enterprises.

8
```
Introduction to Financial

## 3. Comparison Between the Contents of the Course of Financial Management and Other Relevant Courses

We have compared all the knowledge blocs of Financial Management with those of five courses including Management Accounting, Financial Analysis, Securities Investment Theories, Advanced Financial Management, and Financial Accounting. Five influential textbooks are picked for these five courses: *Management Accounting* edited by Zhao Shuanwen published in August, 2011; *Financial Analysis* edited by Jing Xin published in May, 2010; *Securities Investment Theories Advanced Financial Management* edited by Wu Xiaoqiu published in February, 2009; *Advanced Financial Management* edited by Zuo Xiaoping published in September, 2009; *Financial Accounting* edited by Huang Xiaorong.

- There are overlaps between Financial Management and other five courses in terms of values of financial management, basic theories of investment, project investment, securities investment, cash management, inventory management, profit distribution, financial analysis, financial budget, lever principle, prediction of capital requirements and corporate mergers, acquisitions and reorganizations.
- Financial Management and other five courses differ in the contents such as pandect of financial management, overview of various long-term and short-term financing methods, calculation of capital cost and capital structure decisions.

## 4. Suggestions for Reforming Financial Management Curriculum

According to the positioning and the analysis mentioned above of the undergraduate course of application-oriented financial management, we offer our suggestions for reforming the financial management curriculum as follows:

The contents of the application-oriented course of Financial Management are similar to those of other professional courses. It is advisable to incorporate the course into other related courses and enrich and adjust these courses.

Corporate mergers and acquisitions refer to activities of controlling or exerting influence on the target enterprise for purchasing part of its shares or assets. They belong to investment behaviors. We suggest that those universities which have not offered the course of Advanced Financial Management should put this content into the course of Investment Theories.

Corporate restructuring is a process of integration and optimization of existing assets. It belongs to a company's activities of day-to-day business decision-making. We suggest that those universities which have not offered the course of Advanced Financial Management should put this part into the relevant contents of business decisions in the course of Management Accounting.

Accounts receivable are within the range of daily operation decisions. It is better to put this part into the contents related to short-term operating decisions in the course of Management Accounting.

Overview of various long-term and short-term financing methods, calculation of capital cost, lever principle and capital structure decisions are the contents of financing or financing management. What's more, financing is the main direction of employment for graduates of the college major of Application-oriented Financial Management and requires a good mastery of related knowledge. Thus we suggest
```

running an independent course about financing. The School of Business Administration of Haikou College of Economics is among the first to offer the course of Financing Theories and Practices.

To sum up, it is not necessary to include the course of Financial Management any more in the current curriculum of the major of Financial Management. In addition, offering the course of Financial Management can easily lead to confusion between the course and the major. Therefore, we suggest that the course should be cancelled. Meanwhile, we should revise other related courses in order to avoid the omission of knowledge points.

Discussion and Review Questions:
1. What are the fundamental contents of Financial Management?
2. What are the aspects of the financing management bloc? Please make a list.
3. What are the basic theories of the Investment management bloc? Please make a list.
4. What does the operating funds management focus on?
5. Please offer some suggestions for reforming the Financial Management curriculum.

Unit 9

Key Issues in an International Environment

Text

Information

An **international corporation** needs information to coordinate and control its diverse businesses. Reporting and early-warning systems are very important in this environment. Systems that **summarize** sales data and **process accounting information** are necessary, but they only reflect what has happened in the past. These systems represent traditional uses of IT for reporting and control.

Technology offers the international firm many more active tools to help manage the business. Coordination is a major problem for the global firm. IT provides a number of approaches to improving communications and coordination, for example, e-mail and fax. The emergence of **groupware** products is very important to international business. These systems let workers in different locations create a shared, electronic environment. And the manager can use IT in a variety of ways to design the structure of the global organization. We can see that technology plays a crucial part in the design and operation of international firms.

Implementing

The ultimate objective for the global firm is to process data anyplace in the world without having to worry about the type of platform used for processing. What kinds of problems do you **encounter** trying to achieve this objective in an international environment? The following section outlines some of the typical problems faced by a manager of a global organization.

The first problem is managing local development when the foreign unit does not coordinate with **headquarters**. The foreign **subsidiary** may be duplicating development efforts under way in other parts of the world. It also may not have a talented staff, and may end up with poorly **conceived** and designed systems. The question of

94

headquarters – subsidiary coordination and management is a central one in pursuing an international corporate strategy.

The counter argument from the local company is that it knows the needs in its location. A distant headquarters unit cannot set **specifications** for foreign countries. This contention leads to the second development issue. How does the firm develop a set of common systems shared across different countries to take advantage of economies of scale? Headquarters does not want each country to develop its own accounting and sales reporting systems. Different countries have different laws and regulations, so it may be impossible to share programs among foreign locations without making special modifications for unique requirements in each country.

The third development problem is that when designing applications, there are real and perceived unique features in each country. Designers, especially those representing headquarters, must recognize what features are required for a system to work in a country and what features are there as an exercise in local independence. For example, Straub studied the use of e-mail and fax in Japan and the U. S. He found that cultural differences **predisposed** managers in each country to a choice of communications vehicles. Straub suggests that high **uncertainty** avoidance in Japan and structural features of the Japanese language explain why Japanese managers have a lower opinion of the social presence and information richness of e-mail and fax, though American and Japanese managers rated traditional communications media like the telephone and face-to-face communications about the same.

Managers must also be aware that more and more firms want to build a worldwide communications **network** to take advantage of communications and coordination tools to move data freely around the world. This effort can be a major challenge because of different technical standard sand regulations. Certain countries regulate the kind of telecommunications equipment that can be used on their network. In a number of foreign countries PTT (postal, telegraph, and telephone) monopolies regulate communications and may restrict the ability to transmit data. Some underdeveloped countries may not have adequate communications **capabilities** to support private networks. Countries also may prohibit importing certain kinds of computer equipment in order to protect domestic competitors. Different kinds of communications networks and standards can greatly increase the difficulty and cost of building worldwide communications capabilities.

A number of government requirements may impede the development of global information systems:

1. A requirement to purchase specific equipment in the foreign country that may not be compatible with the equipment in other places where the global firm operates.

2. A requirement to do certain kinds of processing in the host country before data can be sent electronically to another country.

3. Restrictions on the use of satellites and special requirements for building private networks.

4. Limited access to flat-rate leased lines or a requirement that all transmission be made on variable cost lines.

A fifth major issue arising from international IT efforts is **transborder data flows**. Moving data across a boundary may be curtailed by government regulation, **ostensibly** to protect its citizens and their privacy. Another impact of regulation is to reduce the economic power of foreign companies or limit the imposition of foreign culture on the host country. Many of the transborder regulations seem to be motivated by a desire to protect local industry. Countries may have a legitimate concern about the **privacy rights** of their citizens. This reason is probably cited most often for instituting data controls. To implement control, a country can establish regulations through its telecommunications ministry, levy tariffs, and/or require formal approval of plans to process data in the country.

Examples of barriers to data flows include:

• Restrictive regulations that require processing of data originating country in that country only, making it difficult to transmit and share data.

• **Exorbitant** pricing of communications services by government owned post, telephone, and telegraph (PTT) ministries. However, a wave of "privatization" is sweeping countries and many PTTs are becoming private or **quasi-private** companies.

• Security. Attacks on computers by various hackers throughout the world have pointed out how difficult it is to secure networked computers.

• As with any international venture , language and cultural differences can also present a challenge to developing IT on a global scale. Time differences can also make communication difficult for different parts of the world, though fax and e-mail have eased this problem considerably. Some firms stress joint development teams with representatives from different countries to avoid problems stemming from developing a system in any one country or language. Foreign subsidiaries may be more willing to adopt an international system developed by across-cultural team.

We can add another important strategy to Roche's list: You need to develop guidelines for when a system should be shared and when a local, autonomous system is more appropriate. The obvious advantages of shared systems are economies of scale and the ability to share data. The problem with shared systems is that they tend to become very large and complex. Also, individual locations and users have special needs which must be incorporated into the system. As the number of exceptions increases, the system becomes more cumbersome and difficult to program.

The advantage of a local system is that it can often be developed quickly in response to a local condition. If it later becomes necessary to coordinate this system with other applications, special interfaces will have to be created. If each location ends up needing a similar system and cannot share this one, the firm have to pay for many systems when possibly one would have sufficed.

There are no firm guidelines for making this kind of decision. Firms have had success and failure with both approaches. Systems development in an international environment (or even a domestic one where there are many locations) leads to this problem. Management has to recognize that the problem exists and compare the alternative of local versus global, shared systems.

Glossary

summarize   *v.*   to give a summary (of) 总结；概述
process   *v.*   to deal with in a routine way 处理；加工

groupware *n.*   software that can be used by a group of people who are working on the same information but may be distributed in space 组合件；群组软件(群件)

encounter *v.*   to meet，esp. unexpectedly 遭遇；偶然遇见

headquarters *n.*   the office that serves as the administrative center of an enterprise 总部；指挥部；司令部

subsidiary *n.*   an assistant subject to the authority or control of another 子公司；辅助者

conceive *v.*   to form in the mind 构思；设想

specification *n.*   a detailed description of design criteria for a piece of work 规格；说明书；详述

predisposed *a.*   made susceptible 先有倾向的，先有意向的

uncertainty *n.*   the quality or state of being unsettled or in doubt or dependent on chance 不确定；不可靠

network *n.*   an interconnected system of things or people 网络

capability *n.*   the quality of being capable-physically or intellectually or legally 才能，能力

ostensibly *ad.*   from appearances alone 表面上

privacy right   the right of a person to be free from intrusion into or publicity concerning matters of a personal nature 隐私权，私生活权

exorbitant *a.*   greatly exceeding bounds of reason or moderation 过高的

quasi-private *a.*   quasi：having something resemblance 准私有的

Key Terms and Concepts

International corporation：It refers to a firm which provides its services or products for worldwide demand and has business operations in at least one country other than its home country. 跨国公司

Accounting information：It refers to the data that is recorded，summarized，analyzed，and interpreted in the process of accounting. 会计信息；会计资料

Transborder data flow：It refers to the transfer of electronic data across national borders. 跨境数据流动

Exercises

I. Discussion and Review Questions

1. What does an international corporation need to coordinate and control its diverse businesses?

2. What is a major problem for a global firm?

3. What is the ultimate goal for a global firm?

4. What are the typical problems a manager of a global organization may face?

5. What can greatly increase the difficulty and cost of building worldwide communications capabilities?

6. Give some examples of barriers to data flows.

II. Vocabulary Review: Without referring to the text, fill in the blanks in the following sentences with the correct words from this list. You may change the tense, number, or form of the words to fit the context. Use each word only once; not all of the words on the list will be used.

accounting information	groupware products	encounter	international corporation
specifications	headquarters	legitimate	networks
subsidiary	conceived		

1. A(n) _____ needs information to coordinate and control its diverse businesses.

2. Systems that summarize sales data and process _____ are necessary.

3. The emergence of _____ is very important to international business.

4. What kinds of problems do you _____ trying to achieve this objective in an international environment?

5. The first problem is managing local development when the foreign unit does not coordinate with _____.

6. The foreign _____ may be duplicating development efforts under way in other parts of the world.

7. A distant headquarters unit cannot set _____ for foreign countries.

8. Some underdeveloped countries may not have adequate communications capabilities to support private _____.

9. Countries may have a(n) _____ concern about the privacy rights of their citizens.

III. Match the terms and expressions on the left with the explanations on the right.

1. summarize   a. software that can be used by a group of people who are working on the same information but may be distributed in space

2. groupware   b. an assistant subject to the authority or control of another

3. headquarters   c. a detailed description of design criteria for a piece of work

4. subsidiary   d. to form in the mind

5. network   e. the offices that serve as the administrative center of an enterprise

6. predisposed   f. made susceptible

7. conceive   g. to give a summary (of)

8. specification   h. an interconnected system of things or people

IV. True and False statements.

1. Systems that summarize sales data and process accounting information are necessary, but they only reflect what will happen in the future. (   )
2. The emergence of groupware products is very important to international business. (   )
3. Certain countries regulate the kind of telecommunications equipment that can be used on their network. (   )
4. A distant headquarters unit can set specifications for foreign countries. (   )
5. Moving data across a boundary may be curtailed by government regulation, ostensibly to protect its citizens and their privacy. (   )
6. Some firms stress joint development teams with representatives from different countries to avoid problems stemming from developing a system in any one country or language. (   )

V. Translate the following into Chinese.

Technology offers the international firm many more active tools to help manage the business. Coordination is a major problem for the global firm. IT provides a number of approaches to improving communications and coordination, for example, e-mail and fax. The emergence of groupware products is very important to international business. These systems let workers in different locations create a shared, electronic environment. And the manager can use IT in a variety of ways to design the structure of the global organization. We can see that technology plays a crucial part in the design and operation of international firms.

The first problem is managing local development when the foreign unit does not coordinate with headquarters. The foreign subsidiary may be duplicating development efforts under way in other parts of the world. It also may not have a talented staff, and may end up with poorly conceived and designed systems. The question of headquarters – subsidiary coordination and management is a central one in pursuing an international corporate strategy.

As with any international venture, language and cultural differences can also present a challenge to developing IT on a global scale. Time differences can also make communication difficult for different parts of the world, though fax and e-mail have eased this problem considerably. Some firms stress joint development teams with representatives from different countries to avoid problems stemming from developing a system in any one country or language. Foreign subsidiaries may be more willing to adopt an international system developed by a cross-cultural team.

VI. Translate the following into English.

1. 协作是全球公司面临的主要问题。
2. 我们可以看到技术在跨国公司的设计和运营中扮演着至关重要的角色。

3. 总公司和分公司协作和管理的问题是追求国际企业战略的中心问题。

4. 时差问题可能使得世界不同地方的沟通变得困难,尽管传真和电子邮件在很大程度上缓解了这一问题。

5. 国外的分公司可能更愿意接受一个跨国文化团队所开发的国际化系统。

Supplemental Reading Material

Managing Information Technology Internationally

Ford Motor Company has business in the U. S., Europe and Asia. It has design centers in Dearborn, Michigan, Ford's headquarters; Valencia, California and five other centers in Cologne, Germany; Dunton, England; Turin, Italy; Hiroshima, Japan; and Melbourne, Australia. Ford has launched a "Studio 2010 Computer Aided Industrial Design" unit in Dearborn. The objective of this project is to establish interactive video links among the seven design centers to facilitate collaboration among its engineers. Designing a new car today costs in the billions of dollars; Studio 2010 is designed to reduce that cost while encouraging collaboration among Ford designers worldwide. Currently there are high speed data links between Dearborn and Valencia, England and Germany.

The company plans to share multimedia information in videoclips and three-dimensional images developed on the computer-aided design workstations.

Ford is a good example of information technology being used to coordinate a global firm; regardless of where an engineer sits or in what time zone he or she works, it is possible to contribute to design project. Linking the world together was a logical step after Ford's engineers had been equipped with computer-aided design workstations. These workstations contributed to the productivity of the team that is working on a design project.

What can the manager do to solve the problems raised above? Some of these impediments to IT require political action or deregulation, for example, the policies of foreign PTT utilities. In other instances, management has to take action to solve problems and managers have to be involved in efforts to develop systems that will be used in multiple countries. It is management that has to sell its vision for the firm's global technological infrastructure and resolve conflicts over IT requirements.

Roche presents a number of strategies for managing information technology in a global environment. See Exhibit 9.1.

Exhibit 9.1   Strategies for Managing Global IT

Concentrate on interorganizational linkages
- Establish global systems development skills
- Build an infra structure
- Take advantage of liberalized telecommunications
- Strive for uniform data
- Develop guidelines for shared versus local systems

There has been a trend toward interorganizational systems—the firm creating linkages with suppliers and customers. This strategy can be extremely effective internationally as well. It can be very difficult to set up these linkages because of differing telecommunications capabilities in different countries. In some regions phone systems do not work well and transmitting data over them is probably not viable. Other countries, like France, have an extremely well-developed infrastructure for business communication, which is discussed later in this section.

There are problems managing IT development projects when all participants are from the same country and work in the same location. Coordinating multinational project teams presents an even greater challenge. Language and distance make it difficult to coordinate. A New York bank has a development team with members in New York, Lexington, Massachusetts and Ireland! In some foreign countries, hiring staff with the appropriate skills to work on technology can be difficult. Interviews with IT managers for multinationals in seven countries found dramatic differences in their accomplishments and their capabilities. Lack of personnel skills can be a major impediment to developing international systems; not all countries have educational programs to prepare individuals for systems analysis or programming jobs.

Justifying expenditures on infrastructure can also be extremely difficult. Infrastructure is the part of technology that does not have an immediate benefit. The easiest example is a worldwide communications network. One money-center bank carefully costed out an international, private network and found that it had a negative net present value. Economic criteria dictate not to undertake the development of the network. However, the bank went ahead and found that the new IT provided a number of benefits that were hard to quantify. Basically, with this network the bank could "plug in" any application to the network and offer any application to the network and offer it anyplace in the world it did business.

The trend toward deregulation in the U. S. is also sweeping foreign countries. France has split Fiance Telecom from the PTT and established it as a quasi-public organization. In the past two decades, France Telecom has replaced an outmoded phone system with a mass market communications network called the Minitelsystem. It is also a leader in providing packet-switched data communications through Transpac. Changes such as these facilitate the development of the international communications networks essential to managing in a global environment.

One of the major problems in sharing data is identifying it. A story is told that a large computer vendor once looked at its logistics systems and found that "ship date" meant six or seven different things depending on the system involved. In one system it might be the promised ship date, and another the date the item left the loading dock. To obtain economies of scale from sharing data and systems, the firm must have a common vocabulary of terms and definitions.

Bill Roberts is the chief information officer for a multinational company. He reports to the company president and has a staff of fifty at headquarters. This group runs systems for the headquarters operation and also tries to provide standards for subsidiaries in foreign countries.

Headquarters has developed a standard library of financial and accounting applications which runs on most of the computers in the subsidiaries. (Bill was successful a few years ago in getting all the subsidiaries except the largest to agree on one model of computer.) Since many of the subsidiaries are not large and have trouble recruiting skilled technology staff members, they are quite happy with the library of programs.

Each country has its own information services department manager, generally reporting to the controller or possibly the president of the subsidiary, Bill and his staff travel extensively to try to help each subsidiary better manage its technology effort.

Bill is facing a major problem in at least two countries; he and his staff think the focal person in charge of information systems is not doing a good job. "After several years of working with the people in charge in two countries, I have come to the conclusion that we really should let them go. However, I have no real responsibility; these people report to a manager in the country, not to me."

How can Bill help the company solve this problem? Do you think they need to reorganize the structure of their IT units? Does it make sense to have foreign operations reporting to Bill? If not, how can he influence what goes on in subsidiaries outside the U.S.?

Discussion and Review Questions:
1. How can Bill help the company solve this problem?
2. Do you think they need to reorganize the structure of their IT units?
3. Does it make sense to have foreign operations reporting to Bill? If yes, why? If not, how can he influence what goes on in subsidiaries outside the U.S.?
4. If you were Bill, what could you do?

Unit 10

Supply-Chain Management and Integration

Text

An individual firm can be involved in multiple supply chains at the same time, and it's important to recognize that expectations and required knowledge can vary across supply chains. For example, food manufacturers may sell to grocery chains, institutional buyers, specialty firms (which might position the food items as gifts), and industrial users (which might use the product as an ingredient in another product that they manufacture). It seems reasonable that the packaging expectations of specialty firms might be more demanding than those of industrial users.

Supply chains are integrated by having various parties enter into and carry out long-term mutually beneficial agreements. These agreements are known by several names, to include **partnerships**, **strategic alliances**, **third-party arrangements**, and **contract logistics.** Whatever they are called, these agreements should be designed to reward all participants when cooperative ventures are successful, and they should also provide incentives for all parties to work toward success. In a similar fashion, the participants should share the consequences when cooperative ventures are less successful than desired.

When an organization enters into a long-term agreement with a source or customer, the organization must keep in mind how this arrangement could affect the rest of the supply chain. Ideally, all participants in the supply chain will meet at one time and work out whatever agreements are necessary to ensure that the entire supply chain functions in the most desirable manner.

In order to integrate a particular supply chain, the various organizations must recognize the shortcomings of the present system and examine channel arrangements as they currently exist and they might be. All of this is done within the framework of the organization's overall strategy, as well as any logistics strategies necessary to support the goals and objectives of the firm's top management.

Broadly speaking, organizations can pursue three primary methods when attempting to integrate their supply chains. One method is through **vertical integration**, where one organization owns multiple participants in the supply chain; indeed, the Ford Motor Company of the 1920s owned forests and steel mills and exercised tight control over its dealers. The most common examples of vertical integration today are some lines of paint and automotive tires. It's important to recognize that there may be regulatory limitations (often in the form of state laws) as to the degree of vertical integration that will be permitted in particular industries.

A second possible method of supply-chain coordination involves the use of *formal contracts* among various participants. One of the more popular uses of contracts is through franchising, which attempts to combine the benefits of tight integration of some functions along with the ability to be very **flexible** while performing other functions. From a supply-chain perspective, a franchiser may exert contractual influence over what products are purchased by a franchisee, acceptable vendors (suppliers) of these products, and the distribution of the product to the franchisee. For example, distribution for many McDonald's franchisees in the United States (e.g, food, beverage, and store supplies) is provided by the Martin-Brower Company.

A third method of supply-chain coordination involves **informal agreements** among the various organizations to pursue common goals and objectives, with control being exerted by the largest organization in the supply chain. While this method offers supply-chain participants flexibility in the sense that organizations can exit unprofitable and/or unproductive arrangements quickly and with relative ease, organizations should be aware of potential shortcomings. For one, the controlling organization may be so powerful that the supply chain becomes more like a **dictatorship** than a partnership. Moreover, the same flexibility that allows for exiting unprofitable or unproductive arrangements also allows parties the ability to switch supply chains when presented with what appears to be a better deal.

Third-Party Logistics

The ultimate supply chain contains several types of organizations (e.g., financial provider, third-party logistics supplier, market research firm) that exist to facilitate coordination among various supply-chain participants. Because this is a logistics textbook, the most relevant **facilitator** for our purposes is the third-party logistics supplier, so it is especially relevant to examine its impact on logistics and supply chains.

Third-party logistics, also called **logistics outsourcing** or contract logistics, continues to be one of the most misunderstood terms in logistics and supply-chain management. As is the case with supply-chain management, here is no commonly accepted definition of third-party logistics (3PL). The general idea behind third-party logistics is that one company (say, a manufacturer) allows a specialist company to provide it with one or more logistics functions (e.g., **warehousing**, outbound transportation). Some well-known 3PL providers include Danzas/AEI/Exel Logistics, Menlo Logistics, Penske Logistics, and C.H. Robinson Logistics, among others.

What we'll call *contemporary* third-party logistics began to emerge in the second half of the 1980s. Its importance in logistics and supply-chain management prompted annual expenditures for contemporary third-party logistics services in the United States of $10 billion in the early 1990s. In the early years of the twenty-first century, annual U.S. 3PL expenditures are approaching $70 billion—which is only about 10 percent of the potential U. S. market for 3PL services. In addition, it has been estimated that by 2005 U. S. 3PL users may be spending about one-third of their total logistics budgets, up from 20 percent in 2000, for 3PL services.

While third-party logistics is not a new idea, several factors distinguish contemporary 3PL from previous **incarnations**. First, there tends to be formal contracts between providers and users that are at least one year (typically three to five years) in duration. Contemporary 3PL also tends to be characterized by a relational (as opposed to a transactional) focus, a focus on mutual benefits, and the availability of **customized** (as opposed to standardized) offerings. Thus, a contemporary 3PL provider views its customer as a party with whom it is going to have a long-term, as opposed to short-term, relationship. In addition, 3PL providers and users actively seek out policies and practices, such as cost reduction, that can benefit both parties. Finally, the nature and scope of customed offerings can be specified in the relevant contract, and they often require both parties to make specific investments in order to fulfill the relationship.

One measure of the **pervasiveness** of third-party logistics in supply-chain management can be seen in the evolution of **fourth-party logistics (4PL)**, or the lead logistics provider (LLP) concept. Because 4PL/LLP is still in its infancy, there is some disagreement as to an exact definition. However, a number of experts currently suggest that a 4PL/LLP should be viewed as a general contractor whose primary purpose is to ensure that various 3PLs are working toward the relevant supply-chain goals and objectives.

At the present time, the 4PL/LLP concept appears best suited for large companies with global supply chains, such as General Motors and Hewlett-Packard. In fact, General Motors is actively engaged in 4PL/LLP through Vector SCM, a joint venture between itself and GNF, Inc. Vector SCM is charged with managing and integrating all of GM's logistics service providers, currently some 2,000 strong. Vector SCM is also charged with reducing GM's $6 billion annual logistics bill, as well as reducing order cycle time from approximately 85 days to the 15-to 20-day range.

Glossary

partnership *n.* a cooperative relationship between people or groups who agree to share responsibility for achieving some specific goal 合伙企业；合作关系

third-party arrangement an arrangement that engages a third party to perform certain functions 第三方协议

flexible *a.* capable of being changed 灵活的

informal agreement a type of agreement that will not require any sort of legal intervention to be considered enforceable 非正式协定

dictatorship *n.* a form of government in which the ruler is an absolute dictator (not restricted by a constitution or laws or opposition etc.) 专制；独裁

facilitator *n.* someone who makes progress easier 服务商

third-party logistics a firm that provides service to its consumers of outsourced logistics services for part, or all of their supply chain management functions 第三方物流

logistics outsourcing the situation where a company hires a third-party provider to manage various parts of their supply chain operations 物流外包

warehouse *n.* a store house for goods and merchandse 仓库 *v.* to store or place in a warehouse 仓储

incarnation **n.** a particular physical form or condition of something or someone that is changing or developing 特殊体现,特殊状态

customized **a.** made according to the specifications of an individual 定制的;用户化的

pervasiveness **n.** the quality of filling or spreading throughout 广泛性;普遍性

fourth-party logistics a model of logistics where manufacturers outsource all of the organization and oversight of their supply chain and logistics to one external provider 第四方物流

Key Terms and Concepts

Supply chain: A system of organizations, people, activities, information, and resources involved in moving a product or service from suppliers to customers. Supply chain activities transform natural resources, raw materials, and components into a finished product that is delivered to the end customer. 供应链

Strategic alliance: An agreement between two or more parties to pursue a set of agreed upon objectives while remaining independent organizations. This form of cooperation lies between mergers & acquisition and organization. 战略联盟

Contract logistics: Contract logistics enterprises think logistics infrastructure investment is not the key, but the construction of work and the communication of information, so they can sign contracts with a variety of storage, transportation, and simple enterprises to ensure it can provide logistics services to clients. This kind of enterprise has a lot of flexibility in operation, and because it is not for the specific management, it can put more focus on improving the logistics service quality. 契约物流

Vertical integration: Absorption into a single firm of several firms involved in all aspects of a product's manufacturer from raw materials to distribution. 纵向一体化

Exercises

I. Discussion and Review Questions.

1. What are supply chains integrated by?

2. Explain the ways to integrate a particular supply chain. What are the three primary methods?

3. What is the general idea behind third-party logistics?

4. What are the most common activities third-party logistics providers can perform?

5. What kind of company is the 4PL concept best suited for? Give an example.

flexible	partnership	facilitator	dictatorship	pervasiveness
warehouse	incarnation	supplemental	customized	logistics
expectation	consequences			

1. One of the more popular uses of contracts is through franchising, which attempts to combine the benefits of tight integration of some functions along with the ability to be very _____ while performing other functions.

2. In a similar fashion, the participants should share the _____ when cooperative ventures are less successful than desired.

3. The most relevant _____ for our purposes is the third-party logistics supplier, so it is especially relevant to examine its impact on logistics and supply chains.

4. For one, the controlling organization may be so powerful that the supply chain becomes more like a(n) _____ than a partnership.

5. One measure of the _____ of third-party logistics in supply-chain management can be seen in the evolution of fourth-party logistics (4PL), or the lead logistics provider (LLP) concept.

6. While third-party logistics is not a new idea, several factors distinguish contemporary 3PL from previous _____.

7. Contemporary 3PL also tends to be characterized by a relational (as opposed to a transitional) focus, a focus on mutual benefits, and the availability of _____ (as opposed to standardized) offerings.

1. partnership   a. capable of being changed
2. flexible   b. someone who makes progress easier
3. dictatorship   c. a cooperative relationship between people or groups who agree to share responsibility for achieving some specific goal
4. facilitator   d. a form of government in which the ruler is an absolute dictator
5. incarnation   e. functioning in a subsidiary or supporting capacity
6. customized   f. a store house for goods and merchandise
7. warehouse   g. made according to the specifications of an individual
8. supplemental   h. the quality of filling or spreading throughout

9. pervasiveness   i. a new personification of a familiar idea

IV. True and False statements.

1. An individual firm can be involved in multiple supply chains at the same time, and it's important to recognize that expectations and required knowledge can vary across supply chains. (   )

2. Supply chains are integrated by having various parties enter into and carry out long-term mutually beneficial agreements. (   )

3. Contract logistics do not require the participants share the consequences when cooperative ventures are less successful than desired. (   )

4. Ideally, all participants in the supply chain will meet at one time and work out whatever agreements are necessary to ensure that the entire supply chain functions in the most desirable manner. (   )

5. It's important to recognize that there may be regulatory limitations (often in the form of state laws) as to the degree of vertical integration that will be permitted in particular industries. (   )

6. A contemporary 3PL provider views its customer as a party with whom it is going to have a short-term, as opposed to long-term, relationship. (   )

V. Translate the following into Chinese.

An individual firm can be involved in multiple supply chains at the same time, and it's important to recognize that expectations and required knowledge can vary across supply chains.

When an organization enters into a long-term agreement with a source or customer, the organization must keep in mind how this arrangement could affect the rest of the supply chain.

Broadly speaking, organizations can pursue three primary methods when attempting to integrate their supply chains. One method is through *vertical integration*, where one organization owns multiple participants in the supply chain; indeed, the Ford Motor Company of the 1920s owned forests and steel mills and exercised tight control over its dealers. A second possible method of supply-chain coordination involves the use of *formal contracts* among various participants. A third method of supply-chain coordination involves *informal agreements* among the various organizations to pursue common goals and objectives, with control being exerted by the largest organization in the supply chain.

A variety of different activities also can be performed by third-party logistics providers, with some of the most common including development of distribution systems, electronic data interchange capability, and freight consolidation. Moreover, some 3PL providers have begun to offer so-called *supplemental* services—such as final product assembly, product installation, and product repair, among others—which are beyond their traditional offerings.

VI. Translate the following into English

1. 一个单一的企业可能同时涉及多个供应链,对于不同的供应链,其期望和要求的知识是不同的,认识到这一点很重要。

2. 许多不同的活动也可以由第三方物流提供者来执行。

3. 当一个组织与一家供应商或一家客户进入长期互利协作关系时,该组织应该对这一安排对供应链其他部分的影响心中有数。

4. 广而言之,一个组织在尝试整合供应链时可以寻求三种主要方法。

5. 协调供应链的第三种办法就是利用不同组织间为寻求共同的目标或目的而签订的非正式协议。

Supplemental Reading Material

Supply-Chain Software

All 3PL customers can demand a number of different activities, with some of the most common involving inbound and outbound transportation, carrier negotiation and contracting, and freight consolidation. Because the services demanded by 3PL customers can vary widely in both nature and scope, it's not possible to discuss a typical 3PL relationship. However, the two actual relationships presented below provide a sense of what they might encompass. Penske Logistics manages the outbound distribution network for the finished appliances of Whirlpool Corporation. Penske's responsibilities involve all relevant activities within Whirlpool's regional and local distribution centers, including warehousing, materials handling, and transportation from the distribution centers to the next party in the supply chain. Exel Logistics developed an interesting relationship with the Harley Owners Group (HOG) concerning the August 2003 celebration of Harley-Davidson's 100th anniversary in Milwaukee, Wisconsin. To allow European members to attend this event, Exel and HOG put together a special package that allowed HOG members to have their motorcycles collected, transported to an airport/port, packaged, and shipped to the United States via either air or water transportation.

A variety of different activities also can be performed by third-party logistics providers, with some of the most common including development of distribution systems, electronic data interchange capability, and freight consolidation. Moreover, some 3PL providers have begun to offer so-called *supplemental* services—such as final product assembly, product installation, and product repair, among others—which are beyond their traditional offerings. These supplemental 3PL services can blur traditional distinctions among supply-chain participants (e. g., product assembly has generally been performed by the manufacturing group). However, this blurring of distinctions may actually facilitate supply-chain integration, in that there is less emphasis on functional issues and more emphasis on cross-functional processes.

It has been pointed out on several occasions that the interorganizational coordination of activities, functions, and processes is a daunting task. A large part of the challenge of interorganizational coordination involves the tremendous amount of data to be transmitted across, and available to, supply-chain participants. To this end, supply-chain software packages have been developed to address the data and informational needs of supply-chain participants. Some of the more prominent supply-chain software companies include EXE Technologies, i2 Technologies, Manhattan Associates, Manugistics, and SAP.

Such a tremendous proliferation of supply-chain software packages has occurred during the past 10 to 15 years that "determining which specific systems and applications can provide a specific supply chain with the greatest benefit is not at all clear". Moreover, because many of these software packages are developed for general application, users may need to modify the packages to address their specific needs and processes, which adds to the costs of purchasing the software.

With so many different types of supply-chain software, it's not possible to provide a comprehensive discussion here about them. As a general rule, the supply-chain software packages look to coordinate and integrate functions, processes, and/or systems across multiple supply-chain participants. Thus, some software packages focus on specific functional areas such as transportation, warehousing, or inventory management. Other software packages focus on specific supply-chain processes, such as customer relationship management (CRM) or collaborative planning, forecasting, and replenishment (CPFR). Still other packages attempt to simultaneously optimize supply-chain processes across organizations.

Estimates of the annual potential savings from supply-chain software—just in the United States—range from approximately $200 billion to $450 billion. While the potential monetary savings from supply-chain software are certainly attractive, the costs of various packages can be quite expensive, ranging from tens of thousands of dollars to millions of dollars, not including installation expenses.

Discussion and Review Questions:
1. What activities can the 3PL customers demand? Please give your opinion.
2. What kind of supplemental services can 3PL providers offer?
3. Why can these supplemental 3PL services blur traditional distinctions among supply-chain participants?
4. What can be brought by this blurring of distinctions?
5. What are the main functions of the supply-chain software packages?

Unit 11

Human Resource Management: An Overview

HUMAN RESOURCE MANAGEMENT AND THE HUMAN RESOURCE MANAGER

The field of **human resource management** changed dramatically during the 1980s, in ways that created a greatly expanded role for the **human resource manager**. In order to understand this development, we must make a distinction between human resource management and the human resource manager.

Human resource management (**HRM**) is the **utilization** of human resources to achieve organizational objectives. Consequently, managers at all levels must concern themselves with human resource management at least to some extent. Basically managers get things done through the efforts of others, which requires effective human resource management. In a manufacturing firm, for instance, the production manager **meshes** physical and human resources to produce goods in sufficient numbers and quality; the marketing manager works through sales **representatives** to sell the firm's products; and the finance manager obtains **capital** and manages investments to ensure sufficient operating funds. These individuals are called "line" managers because they have formal authority and responsibility for achieving their firm's **primary** objectives. Although involved in human resource management, they are not human resource managers. They are responsible primarily for specific functional areas of the business. Carl Edwards, the convenience store **supervisor** in Sacramento, fully understands the challenges that a line manager faces with human resources because he will have to work Friday night if he cannot find a replacement.

A **human resource manager** is an individual who normally acts in an advisory, or "staff" capacity, working with other managers to help them deal with human resource matters. The term "personnel manager" denoted the individual who performed staff functions similar to those now performed by the human resource manager. This evolving change in terminology reflects the expanded role of HRM and an increasing awareness that human resources are the key to a successful organization. Although only **cosmetic** in some instances, this change has been **substantive** in most cases. Thus it reflects a new and continually expanding role for the human resource manager. The current functions of many chief human resource managers is illustrated by Kathryn McKee, senior vice-president, human resources, for First Interstate Bank, Ltd. As she states in *Executive Insights*, "I am now a strategic partner with line management and participate in business decisions which bring human resources perspectives to the general management of the company."

The human resource manager is primarily responsible for coordinating the management of human resources to help the organization achieve its goals. Jane Kay, formerly vice-president of employee relations for Detroit Edison Company, states, "The human resource manager acts more in an advisory capacity, but should be a **catalyst** in proposing human relations policies to be implemented by line managers." William B. Pardue, senior vice-president for American General Life Insurance Company, says, "The real human resource management game is played by the line manager. The human resource manager's role is to develop policies and programs the rules of the game—and to function as a catalyst and **energizer** of the relationship between line management and employees." The distinction between human resource management and the human resource manager is clearly illustrated by the following account:

Bill Brown, the production supervisor for Ajax Manufacturing, has just learned that one of his machine operators **quits**. He immediately calls Sandra Williams, the human resource manager, and says, "Sandra, I just had a Class A machine operator quit down here. Can you find some qualified people for me to interview?" "Sure Bill," Sandra replies. "I'll send two or three down to you within the week, and you can select the one that best fits your needs."

In this instance, both Bill and Sandra are concerned with accomplishing organizational goals, but from different perspectives. Sandra, as a human resource manager, identifies applicants who meet the criteria specified by Bill. Yet, Bill will make the final decision as to who is hired because he is responsible for the machine operator's performance. His primary responsibility is production. Hers is human resources. As a human resource manager, Sandra must constantly deal with the many problems related to human resources Bill and the other managers face. Her job is to help them meet the human resource needs of the entire organization. In some firms her function is also referred to as personnel, employee relations, or industrial relations.

HUMAN RESOURCE MANAGEMENT FUNCTIONS

Today's human resource problems are enormous and appear to be ever expanding. The human resource manager faces a multitude of problems, ranging from motivating a constantly changing work force to coping with the ever-present scores of government regulations. Because of the critical nature of human resource problems, they are receiving increased attention from upper management. Therefore, the human resource executive who is able to deal effectively with those problems often becomes one of the firm's top managers.

Human resource managers develop and work through a human resource management system. Six functional areas are associated with effective human resource management. A major study conducted for the Personnel Accreditation Institute in 1988 confirmed that these areas reveal the way human resource positions are structured regarding knowledge requirements. Sound management practices are required for successful performance in each area. We discuss these functions next.

Human Resource Planning, Recruitment, and Selection

An organization must have qualified individuals in specific jobs at specific places and times in order to accomplish its goals. Obtaining such people involves **human resource planning**, recruitment, and selection.

Human resource planning (HRP) is the process of systematically reviewing human resource requirements to ensure that the required numbers of employees, with the required skills, are available when they are needed. Recruitment is the process of attracting such individuals in sufficient numbers and encouraging them to apply for jobs with the organization. Selection is the process through which the organization chooses, from a group of applicants, those individuals best suited both for open positions, and for the company. Successful accomplishment of these three tasks is vital if the plant is to become operational and accomplish its **mission**.

Human Resource Development

Human resource development (HRD) assists individuals, groups, and the entire organization in becoming more effective. Human resource development is needed because people, jobs, and organizations are always changing. The development process should begin when individuals join the firm and continue throughout their careers. Large-scale HRD programs are referred to as **organization development** (OD). The purpose of OD is to alter the environment within the firm to help employees perform more productively.

Other aspects of HRD include career planning and performance appraisal. Career planning is a process of setting human resource goals and establishing the means to achieve them. Individual careers and organizational needs are not separate and distinct. Organizations should assist employees in career planning so that the needs of both can be satisfied. Through performance appraisal, employees are evaluated to determine how well they are performing their assigned tasks. Performance appraisal affords employees the opportunity to capitalize on their strengths and overcome identified deficiencies, thereby becoming more satisfied and productive employees.

Throughout this text, but especially in the HRD chapters, we use the term "operative" workers or employees. Operative employees are all workers in an organization except managers and professionals such as engineers or accountants. Steel workers, secretaries, truck drivers, and waiters are examples of operative employees.

Compensation and Benefits

The question of what constitutes a fair day's **pay** has **plagued** management, unions, and workers for a long time. A well thought out **compensation** system provides employees with adequate and equitable rewards for their contributions to meeting organizational goals. Compensation includes all rewards that individuals receive as a result of their employment. The reward may be one or a combination of the following:

* ★ **Pay** The money that a person receives for performing a job.
* ★ **Benefits** Additional financial rewards other than base pay, such as paid vacations, sick leave, holidays, and medical insurance.
* ★ Nonfinancial **Nonmonetary rewards**, such as enjoyment of the work performed or a pleasant working environment.

Although compensation is defined as all rewards that individuals receive as a result of their employment, the increasing importance of benefits warrants separate treatment.

Safety and Health

Safety involves protecting employees from injuries caused by work-related accidents. Health refers to employees' freedom from illness and their general physical and mental well-being. These aspects of the job are important because employees who work in a safe environment and enjoy good health are more likely to be productive and yield long-term benefits to the organization. For this reason, progressive managers have long advocated and put in place adequate safety and health programs. Today, because of federal and state legislation, which reflects societal concerns, most organizations have become attentive to their employees' safety and health.

Employee and Labor Relations

In 1987, unions represented 17 percent of all nonfarm workers. By the year 2000, unions will likely represent only 13 percent of all nonfarm workers. Even so, a business firm is required by law to recognize a union and bargain with it in good faith, if the firm's employees want the union to represent them. In the past, this relationship was an accepted way of life for many employers. But according to a recent Conference Board survey of labor-management relations, preventing the spread of unionism and developing effective employee relations systems are now more important to some managers than achieving sound collective bargaining results.

As Judy Lynley, industrial relations manager for Axton Pneumotives, discovered, dealing with a union often presents difficult problems. During the stressful bargaining process, Judy may have tended to agree with the Conference Board survey conclusion. The union placed her in a difficult position: if the workers walk off the job, production steps; agreeing to all the union's demands may result in pricing the firm's products out of the market. Judy must be a skilled negotiator to solve these problems. When a labor union represents a firm's employees, the human resource activity is often referred to as industrial relations.

Human resource managers in union-free organizations are often quite knowledgeable about union goals and activities. Such organizations typically strive to satisfy all reasonable employee work-related needs. Employees often conclude that a union isn't necessary for them to achieve their personal goals. Remaining union free requires a strong commitment by management and a freely communicative and open environment. In many ways, the commitment necessary to maintain a union-free environment is more demanding on the human resources department than is working in a unionized environment. Organizations that do not make and maintain that commitment are vulnerable to union organizing efforts. The old maxim is still true: "Unions don't organize employees, managers do"—through mistakes, neglect, and, unfortunately, plain greed. The human resource manager, therefore, must create and manage an employee relations system that treats employees positively. The system should allow each individual worker to maintain his or her **self-esteem** and grow individually within the organization.

Glossary

utilization *n.*   making (good) use of 利用;使用

mesh *v.*   to connect; be held (together) 接合;相合

representative *n.*   a person acting in place of another person or a group of people 代表;代理

capital *n.*   (a sum of) money used for starting a business 资金

primary *a.*   chief; main 主要的

supervisor *n.*   one who is in charge of a particular department or unit, as in a governmental agency or school system 监督;管理人员

cosmetic *n.*   a preparation such as a face-cream, body-powder, etc., intended to make the skin or hair more beautiful 化妆品

substantive *a.*   important, serious, or related to real facts

insight *n.*   the power of using one's mind to understand something deeply, without help from outside information 洞察力;见识

catalyst *n.*   a person or thing that causes or speeds change 有催化作用的人或物

energizer *n.*   something or somebody that gives energy to 使……活跃的人或物

quit *v.*   *infml* to stop (doing something) and leave (非正式)停止;辞职

recruitment *n.*   the process of finding people to work for a company or become a new member of an organization 招聘,招工

mission *n.*   a group of people, esp. people acting for their country, who are sent abroad for special reason; the duty or purpose for which these people are sent 使团,代表团;任务,使命

plague *v.*   to cause continual discomfort, suffering, or trouble to; to make rather angry 折磨,烦恼;使得灾祸

compensation *n.*   money and other benefits that an employee receives for doing their job 报酬(雇员获得的金钱和其他福利的总和)

self-esteem *n.*   one's good or too good opinion of one's own worth 自尊(心);自大,自负

Key Terms and Concepts

Human resource management（HRM）：Utilization of human resources to achieve organizational objectives. 人力资源管理

Human resource manager：An individual who normally acts in an advisory（staff） capacity when working with other （line）managers regarding human resource matters. 人力资源经理

Human resource planning（HRP）：The process of systematically reviewing human resource requirements to ensure that the required numbers of employees，with the required skills，are available when they are needed. 人力资源规划

Pay：The money that a person receives for performing a job. 工资、薪水

Benefits：Additional financial rewards other than base pay，such as paid vacations，sick leave，holidays，and medical insurance. 财务性奖励

Nonmonetary rewards：Such as enjoyment of the work performed or a pleasant working environment. 非财务性奖励

Exercises

I. Discussion and Review Questions.

1. Who are "line" managers? Why? Can you give an example?

2. What are differences between "human resource manager" and "personnel manager"?

3. What is the human resource manager primarily responsible for? What does Jane Kay state?

4. Can you describe the distinction between human resource management and the human resource manager according to the text?

5. What problems does the human resource manager face? Why are they receiving increased attention from upper management?

6. What is human resource planning(HRP)，recruitment，and selection?

7. Why is human resource development(HRD) needed? And when should the development process begin?

8. What does the compensation include according to the text?

9. What is safety and health? Why have most organizations become attentive to their employees' safety and health?

10. What does human resource managers in union-free organizations often do?

career	appraisal	advisory	utilization	expand	catalyst

1. Human resource management (HRM) is the _____ of human resources to achieve organizational objectives.

2. A human resource manager is an individual who normally acts in a(n) _____, or "staff" capacity, working with other managers to help them deal with human resource matters.

3. The human resource manager acts more in an advisory capacity, but should be a(n) _____ in proposing human relations policies to be implemented by line managers.

4. Today's human resource problems are enormous and appear to be ever _____.

5. _____ planning is a process of setting human resource goals and establishing the means to achieve them.

6. Through performance _____, employees are evaluated to determine how well they are performing their assigned tasks.

1. utilization — a. something or somebody that gives energy to
2. mesh — b. one who is in charge of a particular department or unit, as in a governmental agency or school system
3. representative — c. a person acting in place of another person or a group of people
4. capital — d. to connect; be held (together)
5. supervisor — e. (infml) to stop (doing something) and leave
6. substantive — f. (a sum of) money used for starting a business
7. insight — g. important, serious, or related to real facts
8. catalyst — h. a person or thing that causes or speeds change
9. energizer — i. the power of using one's mind to understand something deeply, without help from outside information
10. quit — j. making (good) use of

1. The field of human resource management changed dramatically during the 1970s, in ways that created a greatly expanded role for the human resource

manager.（　）

2. The human resource manager is primarily responsible for coordinating the management of human resources to help the organization achieve its goals.（　）

3. Large-scale HRD programs are referred to as management development（MD）.（　）

4. Operative employees are all workers in an organization.（　）

5. Health refers to employees' freedom from illness and their general physical well-being.（　）

V. Translate the following into Chinese.

Every human resource management function needs effective research. For instance，research may be conducted to determine the type of workers who will be most successful，or it may be aimed at determining the causes of certain work-related accidents. Numerous quantitative methods are used in human resource research. This function will become increasingly important because，as the work environment becomes more complex，the value of timely and accurate information increases dramatically.

The functional areas of HRM are not separate and distinct; they are highly interrelated. Management must recognize that decisions in one area will have impacts on other areas—and what those impacts are likely to be. For instance，a firm that emphasizes recruiting and training a sales force while neglecting to provide adequate compensation is wasting time，effort，and money. In addition，if management is truly concerned about employee welfare，it must ensure a safe and healthy work environment. An added benefit may be keeping the firm union free. The interrelationships among the HRM functional areas will become more obvious to you as we address each topic in greater detail.

VI. Translate the following into English.

1. 人力资源规划（HRP）是一个系统地掌握人力资源需求，以确保需要时能得到足够数量的、具有合格技能的雇员的过程。

2. 人员招聘是一个吸引足够数量的雇员并鼓励他们申请该组织的工作的过程。

3. 人员选择是从一组申请人中选择出最适合该职位且最适合该公司的雇员的过程。

4. 通过绩效评估，评价出雇员完成受指派任务的优劣程度。

Supplemental Reading Material

Environmental Factors Affecting Human Resource Management

Many interrelated factors affect human resource management. Such factors are part of either the firm's external environment or its internal environment. The firm often has little, if any, control over how the external environment affects management of its human resources. These factors impinge on the organization from outside its boundaries. Moreover important factors within the firm itself also have an impact on how the firm manages its human resources.

Certain interrelationships tend to complicate the management of human resources. Understanding the many interrelationships is essential in order for the human resource professional to help other managers resolve issues and problems. For instance, a production manager may want to give a substantial pay raise to a particular employee. The human resource manager may know that this employee does an exceptional job but should also be aware that granting the raise may affect pay practices in the production department and set a precedent for the entire firm. The human resource manager may have to explain to the production manager that such an action isn't an isolated decision. They may have to consider alternative means of rewarding the employee for superior performance, without upsetting the organization's reward system. Perhaps the human resource manager can point to a higher paying position that the employee is qualified to fill.

◆ THE EXTERNAL ENVIRONMENT

Those factors that affect a firm's human resources from outside its boundaries comprise the external environment. External factors include: the labor force, legal considerations, society, unions, shareholders, competition, customers, and technology. Each—either separately or in combination with others—can place constraints on the human resource manager's job. Thus the HR manager must always try to identify and consider the impact of such factors.

The Labor Force

The capabilities of its employees determine in a large part how well an organization can perform its mission. The labor force is a pool of individuals external to the firm, from which the organization obtains its workers. To some degree, as the labor force changes so will the composition of the work force within the organization. And today's labor force is far different from that of the past.

The projected size of the U. S. labor force in 1995 is about 129 million. This projection represents an increase of about 14 percent from the 1984 level of 114 million. The labor force now includes more working women and older persons.

Companies increasingly hire part-time workers, use temporary and "leased employees", and include disabled people in their workforces. Many new immigrants from developing areas, especially Southeast Asia and Latin America, are also joining the labor force. The breakdown of new entrants in the labor force from 1985 to 2000 are expected to be U. S. born white males, 15 percent; U. S. born white females, 42 percent; U. S. born nonwhite males, 7 percent; U. S. born nonwhite females, 13 percent; immigrant males, 13 percent; and immigrant females, 10 percent.

Women in the Labor Force. Through the mid-1990s, the chief cause of labor-force growth will be the continued, though slower, rise in the number of women seeking jobs. Women are expected to account for more than three fifths of the labor-force growth between 1984 and 1995. As the number of women entering the labor force continues to increase, their problems are becoming of greater concern to human resource managers. In spite of progress made in adapting the workplace to working mothers, most of them must still personally resolve the problems that their working creates.

Older Workers. The U.S. population grew older through the 1980s, a trend which will continue at least through the year 2000. The reason is that the baby-boom generation—born from the end of World War II through 1964—has had only half as many children as their parents did. And life expectancy continues to increase. The trend toward earlier retirement reversed itself in the mid-1980s. Today, many older persons don't want to retire or even to slow down. Some desire semiretirement, preferring part-time work or a less demanding full-time job.

Part-Time Workers. More and more organizations employ part-time workers. In fact, it has been estimated that part-time workers were the fastest growing segment of the workforce after 1970. The use of part-time workers offers a number of advantages. First, it allows access to employees who are available only during certain hours or for a limited number of hours per week. For example, women with small children sometimes work part-time when their children are young. Students may schedule work around their class hours. Second, a company's less than full time need for a skilled person may be filled, saving on both salary and benefits. Third, part-time workers often are not provided with benefits, such as medical insurance and pension programs, thereby saving the company money. However, this advantage has eroded somewhat in recent years. Fourth, part-time workers usually think of their jobs as temporary, so they can be easily hired or laid off as work volume fluctuates. Fifth, if employers restrict employees with demanding family situations to full-time jobs only, the results might include absenteeism, personal business conducted in company time, or loss of good workers.

Temporary and "Leased" Employees. The need for traditional temporary employees increased after the mid 1980s, in part because more women, and a few men, were taking maternity and parenting leave. Also, the corporate takeover fever late in the decade caused many firms to cut work forces to bare minimums. They often filled gaps with temporaries.

A special case of temporary workers is leased employees. Leased employees are individuals provided by an outside firm at a fixed hourly rate, similar to a rental fee, often for extended periods. Employee leasing goes beyond the use of short-term "temps" furnished by such agencies as Kelly Services Inc., and Manpower Inc., to help companies through vacation periods and so forth.

Persons with Disabilities. According to one estimation, there are approximately 36 million disabled employees in the United States, not including mentally handicapped persons. A handicap, or disability, is a disadvantage that limits the amount or kind of work a person can do or makes its achievement unusually difficult.

Laws relating to handicapped workers generally define handicap or disability quite broadly. More common disabilities include limited hearing or sight, limited mobility, mental or emotional deficiencies, and various nerve disorders. Recent studies indicate that disabled workers do as well as the unimpaired in terms of productivity, attendance, and average tenure. In fact, in certain high-turnover occupations, disabled workers had lower turnover rates.

Legal Considerations

Another significant external force affecting human resource management relates to federal, state, and local legislation and the many court decisions interpreting this legislation. In addition, many presidential executive orders have had a major impact on human resource management. These legal considerations affect virtually the entire spectrum of human resource polices.

Society

Society may also exert pressure on human resource management. The public is no longer content to accept, without question, the actions of business. Individuals and special interest groups have found that they can effect change through their voices, votes, and other actions. The influence of activists is obvious by the large number of regulatory laws that have been passed since the early 1960s. To remain acceptable to the general public, a firm must accomplish its purpose while complying with societal norms.

A major point that management must consider is that society includes the firm's employees. For instance, if an organization has 10,000 employees, these individuals will influence a larger number of people who are not connected with the firm, including friends and members of an employee's family. Therefore, it behooves a firm to maintain clear and honest communications with its employees so that they understand and appreciate the firm's position.

The general public's attitude and beliefs can affect the firm's behavior, because those attitudes and beliefs often directly affect profitability. When a corporation behaves as if it has a conscience, it is said to be socially responsible. Social responsibility is the implied, enforced, or felt obligation of managers, acting in their official capacities, to serve or protect the interests of groups other than themselves. Many companies develop patterns of concern for moral and social issues. They do so through policy statements, practices, and the leadership of morally strong employees and managers over time. Open-door policies, grievance procedures, and employee benefit programs often stem as much from a desire to do what is right as from a concern for productivity and avoidance of strife.

Unions

Wage levels, benefits, and working conditions for millions of employees now reflect decisions made jointly by unions and management. A union is a group of employees who have joined together for the purpose of dealing with their employer. Unions are treated as an environmental factor because, essentially, they become a third party when dealing with the company. In a unionized organization, the union rather than the individual employee negotiates an agreement with management.

Shareholders

The owners of a corporation are called shareholders. Because shareholders have invested money in the firm, they may at times challenge programs considered by management to be beneficial to the organization. Managers may be forced to justify the merits of a particular program in terms of how it will affect future projects, costs, revenues, and profits. For instance, $50,000 spent on implementing a management development program may require more justification than saying, "Managers should become more open and adaptive to the needs of employees." Shareholders are concerned with how such expenditure decisions will increase revenues or decrease costs. Thus management must be prepared to explain the merits of a particular program in terms of its economic costs and benefits.

Competition

Unless an organization is in the unusual position of monopolizing the market it serves, other firms will be producing similar products or services. For a firm to succeed, grow, and prosper, it must maintain a supply of competent employees. But other organizations are also striving for that same objective. A firm's major task is to ensure that it obtains and retains a sufficient number of employees in various career fields to allow the firm to compete effectively. A bidding war often results when competitors attempt to fill certain critical positions in their firms. Because of the strategic nature of their needs, firms are sometimes forced to resort to unusual means to recruit and retain such employees.

Customers

The people who actually use a firm's goods and services also are part of its external environment. Because sales are crucial to the firm's survival, management has the task of ensuring that its employment practices do not antagonize the customers it serves. For example, consumer boycotts have been triggered by organizations that limited the number of minorities they employ. If a certain minority or ethnic group purchases a large share of the firm's products, the organization should look closely at including a representative proportion of this group in its workforce.

Customers constantly demand high-quality products and after-purchase service, Therefore, a firm's workforce should be capable of providing quality goods and services. Sales are often lost or gained because of variances in product quality and follow-up service. These conditions relate directly to the skills, qualifications, and motivations of the organization's employees.

Technology

The rate of technological change is accelerating, and as a result, few firms operate today as they did even a decade ago. Of major concern to those in HRM is the effect that technological changes have had, and will have on businesses. Frederick W. Bahl, director of human resource administration for Alumax, inc., believes that "during the next decade, the most challenging area in human resource management will be training employees to stay up with rapidly advancing technology". Products that were not envisioned only a few years ago are now being mass produced, substantially enlarging the tasks of all managers, including human resource managers. New skills are continually needed to meet new technological demands. These skills are typically not in large supply, and recruiting qualified individuals in these areas is often difficult.

◆ THE INTERNAL ENVIRONMENT

The internal environment also exerts considerable pressure on human resource management. Those factors that affect a firm's human resources from inside its boundaries comprise the internal environment. The primary internal factors include the firm's mission, policies, and corporate culture. These factors have a major impact in determining the interaction between HRM and other departments within the organization. This interaction has a major effect on overall organizational productivity, so it is vital that the interaction be positive and supportive of the firm's mission.

Mission

Mission is the organization's continuing purpose or reason for being. Each management level should operate with a clear understanding of the firm's mission. In fact, each organizational unit (division, plant, department) should have clearly understood objectives that coincide with that mission.

The specific company mission must be regarded as a major internal factor that affects the tasks of human resource management. Consider two companies, each having a broadly based mission and envision how certain tasks might differ from one firm to another. Company A's goal is to be an industry leader in technological advances. Its growth occurs through the pioneering of new products and processes. Company B's goal is one of conservative growth, with little risk taking. Only after another company's product or process has proven itself in the marketplace will Company B commit itself.

Policies

A policy is a predetermined guide established to provide direction in decision making. As guides, rather than hard and fast rules, policies are somewhat flexible, requiring interpretation and judgment in their use. They can exert significant influence on how managers accomplish their jobs. For instance, many firms have an "open door" policy, which permits an employee to take a problem to the next higher level in the organization if it can't be solved by the immediate supervisor. Knowing that their subordinates can take problems to a higher echelon tends to encourage supervisors to try harder to resolve problems at their level.

Many larger firms have policies related to every major operational area. Although policies are established for marketing, production, and finance, the largest number of policies often relate to human resource management. Some potential policy statements that affect human resource management are:
  ★ To provide employees with a safe place to work.
  ★ To encourage all employees to achieve as much of their human potential as possible.
  ★ To provide compensation that will encourage a high level of productivity in both quality and quantity.
  ★ To ensure that current employees are considered first for any vacant position for

which they may be qualified.

Corporate Culture

As an internal environmental factor affecting human resource management, corporate culture refers to the firm's social and psychological climate. Corporate culture is defined as the system of shared values, beliefs, and habits within an organization that interacts with the formal structure to produce behavioral norms. An infinite variety of cultures could exist, so we probably should view them as a continuum.

A closed and threatening culture is at one extreme. In this type of culture, decisions tend to be made at higher levels in the organization; management and subordinates lack trust and confidence in each other; secrecy abounds; and workers aren't encouraged to be creative and solve problems. At the other extreme is an open culture in which decisions tend to be made at lower levels in the organization; a high degree of trust and confidence exists between management and subordinates; communication is open; and workers are encouraged to be creative and to solve problems. In all likelihood, the exact nature of any particular corporate culture falls somewhere between these extremes. Regardless of its nature, identification of the corporate culture in a firm is important. It affects job performance throughout the organization and consequently affects profitability.

Discussion and Review Questions:
1. What is the importance of the human resource management (HRM) process?
2. What are the external factors that influence the HRM process?
3. What are the internal factors that influence the HRM process?
4. How does HRM affect all managers?
5. Give a concrete example of human resource management in reality.

Types of Marketing Research

Unit 12

Text

Marketing research provides information to reduce uncertainty. It helps focus decision-making. Sometimes marketing researchers know exactly what their marketing problems are and design careful studies to test specific **hypotheses**. For example, a soft drink company introducing a new clear cola might want to know whether a gold or silver label would make the packaging more effective. This problem is fully defined and an experiment may be designed to answer the marketing question with little preliminary investigation.

In more ambiguous circumstances management may be totally unaware of a marketing problem. For example, McDonald's may notice that Mo's Burgers, a competition in the Japanese market, introduced Mo's Roast Katsu Burger, a roast pork cutlet drenched in traditional Japanese Katsu sauce and topped with shredded cabbage. The managers may not understand much about Japanese consumers' feelings about this menu item. Ordinarily, mine **exploratory research** is necessary to gain insights into the nature of such a problem. To understand the variety of research activity, it is beneficial to categorize types of marketing research.

Marketing research can be **classified** on the basis of either technique or function. Experiments, surveys, and observational studies are just a few common research techniques. **Classifying** research by its purpose or function shows how the nature of the marketing problem influences the choice of methods. The nature of the problem will determine whether the research is (1) **exploratory**, (2) **descriptive**, or (3) **causal**.

Exploratory

Exploratory research is conducted to clarify the nature of ambiguous problems. Management may have discovered a general problem, but it may need research to gain a better understanding of the dimensions of the problem and to aid analysis.

Exploratory research is not intended to provide conclusive evidence from which to determine a particular course of action. Usually exploratory research is conducted with the expectation that subsequent research will be required to provide such conclusive evidence. Rushing into detailed surveys before less expensive and more readily available sources of information have been exhausted can lead to serious mistakes.

For example, suppose a Chinese fast-food restaurant chain is considering expanding its hours and product line with a breakfast menu, exploratory research with a small number of current customers might find a strong negative reaction to eating a spicy vegetable breakfast at a Chinese fast food outlet. Thus, exploratory research might help **crystallize** a problem and **identify** information needed for future research.

Descriptive Research

The major purpose of **descriptive research**, as the name implies, is to describe characteristics of a population. Marketing managers frequently need to determine who purchases a product, portray the size of the market, identify competitors' actions, and so on. Descriptive research seeks to determine the answers to *why*, *what*, *when*, *where*, *and how* questions.

Infiniti learned from descriptive research that Americans generally start to shop for a car by considering six models. They then narrow the field and usually visit three show rooms before they settle on a model. This takes an average of two weeks. However, buyers of luxury cars typically take twice as long to complete the decision and make a purchase. These descriptive findings, combined with knowledge that they faced competition from dozens of luxury models on the market, influenced Infiniti to encourage dealers to emphasize the quality of the consumer's shopping experience. The company made sizable investments in dramatic architecture for showrooms and elegant furnishings such as fountains and indoor bridges. Some Infiniti showrooms have **contemplation** zones—designated areas where customers can sit without harassment to consider car purchases in Zenlike silence.

Magazines typically conduct descriptive surveys to identify the characteristics of their audience. For years *Teen* magazine managers sensed that 12-to-15-year-old girls cared a lot about fragrance, lipstick, and mascara, but they lacked any quantitative evidence. Their descriptive research found that 94.1 percent of 12-to-15-year old girls use cream rinse/conditioner, 86.4 percent use fragrance, and 84.9 percent use lipgloss. Of the girls using fragrance, 73 percent preferred using their own brand, 17 percent shared their brand, and 6 percent used someone else's brand. Results showed that most girls use cosmetics. Brand loyalty begins early, and 12-to-15-year-olds prefer using and choosing their own brands.

Accuracy is of **paramount** importance in descriptive research. While they cannot completely eliminate errors, good researchers strive for descriptive precision. Suppose a study seeks to describe the market potential for personal photocopying machines. If the study does not precisely measure sales volume, it will mislead the managers who are making production scheduling, budgeting, and other decisions based on it.

Unlike exploratory research, descriptive studies are based on some previous understanding of the nature of the research problem. Although the researcher may have a general understanding of the situation, the conclusive evidence that answers questions of fact necessary to determine a course of action has yet to be collected.

Many circumstances require descriptive research to identify the reasons consumers give to explain the nature of things. In other words, a **diagnostic** analysis is performed when consumers answer questions such as "Why do you feel that way?". Although they may describe why consumers feel a certain way, the findings of a descriptive study such as this, sometimes called diagnostic, do not provide causal evidence. Frequently, descriptive research attempts to determine the extent of differences in needs, attitudes, and opinions among subgroups.

Causal Research

The main goal of **causal research** is to identify cause and effect relationships between variables. Exploratory and descriptive research normally precede cause-and-effect relationship studies. In causal studies researchers typically have an expectation about the relationship to be explained, such as **predicting** the influence of price, packaging, advertising, and the like on sales. Thus, researchers must be quite knowledgeable about the subject. Ideally the manager wants to establish that one event (say, a new package) is the means for producing another event (an increase in sales). Causal research attempts to establish that when we do one thing, another thing will follow. The word cause is common in everyday conversation, but from a scientific research perspective, a true causal relationship is impossible to prove. Nevertheless, researchers seek certain types of evidence to help them understand and predict relationships.

A typical causal study has management change one variable (for example, advertising) and then observe the effect on another variable (such as sales). Some evidence for causality comes from the fact that the cause precedes the effect. In other words, having an appropriate causal order of events, or temporal sequence, is one criterion for causality that must be met to be able to measure a relationship. If a consumer behavior theorist wishes to show that an attitude change causes a behavior change, one criterion that must be established is that attitude change must precede the behavior change in time.

In the above example, some evidence of **concomitant variation** exists because advertising and sales appear to be associated. Concomitant variation occurs when two phenomena or events vary together. When the criterion of concomitant variation is not met—that is, when there is no association between the variables—reasoning suggests that no causal relationship exists. If two events vary together, one event may be the cause; however, this by itself is not sufficient evidence for causality because the two events may have a common cause; that is, both may be influenced by a third variable. For instance, a large number of ice cream cones were sold one morning at Atlantic City's beach. That afternoon, a large number of drowning occurred. Most of us would not conclude that eating ice cream causes drowning; more likely, on that day the beach was crowded and the number of people probably influenced both ice cream sales and drowning. The effect could have been produced in other ways. Thus, causation requires more than concomitant variation and a proper time sequence between the occurrences of two events. There may be plausible **alternative** explanations for the observed relationship. A **plurality** of causes is possible.

Consider a presidential candidate who reduces advertising expenditures near the end of the primary campaign race and wins many mom delegates in the remaining primaries. To infer causality that reducing advertising increased the number of delegates might be inappropriate，because the presumed cause of the increase in delegates may not have been the real cause；it is more likely that near the end of the race，**marginal** candidates withdrew. The real cause probably was unrelated to advertising.

In these examples the third variable that is the source of the **spurious** association is a very **salient** factor readily identifiable as the true influence of change. However，within the complex environment in which managers operate，identifying **alternative** or complex causal facts can be difficult.

In summary，research to infer causality should：

1. Establish the appropriate causal order or sequence of events.

2. Measure the concomitant variation between the presumed cause and the presumed effect.

3. Recognize the presence or absence of alternative plausible explanations or causal factors.

Even when these three criteria for causation are present，the researcher can never be certain that the causal explanation is adequate.

Most basic scientific studies in marketing（for example，the development of consumer behavior theory）ultimately seek to identify cause-and-effect relationships. One often associates science with experiments. To predict a relationship between，say，price and perceived quality of a product，causal studies often create statistical experiments with controls that establish contrast groups. A number of marketing experiments are conducted by both theory developers and **pragmatic** business people.

Glossary

hypothesis   *n.*   an idea which is thought suitable to explain the facts about something 假设；假说

classify   *v.*   to arrange or place (animals, plants, books, etc.) into classes; divide according to class 分类；归类

exploratory   *a.*   (of an action) done in order to learn something (指某一措施,举动)探索的；探险的

descriptive   *a.*   that describes 叙述的；描写的

causal   *a.*   of, relating to, or constituting a cause 原因的；因果关系的；表示原因或理由的

crystallize   *v.*   to (cause to) become clear, settled, or fixed in form (使)具体化；使变得明确；定形

identify   *v.*   to recognize someone or something or distinguish them from others 认出，识别

contemplation   *n.*   the act of thinking deeply and quietly; deep thought 思考；沉思

paramount   *a.*   *fml* great above all others; highest in power or importance (正式)至上的；最重要的；最高权力的

diagnostic   *a.*   of or relating to diagnosing 诊断的

predict   *v.*   to see or describe (a future happening) in advance as a result of knowledge, experience, reason, etc. 预言；预测

concomitant   *a.*   *fml* existing or happening together (with something else) (正式)伴随而来的；并存的；连带的

alternative   *a.*   (of two things) that may be used, had, done, etc., instead of another; other (两物中)可用来代替另一个的；其他的

plurality   *n.*   the state of being plural 复数

marginal   *a.*   won or lost by a small number of votes 以少数选票差距取胜或失败的

spurious   *a.*   like something else but falsely so 疑似的；假的

salient *a.*   standing out most noticeably or importantly 显著的；突出的

pragmatic *a.*   dealing with matters in the way that seems best under the actual conditions，rather than following a general principle；practical 实际的；实用主义的

Key Terms and Concepts

Exploratory research：Initial research conducted to clarify and define the nature of problem. 探索性研究

Descriptive research：Research designed to describe characteristics of a population or phenomenon. 描述性研究

Causal research：Research conducted to identify cause-and-effect relationships among variables. 因果关系研究

Concomitant variation：The way in which two phenomena or events vary together. 相随变量，共变因素

Exercises

I. Discussion and Review Questions

1. Sometimes marketing researchers know exactly what their marketing problems are and design careful studies to test specific hypotheses. Can you give an example to explain that?

2. Classify marketing research.

3. What is exploratory research? Can you give an example?

4. What is the major purpose of descriptive research? And what does descriptive research seek to determine?

5. Why is accuracy of paramount importance in descriptive research?

6. Frequently，what does descriptive research attempt to determine?

7. What is the main goal of causal research?

8. What expectation do the researchers typically have in causal studies?

9. Can you give an example to explain that "a typical causal study has management change one variable and then observe the effect on another variable"?

10. What do most basic scientific studies in marketing ultimately seek to identify in causal research?

II. Vocabulary Review: Without referring to the text, fill in the blanks in the following sentences with the correct words from this list. You may change the tense, number, or form of the words to fit the context. Use each word only once.

information	accuracy	function	technique	third	statistical
characteristic	cause	observe	exploratory	conclusive	

1. Marketing research provides _____ to reduce uncertainty.

2. Marketing research can be classified on the basis of either _____ or _____.

3. _____ research is conducted to clarify the nature of ambiguous problems.

4. Usually exploratory research is conducted with the expectation that subsequent research will be required to provide such _____ evidence.

5. The major purpose of descriptive research, as the name implies, is to describe _____ of a population.

6. _____ is of paramount importance in descriptive research.

7. The main goal of causal research is to identify _____ and effect relationships between variables.

8. A typical causal study has management change one variable (for example, advertising) and then _____ the effect on another variable (such as sales).

9. If two events vary together, one event may be the cause; however, this by itself is not sufficient evidence for causality because the two events may have a common cause; that is, both may be influenced by a(n) _____ variable.

10. Causal studies often create _____ experiments with controls that establish contrast groups.

III. Match the terms and expressions on the left with the explanations on the right.

1. hypothesis   a. dealing with matters in the way that seems best under the actual conditions, rather than following a general principle; practical

2. classify   b. to arrange or place (animals, plants, books, etc.) into classes; divide according to class

3. exploratory   c. of or relating to diagnosing

4. descriptive   d. (of an action) done in order to learn something

5. causal   e. to see or describe (a future happening) in advance as a result of knowledge, experience, reason, etc.

6. identify   f. that describes

7. diagnostic   g. to recognize someone or something or distinguish them from others

8. predict   h. (*fml*) existing or happening together (with something

else）

9. concomitant   i. an idea which is thought suitable to explain the facts about something

10. pragmatic   j. of，relating to，or constituting a cause

IV. True and False statements.

1. Exploratory research is intended to provide conclusive evidence from which to determine a particular course of action.（　　）

2. Causal research seeks to determine the answers to *why*，*what*，*when*，*where*，and *how* questions.（　　）

3. While they cannot completely eliminate errors，good researchers strive for descriptive precision.（　　）

4. Like exploratory research，descriptive studies are based on some previous understanding of the nature of the research problem.（　　）

5. When the three criteria for causation are present，the researcher can never be certain that the causal explanation is adequate.（　　）

V. Translate the following into Chinese.

Earlier we discussed some of the managerial benefits of marketing research. Of course，conducting research to obtain these benefits requires expenditure. There are both costs and benefits to conducting marketing research. In any decision-making situation managers must identify alternative courses of action，then weigh the value of each alternative against its costs. Marketing research can be thought of as an investment alternative. When deciding whether to make a decision without research or to postpone the decision in order to conduct research，managers should ask three questions.（1）Will the payoff or rate of return be worth the investment?（2）Will the information gained by marketing research improve the quality of the marketing decision enough to warrant the expenditure?（3）Is the proposed research expenditure the best use of the available funds?

VI. Translate the following into English.

1. 市场营销研究的需求决策取决于：（1）时间的限制，（2）资料的可获得性，（3）决策的性质和（4）与成本比较的信息价值。

2. 从事跨国商业的组织常常发现，当要调查的地域是一个发展中国家时，那些在美国可得到的丰富的商业活动和人口特性数据是不存在的或是贫乏的。

3. 一个不需要大量投资的常规性战术决策可能无法证明将大量经费用于市场营销研究的必要性。

4. 总的来说，战略上的或战术上的决策越重要，实施市场营销研究就越必要。

Supplemental Reading Material

When Is Marketing Research Needed?

Marketing managers confronted with two or more alternative courses of action face the initial decision of whether or not to conduct marketing research. The determination of the need for marketing research centers on (1) time constraints, (2) the availability of data, (3) the nature of the decision to be made, and (4) the value of the research information in relation to costs.

Time Constraints

Systematic research takes time. In many instances management will believe that a decision must be made immediately, allowing no time for research. Decisions sometimes are made without adequate information or thorough understanding of market situations. Although not ideal, sometimes the urgency of a situation precludes the use of research.

Availability of Data

Often managers already possess enough information to make sound decisions with no marketing research. When they lack adequate information, however, research must be considered. Managers must ask themselves. Will the research provide the information needed to answer the basic questions about this decision? Further, if a potential source of data exists, managers will want to know how much it will cost to obtain those data.

If the data cannot be made available, research cannot be conducted. Organizations engaged in international business often find that data about business activity or population characteristics found in abundance when investigating the United States are nonexistent or sparse when the geographic area of interest is a developing country. Imagine the problems facing marketing researchers who wish to investigate market potential in places like the Czech Republic, Yugoslavian Macedonia and other emerging countries.

Nature of the Decision

The value of marketing research will depend on the nature of the managerial decision to be made. A routine tactical decision that does not require a substantial investment may not seem to warrant a substantial expenditure for marketing research. For example, a computer company must update its operator's instruction manual when it makes minor product modifications. The research cost of determining the proper wording for updating the manual is likely to be too high for such a minor decision. The nature of the decision is not totally independent of the next issue to be considered: the benefits versus the costs of the research. In general, however, the more strategically or tactically important the decision, the more likely research will be conducted.

Benefits vs. Costs

Earlier we discussed some of the managerial benefits of marketing research. Of course, conducting research to obtain these benefits requires expenditure. There are both costs and benefits to conducting marketing research. In any decision-making situation managers must identify alternative courses of action, then weigh the value of each alternative against its costs. Marketing research can be thought of as an investment alternative. When deciding whether to make a decision without research or to postpone the decision in order to conduct research, managers should ask three questions. (1) Will the payoff or rate of return be worth the investment? (2) Will the information gained by marketing research improve the quality of the marketing decision enough to warrant the expenditure? (3) Is the proposed research expenditure the best use of the available funds?

For example, *TV-Cable Week* was not test marketed before its launch. Although the magazine had articles and stories about TV personalities and events, its main feature was program listings, channel by channel, showing the exact programs that a particular subscriber could receive. To produce a custom magazine for each individual cable TV system in the country required developing a costly computer system. Since the development necessitated a substantial expenditure. One that could not be scaled down for research, conducting research was judged to be an improper investment. The value of the research information was not positive, because the cost of the information exceeded its benefits, unfortunately. Pricing and distribution problems became so compelling after the magazine was launched that the product was a marketing failure. Nevertheless, managers, without the luxury of hindsight, made a reasonable decision not to conduct research. They analyzed the cost of the information (that is, the cost of test marketing) relative to the potential benefits of the information.

For projects that require considerable investment, the decision whether to conduct research may be made using the Bayesian statistical method for decision-making. This advanced technique requires that the decision maker estimate the probabilities and payoffs associated with each alternative (in this case, making the final decision with or without research).

Discussion and Review Questions:

1. What factors determine whether marketing research is needed?
2. Under what circumstances should not marketing research be conducted?
3. Which types of decisions require marketing research?
4. When deciding whether to make a decision without research or to postpone the decision in order to conduct research, which three questions do managers ask?
5. For projects that require considerable investment, which statistical method can be used to make decisions?

Defining Customer Value and Satisfaction

Text

More than 35 years ago, Peter Drunker insightfully observed that a company's first task is "to create customers". However, creating customers can be a difficult task. Today's customers face a vast **array** of product and brand choices, prices, and suppliers. The company must answer a key question: How do customers make their choices?

The answer is that customers choose the marketing offer that gives them the most value. Customers are value-maximizers, within the bounds of search costs and limited knowledge, **mobility** and income. They form expectations of value and act upon them. Then they **compare** the actual value they receive in consuming the product to the value expected, and this affects their satisfaction and repurchases behavior. We will now examine the concepts of customer value and customer satisfaction more carefully.

Customer Value

Consumers buy from the firm that they believe offers the highest **customer delivered value**— the difference between **total customer value** and **total customer cost** (see Exhibit 13.1). For example, suppose that a large construction firm wants to buy a **bulldozer** to use in residential construction work. It wants a reliable, **durable** bulldozer that performs well. It can buy the bulldozer from either Caterpillar or Komatsu. The sales people for the two companies carefully describe their respective offers to the buyer.

Exhibit 13.1 Customer Delivered Value

	Total customer value	(Product, services, personnel, and image values)
Minus	Total customer cost	(Monetary, time, energy, and psychic costs)
Equals	Customer delivered value	("Profit" to the consumer)

The construction firm now evaluates the two competing bulldozer offers to assess which one offers the greatest value. It adds all the values from four sources—product, services, personnel, and image. First, it judges that Caterpillar's bulldozer provides higher reliability, durability, and performance. It also decides that Caterpillar has better **accompanying** services—delivery, training, and maintenance. The customer views Caterpillar personnel as more knowledgeable and responsive. Finally, it places higher value on Caterpillar's reputation. Thus, the customer decides that Caterpillar offers more total customer value than does Komatsu.

Does the construction firm buy the Caterpillar bulldozer? Not necessarily. The firm also will examine the total customer cost of buying Caterpillar's bulldozer versus Komatsu's. First, the buyer will compare the prices it must pay for each of the competitors' products. If Caterpillar's bulldozer costs a lot more than Komatsu's does, the higher price might **offset** the higher total customer value. Moreover, total customer cost consists of more than just monetary costs. As Adam Smith observed more than two centuries ago, "The real price of anything is the toil and trouble of acquiring it." Total customer cost also includes the buyer's **anticipated** time, energy, and psychic costs. The construction firm will evaluate these costs along with monetary costs to form a complete estimate of its costs.

The buying firm now compares total customer value to total customer cost and determines the total delivered value associated with Caterpillar's bulldozer. In the same way, it assesses the total delivered value for the Komatsu bulldozer. The firm then will buy from the competitor that offers the highest delivered value.

How can Caterpillar use this concept of buyer decision making to help it succeed in selling its bulldozer to this buyer? Caterpillar can improve its offer in three ways. First, Caterpillar can increase total customer value by improving product, services, personnel, or image benefits. Second, Caterpillar can reduce the buyer's **nonmonetary** costs by lessening the buyer's time, energy, and psychic costs. Third, Caterpillar can reduce the buyer's monetary costs by lowering its price, providing easier terms of sale, or, in the longer term, lowering its bulldozer's operating or maintenance costs.

Suppose Caterpillar carries out a customer value **assessment** and concludes that buyers see Caterpillar's offer as worth $200,000. Further suppose that it costs Caterpillar $140,000 to produce the bulldozer. This means that Caterpillar's offer potentially generates $60,000 ($200,000 minus $140,000) of total added value. Caterpillar needs to price its bulldozer between $140,000 and $200,000. If it charges less than $140,000, it won't cover its costs. If it charges more than $200,000, the price will exceed the total customer value. The price Caterpillar charges will determine how much of the total added value will be delivered to the buyer and how much will flow to Caterpillar charges $190,000; it will grant only $10,000 of total added value to the customer and keep $50,000 for itself as profit. Naturally, the lower Caterpillar's price, the higher the delivered value of its offer will be and, therefore, the higher the customer's incentive to purchase from Caterpillar. Delivered value should be viewed as "profit to the customer". Given that Caterpillar wants to win the sale, it must offer more delivered value than Komatsu does.

Some marketers might rightly argue that this concept of how buyers choose among product alternatives is too rational. They might cite examples in which buyers did not choose the offer with an objectively measured highest delivered value. For example, suppose that the Caterpillar salesperson convinces the construction firm that, considering the benefits relative to the purchase price, Caterpillar's bulldozer offer with an objectively measured highest delivered value. The customer still might decide to buy the Komatsu bulldozer. Why would the buyer make this **apparent** nonvalue-maximizing purchase? There are many possible explanations. For example, perhaps the construction firm's buyers enjoy a long-term friendship with the Komatsu salesperson. Or the firm's buyers might be under strict company orders to buy at the lowest price. Or perhaps the construction firm rewards its buyers for short-term performance, causing them to choose the less expensive Komatsu bulldozer, even though the Caterpillar machine will perform better and be less expensive to operate in the long run.

Clearly, buyers operate under various constraints and sometimes make choices that give more weight to their personal benefit than to company benefit. However, the customer-delivered-value framework applies to many situations and yields rich insights. The framework suggests that sellers must first assess the total customer value and total customer cost associated with their own and competing marketing offers to determine how their own offers measure up in terms of customer delivered value. If a seller finds that competitors deliver greater value, it has two alternatives. It can try to increase total customer value by strengthening or **augmenting** the product, services, personnel, or image benefits of the offer. Or it can decrease total customer cost by reducing its price and simplifying the ordering and delivery process.

Customer Satisfaction

Thus, consumers form judgments about the value of marketing offers and make their buying decisions based upon these judgments. Customer satisfaction with a purchase depends on the product's performance relative to a buyer's expectations. A customer might experience various degrees of satisfaction. If the product's performance falls short of expectations, the customer is **dissatisfied**. If performance matches expectations, the customer is satisfied. If performance exceeds expectations, the customer is highly satisfied or delighted.

But how do buyers form their expectation? Expectations are based on the customer's past buying experiences, the opinions of friends and associates, and marketer and competitor information and promises. Marketers must be careful to set the right level of expectations. If they set expectations too low, they may satisfy those who buy but fail to attract enough buyers. In contrast, if they raise expectations too high, buyers are likely to be disappointed. For example, Holiday Inn ran a campaign a few years ago called "No Surprises", which promised **consistently** trouble-free accommodations and service. However, Holiday Inn guests still encountered a lot of problems, and the expectations created by the campaign only made customers more dissatisfied. Holiday Inn had to withdraw the campaign.

Still, some of today's most successful companies are raising expectations—and delivering performance to match. These companies embrace total customer satisfaction. For example, Honda claims, "One reason our customers are so satisfied is that we aren't." And Cigna **vows** "We'll never be 100 percent satisfied until you are, too." These companies aim high because they know that customers who are only satisfied will still find it easy to **switch** suppliers when a better offer comes along. For example, a study by AT&T showed that 70 percent of customers who say they are satisfied with a product or service would still be willing to switch to a competitor. In contrast, customers who are highly satisfied are much less ready to switch. One study showed that 75 percent of Toyota buyers were highly satisfied and about 75 percent said they intended to buy a Toyota again. Thus, customer delight creates an emotional **affinity** for a product or service, not just a rational preference, and this creates high customer loyalty.

Today's winning companies track their customers' expectations, perceived company performance, and customer satisfaction. However, customer satisfaction measures are meaningful only in a competitive context. For example, a company might be pleased to find that 80 percent of its customers say they are satisfied with its products. However, if a competitor is attaining 90 percent customer satisfaction and aiming for 100 percent, the company may find that it is losing customers to the competitor. Thus, companies must **monitor** both their own and competitors' customer satisfaction performance.

Glossary

array *n.*   an impressively large number, as of persons or objects 令人瞩目的大数量,如人或物

mobility *n.*   the quality or state of being mobile 易动性,易动的性质或状态

compare *v.*   to draw comparisons 比较,区别

durable *a.*   lasting; stable 持久的;稳定的

bulldozer *n.*   a heavy, driver-operated machine for pushing earth and stones away and for making areas of ground flat, usually having continuous treads and a broad hydraulic blade in front 推土机,用来清除和平整土方的、重型的、由驾驶员操作的机器,常有连续的履带,前部有宽的液压铲刀

accompanying *a.*   appearing or going with someone or something else 陪伴的,附随的

offset *v.*   to counterbalance, counteract, or compensate for 平衡、中和或补偿

anticipated *a.*   expected or looked-forward to 预先的

nonmonetary *a.*   not relating to money or consisting of money 非货币的,非金融的

assessment *n.*   the act of assessing; appraisal 评估,估价,估价的行为;评估

apparent *a.*   readily understood; clear or obvious 显然的;明明白白的

augment *v.*   to make (something already developed or well under way) greater, as in size, extent, or quantity 扩大,增加,加强,使(已经发展的或稳妥进行的事物)在尺寸、程度或数量方面增大

dissatisfied *a.*   feeling or exhibiting a lack of contentment or satisfaction 不满意的

consistently *ad.*   in a way that does not change 一贯地,一向,始终如一地

vow *v.*   to declare or assert 宣称或断言

switch *v.*   to shift, transfer, or divert 转变、转移或改换

affinity *n.*   a natural attraction or feeling of kinship 共鸣,吸引,自然的吸引或亲密的感情

monitor *v.*   to test or sample on a regular or ongoing basis 定期或持续地测试或进行抽样调查

Key Terms and Concepts

Customer delivered value: The consumer's assessment of the product's overall capacity to satisfy his or her needs. The difference between total customer value and total customer cost of a marketing offer—"profit" to the customer. 顾客让渡价值

Total customer value: The total of all of the product，services，personnel，and image values that a buyer receives from a marketing offer. 总顾客价值

Total customer cost: The total of all the monetary，time，energy，and psychic costs associated with a marketing offer. 总顾客成本

Exercises

I. Discussion and Review Questions.

1. What do customers have to face today?
2. How do customers make their choices?
3. What is customer value?
4. What is customer satisfaction?
5. Cite an example for customer value.
6. What does customer satisfaction with a purchase depend upon?
7. How do buyers form their expectation?
8. Must companies monitor both their own and competitors' customer satisfaction performance?

II. Vocabulary Review: Without referring to the text，fill in the blanks in the following sentences with the correct words from this list. You may change the tense，number，or form of the words to fit the context. Use each word only once; not all of the words on the list will be used.

| affinity | mobility | accompanying | assessment | dissatisfied | monitor |
| array | compare | anticipate | augment | vow | |

1. Today's customers face a vast _____ of product and brand choices，prices，and suppliers.

2. Customers are value-maximizers，within the bounds of search costs and limited knowledge，_____ ，and income.

3. Total customer cost also includes the buyer's _____ time，energy，and psychic costs.

4. Suppose Caterpillar carries out a customer value _____ and concludes that buyers see Caterpillar's offer as worth $200,000.

5. It can try to increase total customer value by strengthening or _____ the product，services，personnel，or image benefits of the offer.

6. If the product's performance falls short of expectations，the customer

is _____ .

7. Thus, customer delight creates an emotional _____ for a product or service, not just a rational preference, and this creates high customer loyalty.

8. Thus, companies must _____ both their own and competitors' customer satisfaction performance.

9. Then they _____ the actual value they receive in consuming the product to the value expected, and this affects their satisfaction and repurchase behavior.

III. Match the terms and expressions on the left with the explanation on the right.

1. array	a. to draw comparisons	
2. compare	b. the quality or state of being mobile	
3. vow	c. lasting; stable	
4. affinity	d. to counterbalance, counteract, or compensate for	
5. mobility	e. a natural attraction or feeling of kinship	
6. durable	f. readily understood; clear or obvious	
7. offset	g. an impressively large number, as of persons or objects	
8. apparent	h. to declare or assert	

IV. True and False statements.

1. Customers are value-maximizers, within the bounds of search costs and limited knowledge, mobility, and income. (   )

2. Some marketers might rightly argue that this concept of how buyers choose among product alternatives is too rational. (   )

3. In contrast, if marketers set expectations too low, buyers are likely to be disappointed. (   )

4. Still, some of today's most successful companies are raising expectations—and delivering performance to match. (   )

5. Today's customers face a few product and brand choices, prices, and suppliers. (   )

6. If a product's performance falls short of expectations, customers are satisfied. (   )

V. Translate the following into Chinese.

Thus, consumers form judgments about the value of marketing offers and make their buying decisions based upon these judgments. Customer satisfaction with a purchase depends on the product's performance relative to a buyer's expectations. A customer might experience various degrees of satisfaction. If the product's performance falls short of expectations, the customer is dissatisfied. If performance matches expectations, the customer is satisfied. If performance exceeds expectations, the customer is highly satisfied or delighted.

But how do buyers form their expectation? Expectations are based on the customer's past buying experiences, the opinions of friends and associates, and marketer and competitor information and promises. Marketers must be careful to set the right level of expectations. If they set expectations too low, they may satisfy those who buy but fail to attract enough buyers. In contrast, if they raise expectations too high, buyers are likely to be disappointed. For example, Holiday Inn ran a campaign a few years ago called "No Surprises", which promised consistently trouble-free accommodations and service. However, Holiday Inn guests still encountered a lost of problems, and the expectations created by the campaign only made customers more dissatisfied. Holiday Inn had to withdraw the campaign.

Still, some of today's most successful companies are raising expectations—and delivering performance to match. These companies embrace total customer satisfaction. For example, Honda claims, "One reason our customers are so satisfied is that we aren't." And Cigna vows "We'll never be 100 percent satisfied until you are, too." These companies aim high because they know that customers who are only satisfied will still find it easy to switch suppliers when a better offer comes along. For example, a study by AT&T showed that 70 percent of customers who say they are satisfied with a product or service would still be willing to switch to a competitor. In contrast, customers who are highly satisfied are much less ready to switch. One study showed that 75 percent of Toyota buyers were highly satisfied and about 75 percent said they intended to buy a Toyota again. Thus, customer delight creates an emotional affinity for a product or service, not just a rational preference, and this creates high customer loyalty.

VI. Translate the following into English.

1. 如今的消费者要面对大量的产品、品牌、价格和厂商。
2. 通过强化或增加产品、服务、人员和利益供应来增加顾客总价值。
3. 顾客的期望值是基于顾客以往的购买经验、朋友或同事的观点、经销商及其竞争者的信息或承诺而形成的。
4. 相对于购买者的期望值来说,顾客的满意度更依赖于产品的性能。
5. 顾客总价值通常包括消费者预先付出的时间、体力和精神价值。
6. 如果产品的性能达不到期望值的要求,就会令顾客失望。

Supplemental Reading Material

Marketing Management Philosophies

There are five competing concepts under which organizations can choose to conduct their marketing activities: the production concept, the product concept, the selling/sales concept, the marketing concept, and the societal marketing concept.

The Production Concept

The production concept is one of the oldest concepts in business. It holds that consumers will favor those products that are widely available and low in cost. Managers of production-oriented organizations concentrate on achieving high production efficiency and wide distribution. The assumption that consumers are primarily interested in product availability and low price holds in at least two situations. The first is where the demand for a product exceeds supply, as in many developing countries. Here consumers are more interested in obtaining the product than in its fine points, and suppliers will concentrate on finding ways to increase production. The second situation is where the product cost is high and has to be decreased to expand the market.

The Product Concept

Other businesses are guided by the product concept. It holds that consumers will favor those products that offer the most quality performance or innovative features. Managers in product-oriented organizations focus their energy on making superior products and improving them over time. Under the concept, managers assume that buyers admire well-made products and can appraise product quality and performance. However, these managers are sometimes caught up in a love affair with their product and do not realize that the market may be less "turned on". Product-oriented companies often design their products with little or no customer input. They trust that their engineers will know how to design or improve the product. Very often they will not even examine competitors' products.

The Selling Concept/Sales Concept

The selling concept is another common approach. It holds that consumers, if left alone, will ordinarily not buy enough of the organization's products. The organization must therefore undertake an aggressive selling and promotion effort. This concept assumes that consumers typically show buying inertia of resistance and must be coaxed into buying. It also assumes that the company has available a whole battery of effective selling and promotion tools to stimulate more buying. The selling concept is practiced most aggressively with unsought goods, those goods that buyers normally do not think of buying, such as insurance, encyclopedias, and funeral plots. These industries have perfected various sales techniques to locate prospects and hard-sell them on their product's benefits. Most firms practice the selling concept when they have overcapacity. Their aim is to sell what they make rather than make what the market wants.

The Marketing Concept

The marketing concept is a business philosophy that challenges the three concepts we just discussed. Its central tenets crystallized in the mid-1950s. It holds that the key to achieving organizational goals consists of being more effective than competitors in integrating marketing activities toward determining and satisfying the needs and wants of target markets. The selling concept takes an inside-out perspective. It starts with the factory, focuses on the company's existing products, and calls for heavy selling and promoting to produce profitable sales. The marketing concept takes an outside-in perspective. It starts with a well-defined market, focuses on customer needs, integrates all the activities that will affect customers, and produces profits by satisfying customers.

The Societal Marketing Concept

In recent years, some have questioned whether the marketing concept is an appropriate philosophy in an age of environmental deterioration, resources shortages, explosive population growth, world hunger and poverty, and neglected social services. Are companies that do an excellent job of satisfying consumer want necessarily acting in the best long-run interests of consumers and society? The marketing concept sidesteps the potential conflict among consumer want, consumer interests, and long-run societal welfare. The societal marketing concept holds that the organization's task is to determine the needs, wants more efficiently than competitors in a way that preserves or enhances the consumer's well-being. It calls upon marketers to build social and ethical considerations into their marketing practices. They must balance and juggle the often conflicting criteria of company profits, consumer want satisfaction, and public interest.

Discussion and Review Questions:

1. According to which concepts can an organization choose to conduct marketing activities?

2. What kind of products does the production concept think consumers prefer?

3. What does the product concept say consumers like?

4. How does the selling concept view assume consumers?

5. What is the view of the societal marketing concept?

Integrated Logistics Management

Text

Today, more and more companies are adopting the concept of **integrated logistics management**. This concept recognizes that providing better customer service and **trimming** distribution costs requires **teamwork**, both inside the company and among all the marketing channel organizations. Inside the company, the various functional departments must work closely together to maximize the company's own logistics performance. The company must also integrate its logistics system with those of its suppliers and customers to maximize the performance of the entire distribution system.

Cross-Functional Teamwork Inside the Company

In most companies, responsibility for various logistics activities is assigned to many different functional units—marketing, sales, finance, manufacturing, purchasing. Too often, each function tries to optimize its own logistics performance without regard for the activities of the other functions. However, transportation, inventory, **warehousing**, and order processing activities **interact**, often in an **inverse** way. For example, lower inventory levels reduce inventory carrying costs, from **stock-outs**, backorders, special production runs, and costly fast-freight shipments. Because distribution activities involve strong **trade-offs**, decisions by different functions must be coordinated to achieve superior overall logistics performance.

Thus, the goal of integrated logistics management is to **harmonize** all of the company's distribution decisions. Close working relationships among functions can be achieved in several ways. Some companies have created permanent logistics committees made up of managers responsible for different physical distribution activities. These committees meet often to set policies for improving overall logistics performance. Companies can also create management positions that link the logistics activities of functional areas. For example, Procter & Gamble has created "supply managers" who manage all of the supply chain activities for each of its product categories. Many companies have a vice-president of logistics with cross-functional authority. In fact, according to one logistics expert, three-fourths of all major wholesalers and retailers, and a third of major manufacturing companies, have senior logistics officers at the vice-president or higher level. The location of the logistics functions within the company is a secondary concern. The important thing is that the company coordinates its logistics and marketing activities to create high market satisfaction at a reasonable cost.

Building Channel Partnerships

The members of a distribution channel are linked closely in delivering customer satisfaction and value. One company's distribution system is another company's supply system. The success of each channel member depends on the performance of the entire supply chain. For example, Wal-Mart can charge the lowest prices at retail only if its entire supply chain, consisting of thousands of merchandise suppliers, transport companies, warehouses, and service providers, operates at maximum efficiency.

Companies must do more than improve their own logistics. They must also work with other channel members to improve whole-channel distribution. For example, it makes little sense for Levi Strauss to ship finished jeans to its own warehouse, then from these warehouses to JC Penney's stores. If the two companies can work together, Levi Strauss might be able to ship much of its merchandise directly to JC Penney's stores, saving time, inventory, and shipping costs for both. Today, smart companies are coordinating their logistics strategies and building strong partnerships with suppliers and customers to improve customer service and reduce channel costs.

These channel partnerships can take many forms. Many companies have created cross-functional, cross-company teams. For example, Procter & Gamble has a team of almost 100 people living in Bentonville, Arkansas, home of Wal-Mart. The P & Gers work with their **counterparts** at Wal-Mart to jointly find ways to squeeze costs out of their distribution system. Working together benefits not only P & G and Wal-Mart, but also their final consumers. Haggar **Apparel** Company has a similar system called "multiple points of contact", in which a Haggar team works with JC Penney people at corporate, divisional, and store levels. As a result of this partnership, Penney now receives Haggar merchandise within 18 days of placing an order—10 days fewer than its next best supplier. And Haggar ships the merchandise "floor ready"—hangered and pre-tagged—reducing the time it takes Penney to move the stock from receiving **docks** to the sales floor from four days to just one.

Other companies partner through shared projects. For example, many larger retailers are working closely with suppliers on in-store programs. Home Depot allows key suppliers to use its stores as a testing ground for new merchandising programs. The suppliers spend time at Home Depot stores watching how their product sells and how customers relate to it. They then create programs specially **tailored** to Home Depot and its customers. Western Publishing Group, publisher of "Little Golden Books" for children, formed a similar partnership with Toys"R"Us. Western and the giant toy retailer coordinated their marketing strategies to create mini-bookstore sections—called Books"R" Us—within each Toys"R" Us store. Toys"R" Us provides the locations, space, and customers, Western serves as **distributor**, **consolidator**, and servicer for the Books"R"Us program. Clearly, both the supplier and customer benefit from such partnerships.

Channel partnerships may also take the form of information sharing and continuous inventory **replenishment** systems. Companies manage their supply chains through information. Suppliers link up with customers through electronic data interchange (EDI) systems to share information and coordinate their logistics decisions. Here are just two examples:

Information sharing is at the heart of supplier-customer relationships. Increasingly, high-performance retailers are sharing point-of-sale scanner data with their suppliers through electronic data interchange. Wal-Mart was one of the first companies to provide suppliers with timely sales data. With its Retail Link system, major suppliers have "earth stations" installed by which they are directly connected to Wal-Mart's information network. Now, the same system that tells Wal-Mart what customers are buying lets suppliers know what to produce and where to ship the goods. Thus, when a teenager buys a size 10 Nike running shoe, the information goes directly to Nike's computers, triggering replacement or production. Wal-Mart no longer issues purchase orders to some of its most reliable suppliers. These suppliers automatically replenish Wal-Mart's inventory based on the retailer's scanner data and their knowledge of Wal-Mart's operations.

Bailey Controls, a manufacturer of control systems for big factories, from steel and paper mills to chemical and pharmaceutical plants, treats some of its suppliers almost like departments of its own plants. Bailey has plugged two of its main electronics suppliers into itself. Future Electronics is hooked on through an electronic data interchange system. Every week, Bailey electronically sends Future its latest forecasts of what materials it will need for the next six months, so that Future can **stock up** in time. Bailey itself stocks only enough inventory for a few days of operation, as opposed to the three or four months worth it used to carry. Whenever a **bin** of parts falls below a **designated** level, a Bailey employee passes a laser scanner over the bin's **bar code**, instantly alerting Future to send the parts at once. Arrow Electronics is plugged in even more closely: It has a warehouse in Bailey's factory, stocked according to Bailey's twice-a-month forecasts. Bailey provides the space, Arrow the warehouseman and the $500,000 of inventory.

Today, as a result of such partnerships, many companies have switched from anticipatory-based distribution systems to response-based distribution systems. In anticipatory distribution, the company produces the amount of goods called for by a sales forecast. It builds and holds stock at various supply points such as the plant, distribution centers, and retail outlets. Each supply point reorders automatically when its order point is reached. When sales are slower than expected, the company tries to reduce its inventories by offering discounts, rebates, and promotions. For example, the American auto industry produces cars far in advance of demand, and these cars often sit for months on inventory until the companies undertake aggressive promotion.

A response-based distribution system, in contrast, is customer-triggered. The producer continuously builds and replaces stock as orders arrive. It produces what is currently selling. For example, Japanese car makers take orders for cars, then produce and ship them within four days. Some large appliance manufacturers, such as Whirlpool and GE, are moving to this system. Benetton, the Italian fashion house, uses a quick-response system, dyeing its sweaters in the colors that are currently selling instead of trying to guess long in advance which colors people will want. Producing for order rather than for forecast substantially cuts down inventory costs and risks.

Glossary

logistics *n.* a study encompassing planning, overseeing, coordinating and managing the flow of materials, transportation, production systems, etc. 物流学

trimming *n.* the act of one that trims 整理, 调整

teamwork *n.* cooperative effort by the members of a group or team to achieve a common goal 协同工作

warehousing *n.* the act or process of placing or storing in a warehouse, esp. in a bonded or government warehouse 仓库贮存

interact *v.* to act on each other 互相作用

inverse *a.* reversed in order, nature, or effect 相反的

stockout *n.* a situation where no goods of a particular kind is available for sale 脱销

trade-off *n.* a situation where two opposing situations or qualities are balanced 权衡; 协调

harmonize *v.* to bring or come into agreement or harmony 使协调一致

counterpart *n.* one that has the same functions and characteristics as another; an opposite number 对手方, 相应的人或物

apparel *n.* clothing, especially outer garments; attire 服饰

dock *n.* a pier; a wharf 码头

tailored *a.* made by a tailor; custom-made 剪裁讲究的, 定制的

distributor *n.* one that markets or sells merchandise, especially a wholesaler 发行者, 销售者

consolidator *n.* a transport company that arranges for goods sent by different companies to be stored and transported together 集运商

replenishment *n.* the act of filling something up again 补给, 补充

stock up to buy a large quantity of something 采购, 囤积

bin *n.* a container or enclosed space for storage 箱柜

designated *a.* to point out or call by a special name 指定的

bar code a code representing characters by sets of parallel bars of varying thickness and separation that are read optically by transverse scanning 条形码

Key Terms and Concepts

Integrated logistics management: Integrated logistics management is a logistics concept that emphasizes the teamwork, both inside the company and along all the marketing channel organizations, in order to maximize the performance of the entire distribution system. 综合物流管理

Supply chain management: Supply chain management is the integration of all the facilities，functions，and processes associated with the production of goods and services all the way from suppliers to customers or end-users. 供应链管理

Exercises

I. Discussion and Review Questions

1. Please define the integrated logistics briefly.
2. Are the transportation，inventory，warehousing，and order processing in an inverse way? Give an example.
3. What is the goal of integrated logistics?
4. What are the functions of the logistics committees?
5. What does the success of each channel member depend on?
6. How many forms can these channel partnerships take?
7. Do the companies manage their supply chains through information?
8. How have the companies switched as a result of such partnerships today?

II. Vocabulary Review: Without referring to the text，fill in the following sentences with the correct words from the list. You may change the tense，number，or form of the words to fit the context. Use each word only once; not all of the words on the list will be used.

| logistics | teamwork | tailored | replenishment | counterpart | stock up |
| designated | harmonize | dock | interact | bin | apparel |

1. Thus，the goal of integrated logistics management is to _____ all of the company's distribution decisions.
2. Whenever a bin of parts falls below a(n) _____ level，a Bailey employee passes a laser scanner over the bin's bar code，instantly alerting Future to send the parts at once.
3. They then create programs specially _____ to Home Depot and its customers.
4. Today，more and more companies are adopting the concept of integrated _____ management.
5. The P & Gers work with their _____ at Wal-Mart to jointly find ways to squeeze costs out of their distribution system.
6. However，transportation，inventory，warehousing，and order processing activities _____ ，often in an inverse way.
7. Every week，Bailey electronically sends Future its latest forecasts of what

materials it will need for the next six months, so that Future can _____ in time.

8. Channel partnerships may also take the form of information sharing and continuous inventory _____ systems.

9. And Haggar ships the merchandise "floor ready"—hangered and pretagged—reducing the time it takes Penney to move the stock from receiving _____ to the sales floor from four days to just one.

10. This concept recognizes that providing better customer service and trimming distribution costs requires _____ , both inside the company and among all the marketing channel organizations.

III. Match the terms and expressions on the left with the explanations on the right.

1. teamwork
2. warehousing
3. designated

4. inverse
5. replenishment
6. tailored

7. interact
8. harmonize

a. reversed in order, nature, or effect
b. to bring or come into agreement or harmony
c. the act or process of placing or storing in a warehouse, esp. in a bonded or government warehouse
d. to act on each other
e. to point out or call by a special name
f. cooperative effort by the members of a group or team to achieve a common goal
g. made by a tailor; custom-made
h. the act of filling something up again

IV. True and False statements.

1. The company must also integrate its logistics system with those of its suppliers and customers to maximize the performance of the entire distribution system. (   )

2. The goal of integrated logistics management is to harmonize some of the company's distribution decisions. (   )

3. These committees meet often to set policies for improving overall logistics performance. Companies can also create management positions that link the logistics activities of functional areas. (   )

4. The location of the logistics functions within the company is a secondary concern. (   )

5. One company's distribution system is another company's demand system. (   )

6. Channel partnerships may also take the form of information sharing and continuous inventory replenishment systems. (   )

IV. Translate the following into Chinese.

In most companies, responsibility for various logistics activities is assigned to many different functional units—marketing, sales, finance, manufacturing, purchasing. Too often, each function tries to optimize its own logistics performance without regard for the activities of the other functions. However, transportation, inventory, warehousing, and order processing activities interact, often in an inverse way. For example, lower inventory levels reduce inventory carrying costs from stockouts, backorders, special production runs, and costly fast-freight shipments. Because distribution activities involve strong trade-offs, decisions by different functions must be coordinated to achieve superior overall logistics performance.

Thus, the goal of integrated logistics management is to harmonize all of the company's distribution decisions. Close working relationships among functions can be achieved in several ways. Some companies have created permanent logistics committees made up of managers responsible for different physical distribution activities. These committees meet often to set policies for improving overall logistics performance. Companies can also create management positions that link the logistics activities of functional areas. For example, Procter & Gamble has created "supply managers" who manage all of the supply chain activities for each of its product categories. Many companies have a vice-president of logistics with cross-functional authority. In fact, according to one logistics expert, three-fourths of all major wholesalers and retailers, and a third of major manufacturing companies, have senior logistics officers at the vice president or higher level. The location of the logistics functions within the company is a secondary concern. The important thing is that the company coordinates its logistics and marketing activities to create high market satisfaction at a reasonable cost.

VI. Translate the following into English.

1. 现在,越来越多的企业采用了综合性物流管理这个概念。
2. 综合性物流管理的目标是协调公司所有的经销策略。
3. 每个营销渠道成员的成功都要依靠整个供应链的运作。
4. 他们也必须同渠道内其他的成员进行协作,以提高整个渠道的经营能力。
5. 渠道内的合伙企业,可以采用信息共享和连续盘存补给系统的形式进行合作。
6. 一旦达到了订购指标,每个供应点会自动重新订货。

Supplemental Reading Material

Managing the Channel

After deciding on the channel design, the actual channel participants are identified, evaluated, and recruited. Finding competent and motivated intermediaries is critical to successfully implementing the channel strategy. Channel management activities include choosing how to assist and support intermediaries, developing operating policies, providing incentives, selecting promotional programs, and evaluating channel results. These activities consume much of management's time, since the channel design is not modified frequently. Importantly, changes in channel design may have serious consequences for the members. To gain a better insight into channel management, we will discuss channel leadership, management structure and systems, physical distribution management, channel relationships, conflict resolution, channel performance, and legal and ethical considerations.

Some form of inter-organization management is needed to assure that the channel has satisfactory performance as a competitive entity. One firm may gain power over other channel organizations because of its specific characteristics (e.g. size), experience, and environmental factors, and its ability to capitalize on such factors. Thus the channel leader's power depends on its competitive advantages and its environment. Performing the leadership role may also lead to conflicts arising from differences in the objectives and priorities of channel members. The organization with the most power may make decisions that are not considered favorable by other channel members.

Channel coordination and management are often the responsibility of the sales organization. For example, a manufacturer's salespeople develop buyer-seller relationships with wholesalers and/or retailers. The management structure and systems may be from informal arrangements to highly structured operating systems. It may include operating policies and procedures information system linkages, various supporting services to channel participants, and performance targets.

Physical distribution management has received considerable attention from logistics, marketing, manufacturing, and transportation professionals. The objective is to improve the distribution of supplies, goods in process, and finished products. The decision whether to integrate physical distribution with other channel functions or to manage it separately is a question that must be resolved by a particular organization. There are instances when either approach may be appropriate. Physical distribution is a key channel function and thus an important part of channel strategy and management. Management needs to first select the appropriate channel strategy, considering the physical distribution function and other essential channel activities. Once the strategy is selected, physical distribution management alternatives can be examined for the channel network.

Channel relationships are often transactional in conventional channels but become more collaborative now. The extent of collaboration is influenced by the complexity of the product, the potential benefits of collaboration, and the willingness of channel members to work together as partners. Just-in-time inventory programs and other total quality management activities encourage collaboration between suppliers and producers. The commitment and trust of channel organizations is likely to be higher compared to conventional channels. For example, a contractual arrangement is a commitment to work together. Yet, the strength of the commitment may vary depending on the contract terms. Highly collaborative relationships among channel members call for a considerable degree of trust between the partners. The cooperating organizations provide access to confidential product plans, market data, and other trade secrets. Trust normally develops as the partners learn to work with each other and find the relationship to be favorable to partner's objectives.

Conflicts are certain to occur between the channel members because of differences in objectives, priorities, and corporate cultures. Looking at a proposed channel relationship by each participating organization may identify areas that may lead to major conflicts. In such situations, management may decide to seek another channel partner. Effective communications before and after establishing the channel relationships can also help to eliminate or reduce conflicts. Several methods are used to resolve actual and potential conflicts. One useful approach is to involve channel members in the decisions that will affect the members. Another helpful method of resolving or reducing conflict is developing effective communications channels between channel members. Pursuing objectives that are important to all channel members is also a useful approach to reducing conflict. Finally, it may be necessary to establish methods for mediation and arbitration.

The performance of the channel is important from two points of view. First, each member is interested in how well the channel is meeting the member's objectives. Second, the organization that is managing or coordinating the channel is concerned with its performance and the overall performance of the channel. Tracking performance for the individual channel members includes various financial and market measures such as profit contribution, revenues, costs, market share, customer satisfaction, and rate of growth. Companies gain a strategic advantage by improving distribution productivity. Reducing distribution costs and the time in moving products to end-users are high-priority action areas in many companies. The opportunity to lower costs may be substantial. These costs may account for one-third or more of total product costs.

Discussion and Review Questions:
1. What are the keys to successful channel strategy implementation?
2. What does channel management include?
3. How does a firm acquire the power over other channel organizations?
4. What factors affect the extent of collaboration?
5. Why is the performance of the channel important?

Unit 15

Understanding Services

Text

Distinctive Aspects of Service Management

As consumers, we use services every day. Businesses and other organizations also use a wide array of services, usually purchasing on a much larger scale than do individuals or households. The institution at which you are studying is itself a complex service organization. In addition to educational services, the facilities at today's colleges and universities usually **comprise** libraries and cafeterias, counseling services and placement offices, a bookstore, copy services, telephones and Internet connections, and maybe even a bank.

Unfortunately, people complain about late deliveries, rude or incompetent personnel, inconvenient service hours, poor performance, needlessly complicated procedures, and a host of other problems. They **grumble** about the difficulty of finding sales assistants to help them in shops, express frustration about mistakes on their credit card bills or bank statements, shake their heads over the complexity of new self-service equipment, mutter about poor value, and sigh as they are forced to wait for service or stand in lines almost everywhere they go.

Suppliers of services often seem to have a very different set of concerns. Many complain about how difficult it is to make a profit, how hard it is to find skilled and motivated employees, or how difficult to please customers it has become. Some firms seem to believe that the surest route to financial success lies in cutting costs and eliminating what they believe to be unnecessary **frills**. A few even give the impression that they could run a much more efficient operation if it weren't for all the stupid customers who keep making unreasonable demands and messing things up!

Happily, in almost every field of endeavor there are service suppliers who know how to please their customers while also running a productive, profitable operation, staffed by pleasant and competent employees.

Services in the Modern Economy

Around the world, the service sector of the economy is going through a period of almost revolutionary change in which established ways of doing business continue to be shunted aside. At the beginning of a new **millennium**, we are seeing the manner in which we live and work being transformed by new developments in services. Innovators continually launch new ways to satisfy our existing needs and to meet needs that we did not even know we had. The same is true of services directed at corporate users.

What Is a Service?

The group of services described earlier is remarkably diverse yet represents only a fraction of the many different industries found in the service sector. Because of this diversity, services have traditionally been difficult to define. Complicating matters further is the fact that the way in which services are created and delivered to customers is often hard to grasp because many inputs and outputs are **intangible.** Most people have little difficulty defining manufacturing or mining or agriculture, but defining service can elude them. Here are two approaches that capture the essence:

- A service is an act or performance offered by one party to another. Although the process may be tied to a physical product, the performance is essentially intangible and does not normally result in ownership of any of the factors of production.
- Services are economic activities that create value and provide benefits for customers at specific times and places as a result of bringing about a desired change in—or on behalf of—the recipient of the service.

More amusingly, services have been described as "something that may be bought and sold, but which can not be dropped on your foot".

Marketing Services vs. Physical Goods

The dynamic environment of services today places a **premium** on effective marketing. Among the keys to competing effectively in this new and challenging environment are skills in marketing strategy and execution—areas in which many service firms have traditionally been weak.

Marketing can be described in several ways. It can be seen as a **strategic thrust** pursued by top management, as a set of functional activities performed by **line managers**, or as a customer-driven orientation for the entire organization.

Although it's still very important to run an efficient operation, that orientation no longer **suffices** for success. Employees must be customer service oriented as well as concerned about efficiency. The service product must be tailored to customer needs, priced realistically, distributed though convenient channels, and actively promoted to customers. Today, many new market **entrants** are positioning their services to appeal to specific market segments through their pricing, communication efforts and service delivery, rather than trying to be all things to all people.

All *products*—a term that we use in this book to describe the core output of any type of industry—deliver benefits to the customers who purchase and use them. Goods can be described as physical objects or devices, whereas services are actions or performances. Early research into services sought to differentiate them from goods, focusing particularly on four **generic** differences, referred to as *intangibility, heterogeneity (or variability), perishability of output, and simultaneity of production and consumption*. Although these characteristics are still cited, they over-simplify the real-world environment. Worse, they simply don't apply to all services.

No Customer Ownership of Services

Perhaps the key distinction between goods and services lies in the fact that customers usually derive value from services without obtaining ownership of any tangible elements (exceptions include food services and installation of spare parts during delivery of repair and maintenance services). In many instances, service marketers offer customers the opportunity to rent the use of a physical object such as a rental car or hotel room, to hire the labor and expertise of people whose skills range from brain surgery to knowing how to clean your home quickly and effectively, or to rent (as a loan) a sum of money.

A key implication for marketers concerns pricing. When the firm rents out usage of its physical, human, or intangible assets, time becomes an important denominator; in particular, determining the relevant costs requires time-based calculations. Another important issue concerns what criteria drive customer choice behavior for a rental, which tends to be short term in nature. Marketing a car rental service to a customer, for instance, is very different from attempting to sell a car at an automobile dealership to that same person, who may intend keeping it for at least three to five years. People usually rent cars for a period of 1 to 14 days when they are away from home.

In most instances, people reserve a particular class or category of vehicle (such as compact, intermediate, or full-size) rather than a specific brand and model. Instead of worrying about such physical characteristics as colors and **upholstery**, customers focus on such elements as the location and appearance of pickup and delivery facilities, hours when facilities are open, extent of insurance coverage, cleanliness and maintenance of vehicles, provision of free shuttle buses at airports, availability of 24-hour reservations service, and quality of service provided by customer-contact personnel.

Service Products as Intangible Performances

Although services often include tangible elements—such as sleeping in a hotel bed, working out at a health club, having your teeth cleaned at the dentist, or getting damaged equipment repaired—the service performance itself is basically an intangible. In services, the benefits come from the nature of the performance, which requires a different marketing emphasis from marketing tangible goods, including a need to employ tangible images and metaphors to demonstrate the competencies of the service firm and to illustrate the benefits resulting from service delivery.

An interesting way to distinguish between goods and services is to place them on a scale from tangible-dominant to intangible-dominant. Kotler proposes five categories of market offer:

- Pure tangible good (such as soap or salt)
- Tangible good with accompanying services (for example, cars or computers)
- Hybrid (e.g.,a restaurant) combining roughly equal parts of good and services
- Major service with accompanying minor goods and services (e.g., air travel)
- Pure service (such as babysitting or psychotherapy)

Sasser, Olsen, and Wyckoff suggest that an acid test of whether a product is a good or a service is to determine whether more than half the value comes from the service elements. At a restaurant, for example, the cost of the food itself may account for as little as 20 to 30 percent of the price of the meal; the balance of the value added comes from food preparation; cooking; table service; extras such as parking, coatroom, and toilets; and the restaurant environment itself.

The notion of service as a performance that cannot be touched, wrapped, or taken away leads to the use of a theatrical metaphor for service management that likens service delivery to the staging of a play, with service personnel as the actors and customers as the audience. The reading "Service Theater: An Analytical Framework for Services Market" by Stephen Grove and Raymond Fisk describes both the theoretical constructs and practical implication of what is often referred to as **dramaturgy**.

Customer Involvement in the Production Process

Performing a service involves assembling and delivering the output of a mix of physical facilities and mental or physical labor. Many services require customers to participate in creating the service product (expectations include a wide array of services in which production is left entirely to the service provider, such as office cleaning, weather forecasting, car repair, and life insurance). **Customer involvement** in helping to create the service product can take the form of self-service—as in using a laundromat or withdrawing money from an automated teller machine (ATM)—or cooperation with service personnel in settings such as hairdressers, hotels, colleges, or hospitals. Under such circumstance, customers can be thought of as partial employees, and service firms have much to gain from trying to train their customers so as to make them more competent and productive.

Changing the nature of the production process often affects the role that customers are asked to play in that process. In your own role as a service consumer, you know that although your main interest is in the final output, the way in which you are treated during service delivery can also have an important impact on your satisfaction. When customers are required to visit the service delivery site, that facility should be sited in a convenient location and open at times that suit customers' needs. Customers are more likely to return if they find that buildings and equipment are designed in ways that make them user-friendly and reasonably attractive to visit.

People as Part of the Product

It can be a challenging task to manage service encounters between customers and service personnel in ways that will create a satisfactory experience. Similarly, the type of customers who **patronize** a particular service business helps to define the nature of the service experience. If you attend a sporting event, the behavior of the fans can be a big plus and add to the excitement of the game if they are enthusiastic but well behaved. But if some of them become rowdy and abusive, it can detract from the enjoyment of other spectators at the stadium. For good or ill, other customers become part of the product in many services.

Greater Variability in Operational Inputs and Outputs

The presence of employees and other customers in the operational system makes it difficult to standardize and control variability in both service inputs and outputs. Manufactured goods can be produced under controlled conditions that have been designed to optimize both productivity and quality and then checked for conformance with quality standards long before they reach the customer. The same is true for services performed while the customer is absent, such as processing bank checks, repairing cars, or cleaning offices at night. But for those services that are consumed as they are produced, final "assembly" must take place under real-time conditions, which may vary from customer to customer and even from one time of the day to another. As a result, mistakes and shortcomings are both more likely and harder to conceal. These factors make it difficult for service organizations to improve productivity, control quality, and offer a consistent product.

Difficulty of Customer Evaluation

Most physical goods tend to be relatively high in "search properties", the characteristics of the product that a customer can determine prior to purchasing it, such as color, style, shape, price, fit, feel, hardness, and smell. Other goods and some services, by contrast, may emphasize experience properties that can be discerned only after purchase or during consumption, such as taste, wearability, ease of handling, quietness, and personal treatment. Finally, there are "credence properties"—characteristics that customers find hard to evaluate even after consumption. Examples of services in which credence properties predominate include surgery, professional services such as accountancy, and many technical repairs.

No Inventories for Services after Production

Because a service is a deed or performance, rather than a tangible item that the customer keeps, it is, in a sense, perishable and cannot be physically stocked for sale after production is completed. Of course, the necessary facilities, equipment, and labor can be held in readiness to create the service, but these simply represent productive capacity, not the product itself. Having unused capacity in a service business is rather like running water into a sink without a plug. The flow is wasted unless customers (or possessions requiring service) are present to receive it. When demand exceeds capacity, customers may be sent away disappointed unless they are prepared to wait.

Importance of the Time Factor

Many services are delivered in real time. Customers have to be physically present to receive service from organizations. People are willing to spend only a limited amount of time at the service "factory"—particularly if it involves just waiting in line—so service must be delivered with acceptable speed. Increasingly, busy customers expect service to be available at times when it suits them—rather than when it suits the service company. In response, more and more firms are offering extended hours and even going to 24/7 service (available 24 hours a day, seven days a week).

Different Distribution Channels

Unlike manufacturers, many service businesses use electronic channels (as in broadcasting or electronic funds transfer). Alternatively, they may choose to combine the service factory, retail outlet, and point of consumption at a single location, thus requiring them to get involved in site selection, building design and maintenance, and management of customer contact personnel. Sometimes, as in banking, firms offer customers a choice of distribution channels, ranging from visiting the bank in person to conducting home banking on the Internet.

Glossary

comprise *v.* to be composed of 包含;由……组成

grumble *v.* to show one's unhappiness or critical attitude 抱怨;嘟囔

frills *n.* extra things that are added to something to make it more pleasant or more attractive, but that are not necessary 不必要的装饰,虚饰

millennium *n.* a span of 1,000 years 千年期,千禧年;一千年

intangible *a.* (of especially business assets) not having physical substance or intrinsic productive value 无形的,触摸不到的

premium *n.* payment for insurance 额外费用;奖金;保险费;(商)溢价

strategic thrust the force of strategy used in pushing 战略主推力

suffice *v.* to be enough 使满足;足够……用

entrant *n.* any new participant in some activity 进入者

generic *a.* relating to or being a product that is sold or distributed without any brand name or without a widely known brand name 通用的,无厂家商标的

upholstery *n.* covering (padding and springs and webbing and fabric) on a piece of furniture 垫衬物

dramaturgy *n.* the art of writing and producing plays 演出法;戏剧作法

patronize *v.* to assume sponsorship; do business with 经常光顾,惠顾;资助

Key Terms and Concepts

Nonprofit organization: An organization chartered for other than profit-making activities. 非营利组织

Line manager: Line manager is the person at work who is in charge of department, group，or project. 直线管理人员

Customer involvement：Customer involvement refers to ways which customers become part of the process and the extent of their participation. This is particularly important if your business involves a high level of customer contact. 客户参与

Exercises

1. What is a service?
2. What characteristics make services different from goods?
3. Why is it important to examine service marketing in the broader framework of integrated service management?
4. What are the major changes occurring in the service sector?
5. Why do service businesses need to integrate the marketing，operations，and human resource functions?

millennium	thrust	entrant	intangible	headquartered
patronize	frill	premium	suffice	

1. Some firms seem to believe that the surest route to financial success lies in cutting costs and eliminating what they believe to be unnecessary _____.
2. At the beginning of a new _____ , we are seeing the manner in which we live and work being transformed by new developments in services.
3. The dynamic environment of services today places a(n) _____ on effective marketing.
4. It can be seen as a strategic _____ pursued by top management, as a set of functional activities performed by line managers (such as product policy, pricing, delivery, and communications), or as a customer-driven orientation for the entire organization.
5. Although it's still very important to run an efficient operation，that orientation no longer _____ for success.
6. Today，many new market _____ are positioning their services to appeal to specific market segments through their pricing，communication efforts and

service delivery, rather than trying to be all things to all people.

7. Similarly, the type of customers who _____ a particular service business helps to define the nature of the service experience.

8. Complicating matters further is the fact that the way in which services are created and delivered to customers is often hard to grasp because many inputs and outputs are _____ .

9. _____ in the United Kingdom, it rents mobile electricity generators and temperature control equipment from 70 depots in 20 countries.

III. Match the terms and expressions on the left with the explanations on the right.

1. grumble	a. extra things that are added to something to make it more pleasant or more attractive, but that are not necessary
2. frills	b. acting or arriving or performed exactly at the time appointed.
3. millennium	c. not having physical substance or intrinsic productive value
4. punctual	d. the art of writing and producing plays
5. intangible	e. to show one's unhappiness or critical attitude
6. premium	f. payment for insurance
7. dramaturgy	g. a span of 1,000 years

IV. True and False statements.

1. Businesses and other organizations also use a wide array of services, usually purchasing on a much smaller scale than do individuals or households. (   )

2. Are the marketing concepts and practices that have been developed in manufacturing companies directly transferable to service organizations? The answer is often yes. (   )

3. In services, the benefits come from the nature of the performance, which requires a different marketing emphasis from marketing tangible goods, including a need to employ tangible images and metaphors to demonstrate the competencies of the service firm and to illustrate the benefits resulting from service delivery. (   )

4. In your own role as a service consumer, you know that although your main interest is in the final output, the way in which you are treated during service delivery can also have an important impact on your satisfaction. (   )

5. Service firms need to devote normal care to selecting, training, and motivating those employees who will be serving customers directly. (   )

6. However, not all variations in service delivery are necessarily negative, and modern service businesses are coming to recognize the value of customizing at least some aspects of the service offering to the needs and expectations of individual customers. (   )

7. Increasingly, busy customers expect service to be available at times when it suits them—rather than when it suits the service company. (   )

8. Like manufacturers, which produce their products in one location and require physical distribution channels to move goods from factory to customers, many service businesses use electronic channels. (   )

Most physical goods tend to be relatively high in "search properties", the characteristics of the product that a customer can determine prior to purchasing it, such as color, style, shape, price, fit, feel, hardness, and smell. Other goods and some services, by contrast, may emphasize experience properties that can only be discerned after purchase or during consumption, such as taste, wearability, ease of handling, quietness, and personal treatment. Finally, there are "credence properties"—characteristics that customers find hard to evaluate even after consumption. Examples of services in which credence properties predominate include surgery, professional services such as accountancy, and many technical repairs.

Service marketers can help customers overcome some of the unease that they reel before purchasing a service by helping them to match their needs to specific service features and educating them as to what to expect both during and after service delivery. A firm that develops a reputation for considerate and ethical treatment of its customers will gain the trust of its existing customers and benefit from positive word-of-mouth referrals.

1. 很多人抱怨服务业很难赚取利润,很难找到经验丰富、有进取心的员工,很难使顾客满意。

2. 在世界范围内,服务经济正经历革命性的变化时期,在此期间,企业经营的现有方法继续受到排挤。

3. 服务是一方向另一方提供的行为或活动。尽管这个过程可能会涉及有形产品,但是服务本质上是无形的,并且一般不会涉及任何生产要素的所有权变化。

4. 在很多国家,服务业十分多样化,包括一系列不同的行业,这些行业不仅为个体消费者和商业用户提供服务,还有政府机构和非营利组织。

5. 服务业的营销职能比传统营销部门的活动和产出更广泛,要求营销人员与负责运营和人力资源的管理者紧密合作。

6. 当企业出租其有形资产、人力资源或无形资产时,时间成为重要的分母;特别是,确定相关成本需要基于时间计算。

Supplemental Reading Material

Service Managerial Focus of Logistics Enterprises Based on GRA

1. Introduction

The logistics industry in the developed countries was known as "accelerator" of economic development. For a long time, due to the subordinate position in the production and circulation, logistics service didn't get the attention it deserves. With the arrival of the period of market segmentation, logistics service has become one of the most important aspects of the logistics enterprises. Implementing differentiation marketing strategy, in this case, to determine the optimum logistics service level is particularly important for logistics enterprises. First, market demand has decentralized and diversified characteristics. According to different types, different levels of market demand, only by providing the appropriate logistics service can enterprises rapidly and effectively meet the customers demand, survive and develop in the fierce competition and in a changing market. Second, determining the level of logistics services has a significant impact on business performance. The appropriate logistics service level of logistics enterprises can make for a larger income and low cost, in order to achieve maximum profits.

In the field of research, the importance of logistics service quality has been recognized for a long time. Logistics service quality is closely related with service performance. The improvement of logistics services quality helps to improve the customer satisfaction and loyalty, and to enlarge market share. Logistics service is defined based on the customer satisfaction. The latest rescrach of logistics service quality is the research results of the University of Tenessee in 2001. The research used customer satisfaction as the core variable to reflect logistics enterprise service performance. Through a survey of logistics enterprises and customers, they summed up nine indicators: staff communication quality, order release quantity, ordering process, the accurate rate, the intact rate of good and so on. But the research ignored the logistics service process and service time, and the correlation among the various indicators.

To raise the level of logistics services, one needs to improve enterprises' management of logistics service. The influence of service management to service level is mainly reflected in the logistics enterprise's service ability. Service ability is the strategic priority for logistics enterprises to gain competitive advantage, and also the important characteristic to maintain their dominant position in market competition and long-term prosperity. In the logistics research field, some literature defines logistics capability and logistics service capability. Daugherty and Stank, etc. study the relationship between logistics service capability, customer satisfaction, loyalty and the market share. They give 11 logistics service capability indexes from the point of logistics distribution. Finland scholars Jukka and Markku use analytic hierarchy process (AHP) to study the third party logistics service quality evaluation, taking reliability, emergency power, order cycle, price and value-added service quality as evaluation indicators. Kee-hung Lai defines logistics enterprise service capacity as "the ability of creation and allocation of resources to meet the customer's logistics demand and the pursuit of better service performance". Mentzer, Myers and Mee-shew Cheung successively put forward two-stage logistics service quality definition and customer-orientated logistics service quality model based on service process. They also study the role of logistics service quality in global market segmentation.

In conclusion, many researchers attach importance to service quality management. However, less literature refers to this question: which parts are more important in improving the service quality of logistics enterprises? That is what this paper wants to discuss in detail.

2. The Problems of Logistics Enterprise Service Management

2.1. Lack of Service Quality Standard System

According to the survey, the logistics industry is in lack of unified standards in the service quality management. Most logistics enterprises have not necessary service specifications and regulations with extensive management, which makes it difficult to provide standardized services.

2.2. Low level in Logistics Informatization

A large number of small and medium-sized logistics enterprises only rely on a telephone and a few vans to start the service, with phones and shipping documents as the main means. Even with enterprise information system, its information demand still belongs to the low level demand, more concentrated in the local link such as warehousing, transportation and order management.

2.3. Lack of High-quality Talents in the Field of Logistics Services

The logistics practitioners' quality of many logistics enterprises is generally low. On-the-job education and on-the-job training's effect is not good, and effective training mechanism has not been effectively utilized.

2.4. Lack of Time Consciousness

Many logistics enterprises do not pay enough attention to quick response in delivery and solving basic services demands such as consulting, customer difficulty and so on.

2.5. Poor Reliability

Logistics enterprises should have the ability to complete all operations related to the delivery of the goods, which makes consumers feel assured. But some enterprises fail to do that, often making mistakes here and there, which damages customers' confidence in them.

2.6. Less Logistics Value-added Services

Most logistics enterprises passively comply with the instructions and requirements of users, and engage in a elementary transport, warehousing and distribution function. Few of them can provide logistics planning, organizing or go deep into the enterprise's internal production areas for the value-added service.

3. Service Quality Focus of the Logistics Enterprises

The evaluation of the level of the service management for a logistics enterprise shall be based on the evaluation of its quality of service; and to some extent the quality of service can represents the enterprise's service management level.

This article will mainly study the measure of the level of service management of logistics enterprises through the study of factors influencing the level of their logistics service quality. Therefore, in order to build an evaluation system for the service quality of logistics enterprises, totally 5 classes and 16 specific indexes can be given.

3.1. The Reliability of the Logistics Service

This index evaluates whether an enterprise can fulfill its service promises reliably and accurately. Reliable service means that services can be achieved on time without mistakes, which is obviously desired by customers. The writer selects three secondary indexes to assess the reliability of logistics services:

- Evaluate the accuracy of providing the necessary services.
- Evaluate the accuracy of fulfilling promises.
- Evaluate the quality of after-sales services.

3.2. The Response Speed of the Logistics Service

This index evaluates whether an enterprise is well ready to help customers and provides fast and efficient services. This index also includes three secondary indexes:

- Evaluate the preparation time from getting the order to implementing it, which reflects the response ability.
- Evaluate the distribution time, which reflects the distribution efficiency of the enterprise.
- Evaluate whether the after-sales services are in time.

Clearly, no customer is ready to wait for a long time after ordering, especially waiting for no reason. Upon receiving orders, the logistic enterprise should start to arrange logistics services.

3.3. The Security Conditions of Services

This index reflects the staff's ability to achieve the services. This index includes three secondary indexes:

- Evaluate the professional knowledge of the staff, which reflects the service personnel's working ability of the enterprise.
- Evaluate rules and regulations for service management, which reflects the enterprise's degree of the attention to the service quality.
- Evaluate whether communication with customers is effective, which reflects the service methods.

3.4. The Service Attitudes of the Staff

This index reflects whether the staff put themselves in customers' positions and pay special attention to customers. This index includes three secondary indexes:

- Evaluate whether the staff are sincere to customers, which reflects the attention degree to customers.
- Evaluate the personalized service level, which reflects the quality of the value-added service to customers.
- Evaluate whether the staff are polite and respectful to customers, which reflects the basic literacy of the employees.

3.5. Hardware Conditions of Logistics Enterprises

This index refers to the facilities and equipment. Hardware conditions are the basis upon which a logistics enterprise provides customers with qualified logistics services. Its evaluation indexes include the following aspects:

- Evaluate the informatization level, which reflects the modernization level.
- Evaluate the facility level, which reflects the logistics enterprise's service

ability.

● Evaluate the vehicle quantities, which reflects the logistics enterprise's transport ability.

● Evaluate the storage equipment, which reflects the logistics enterprise's storage ability.

Discussion and Review Questions:

1. Why was the logistics industry in developed countries known as "accelerator" of economic development?

2. How to determine the optimum logistics service level for logistics enterprises?

3. What are the problems of logistics enterprises' service management?

4. What is the service quality focus of logistics enterprises? Please give your opinion.

5. What are the evaluation indexes of hardware conditions of logistics enterprises?

Unit 16

How to Set a Price on a Product

Text

Price is one of the most important marketing variables in the marketing mix. Generally speaking, setting the right price on a product is a four-step process (see Exhibit 16.1):

1. Establish pricing goals.
2. Estimate demand, costs, and profits.
3. Choose a **price strategy** to help determine a **base price**.
4. Fine-tune the base price with pricing tactics.

These four steps are discussed next.

The first step in setting the right price is to establish pricing goals. Generally speaking, the pricing objectives fall into three categories: profit **oriented**, sales oriented, and **status quo**. These goals are derived from the firm's overall objectives.

A good understanding of the marketplace and of the consumer can sometimes tell a manager very quickly whether a goal is realistic. For example, if firm A's objective is a 20 percent target return on investment (ROI), and its product development and implementation costs are $5 million, the market must be rather large or must support the price required to earn a 20 percent ROI. Assume that company B has a pricing objective that all new products must reach at least 15 percent market share within three years after their introduction. A thorough study of the environment

Exhibit 16.1   Steps in Setting the Right Price on a Product

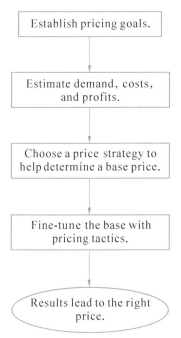

165

may convince the marketing manager that the competition is too strong and the market share goal can't be met.

All pricing objectives have trade-offs that managers must weigh. A profit **maximization** objective may require a bigger initial investment than the firm can commit or wants to commit. Reaching the desired market share often means sacrificing short-term profit, because without careful management, long-term profit goals may not be met. Meeting the competition is the easiest pricing goal to implement. However, can managers really afford to ignore demand and costs, the life cycle stage, and other considerations? When creating pricing objectives, managers must consider these trade-offs in light of the target customer and the environment.

Estimate Demand, Costs, and Profits

Theoretically, total revenue is a function of price and quantity demanded and that quantity demanded depends on **elasticity**. After establishing pricing goals, managers should estimate total revenue at a variety of prices. Next, they should determine corresponding costs for each price. They are then ready to estimate how much profit, if any, and how much market share can be earned at each possible price. These data become the heart of the developing price policy. Managers can study the options in light of revenues, costs, and profits. In turn, this information can help determine which price can best meet the firm's pricing goals.

Choose a Price Strategy

The basic, long-term pricing framework for a product or service should be a logical extension of the pricing objectives. The marketing manager's chosen price strategy defines the initial price and gives direction for price movements over the product life cycle.

The price strategy sets a competitive price in a specific market segment, based on a well-defined positioning strategy. Changing a price level from premium to superpremium, may require a change in the product itself, the target customers served, the promotional strategy, or the distribution channels. Thus, changing a price strategy can require dramatic **alternations** in the marketing mix. A carmaker cannot successfully compete in the superpremium category if the car looks and drives like an economy car.

A company's freedom in pricing a new product and devising a price strategy depends on the market conditions and other elements of the marketing mix. If a firm launches a new item resembling several others already on the markets, its pricing freedom will be restricted. To succeed, the company will probably have to charge a price close to the average market price. In contrast, a firm that introduces a totally new product with no close substitutes will have considerable pricing freedom.

The three basic strategies for setting a price on a good or service are **price skimming**, **penetration pricing**, and status quo pricing. A discussion of each type follows.

Price Skimming Price skimming is sometimes called a "market-plus" approach to pricing, because it denotes a high price relative to the prices of competing products, Radius Corporation produces unique oval-headed toothbrushes made of black **neoprene** that look like a **scuba**-diving accessory. Radius uses a skimming policy, pricing the toothbrushes at $9.95, compared to around $2.00 for a regular toothbrush.

The term price skimming is derived from the phrase "skimming the cream off the top". Companies often use this strategy for new products when the product is perceived by the target market as having unique advantages. For example, Caterpillar sets premium prices on its construction equipment to support and capture its high perceived value. Genzyme Corporation introduced Ceredase as the first effective treatment for Gaucher's disease. The pill allows patients to avoid years of painful physical **deterioration** and lead normal lives. A year's supply for one patient can exceed $300,000.

As a product progresses through its life cycle, the firm may lower its price to successfully reach larger market segments. Economists have described this type of pricing as "sliding down the demand curve". Not all companies slide down the curve. Genentech's TPA, a drug that clears blood **clots**, was still priced at $2,200 a dose four years after its introduction, despite competition from a much lower priced competitor.

Price skimming works best when the market is willing to buy the product even though it carries an above-average price. If, for example, some purchasing agents feel that Caterpillar equipment is far superior to competitors' products, then Caterpillar can charge premium prices successfully. Firms can also effectively use price skimming when a product is well protected legally, when it represents a technological **breakthrough**, or when it has in some other way blocked entry to competitors. Managers may follow a skimming strategy when production cannot be expanded rapidly because of technological difficulties, shortages, or constraints imposed by the skill and time required to produce a product. As long as demand is greater than supply, skimming is an **attainable** strategy.

A successful skimming strategy enables management to recover its product development or "educational" costs quickly. (Often, consumers must be "taught" the advantages of a radically new item, such as high-definition TV.) Even if the market perceives an introductory price as too high, managers can easily correct the problem by lowering the price. Firms often feel it is better to test the market at a high price and then lower the price if sales are too slow. They are **tacitly** saying, "If there are any premium-price buyers in the market, let's reach them first and maximize our revenue per unit." Successful skimming strategies are not limited to products. Well-known athletes, entertainers, lawyers, and **hairstylists** are experts at price skimming. Naturally, a skimming strategy will encourage competitors to enter the market.

Penetration Pricing   Penetration pricing is at the end of the **spectrum**, opposite to skimming. Penetration pricing means charging a relatively low price for a product as a way to reach the mass market. The low price is designed to capture a large share of a substantial market, resulting in lower production costs. If a marketing manager has made obtaining a large market share the firm's pricing objective, penetration pricing is a logical choice.

Penetration pricing does mean lower profit per unit, however. Therefore, to reach the break-even point, it requires higher volume sales than would a skimming policy. If reaching a high volume of sales takes a long time, then the recovery of product development costs will also be slow. As you might expect, penetration pricing tends to discourage competition.

A penetration strategy tends to be effective in a **price-sensitive market**. Price should decline more rapidly when demand is elastic, because the market can be expanded through a lower price. Also, price sensitivity and greater competitive pressure should lead to relatively slow decline in the price later. Southwest Airlines' success is based on penetration pricing. By flying only the Boeing 737, it realizes efficiencies in stocking parts and training pilots and mechanics. It also saves by avoiding a costly computer reservation system, such as Apollo or SABRE, and by not serving meals. Southwest has a cost per seat mile of 7.0¢ —the lowest in the industry. Costs per seat mile for other major carriers are USAir, 10.8¢; United, 9.6¢; Delta, 9.4¢; Northwest, 9.1¢; and American, 8.9¢.

If a firm has a fixed cost structure and each sale provides a large contribution to those fixed costs, penetration pricing can boost sales and provide large increases to profits—but only if the market size grows or if competitors choose not to respond. Low prices can draw additional buyers to enter the market. The increased sales can justify production expansion or the adoption of new technologies, both of which can reduce costs. And, if firms have excess capacity, even low-priced business can provide incremental dollars toward fixed costs.

Penetration pricing can also be effective if a large experience curve causes costs per unit to drop significantly. The experience curve proposes that per-unit costs will go down as a firm's production experience increases. On average, for each doubling of production, a firm can expect per-unit costs to decline by roughly 20 percent. Cost declines can be significant in the early stages of production. Manufacturers who fail to take advantage of these effects will find themselves at a competitive cost disadvantage relative to others who are further along the curve.

The big advantage of penetration pricing is that it typically discourages or blocks competition from entering a market. The disadvantage is that penetration means gearing up mass production to sell a large volume at a low price. What if the volume fails to **materialize**? The company is faced with huge losses from building or converting a factory to the failed product. Skimming, in contrast, lets a firm "stick its toe in the water" and see if the limited demand exists at the high price. If not, the firm can simply lower the price. Skimming lets a company start out with a small production facility and expand it **gradually** as price falls and demand increases.

Another problem with penetration pricing is when a **prestige** brand moves to penetration pricing to gain market share and fails. When Omega—once a brand more **prestigious** than Rolex—was trying to improve market share, it adopted a penetration pricing strategy that succeeded in destroying the watch's brand image by flooding the market with lower-priced products. Omega never gained sufficient share on the lower price/lower image competitors to justify destroying its brand image and high-priced position with upscale buyers. Similar out-comes were experienced by the Candillac Cimarron and Lacoste clothing.

Sometimes marketers use unusual pricing schemes to reach their pricing goals.

Managers must understand both the legal and marketing consequences of price strategies; they should set a base price, the general price level at which the company expects to sell the good or service. The general price level is correlated with the pricing policy: above the market (price skimming), at the market (status quo pricing), or below the market (penetration pricing). The final step, then, is to fine-tune the base price.

Fine-tuning techniques are short-run approaches that do not change the general price level. They do, however, result in changes within a general price level. These pricing tactics allow the firm to adjust for competition in certain markets, meet ever-changing government regulations, take advantage of unique demand situations, and meet promotional and positioning goals. Fine-tuning pricing tactics include various sorts of discounts, geographic pricing, and special pricing tactics.

Glossary

oriented *a.* directed towards something 以……为方向(目的)的，面向的

status quo *n.* the existing condition or state of affairs 现状，现存情况或事态

maximization *n.* the process of making something as great in amount, size, or importance as possible 最大值化，极大值化

elasticity *n.* the condition or property of being elastic；flexibility 有弹性的状态或性质；弹性

alternation *n.* successive change from one thing or state to another and back again 交替从一种事物或状态变为另一种事物或状态并再变回来的一系列变化

skimming *n.* the practice of charging a high price for a new product in order to make as much profit as possible before other similar products become available and prices fall 撇脂定价

penetration *n.* the act or process of piercing or penetrating something 渗透，穿透或渗透的行为或过程

neoprene *n.* a synthetic rubber produced by polymerization of chloroprene and used in weather-resistant products, adhesives, shoe soles, paints, and rocket fuels 氯丁橡胶，由氯丁橡胶聚合而生产的合成橡胶，用于抗风化产品、粘胶鞋底、涂料和火箭燃料

scuba *n.* a portable apparatus containing compressed air and used for breathing under water 自携式水下呼吸器，包括压缩空气和在水下用于呼吸的便携式仪器

deterioration *n.* the fact or process of becoming worse 恶化；变坏；退化

clot *n.* a thick, viscous, or coagulated mass or lump, as of blood 凝块，稠的、黏的或凝结的团或块，如血液的凝块

breakthrough *n.* a major achievement or success that permits further progress, as in technology 重大成就，允许进一步发展的主要成就或成功，如在技术上

attainable *a.* possible to achieve 可达到的；可得到的

tacitly *ad.* without expressing something directly 心照不宣地，沉默地

hairstylist *n.* someone whose job is to cut and arrange people's hair 发式专家，发型师

spectrum *n.* a range of different positions, opinions, etc. between two extreme points (看法、感觉等的)范围

price-sensitive market market in which the sales of a product or service are influenced by price rather than quality 价格不稳定的市场

materialize *v.* to become actual fact, to happen 实现，成为现实

gradually *ad.* advancing or progressing by regular or continuous degrees 逐级地，逐步地，规则地或连续地发展或前进的

prestige *a.* causing admiration because of being connected with being rich or powerful 有威望的，有威信的

prestigious *a.* having prestige；esteemed 有威望的；受尊敬的

Key Terms and Concepts

Price strategy：A basic, long-term pricing framework, which establishes the initial price for a product and the intended direction for price movements over the product life cycle. 价格策略

Base price：The general price level at which the company expects to sell a product or service. 基础价格

Price skimming：A pricing policy whereby a firm charges a high introductory price，often coupled with heavy promotion. 撇脂定价

Penetration pricing：A pricing policy whereby a firm charges a relatively low price for a product initially as a way to reach the mass market. 渗透定价

Exercises

I. Discussion and Review Questions.

    1. What is the first step in setting a right price?

    2. What are the three categories about the pricing objectives?

    3. What should the managers do after establishing pricing goals?

    4. What are the three basic strategies for setting a price on a product or service?

    5. Try to explain how to choose a price strategy. Give an example.

    6. Please define the price skimming strategy.

    7. What is penetration pricing?

    8. When does a prestige brand move to gain market share and fail?

II. Vocabulary Review: Without referring to the text，fill in the blanks in the following sentences with the correct words from this list. You may change the tense，number，or form of the words to fit the context. Use each word only once；not all of the words on the list will be used.

price-sensitive	market	alternation	scuba	breakthrough
attainable	prestige	elasticity	hairstylist	clot
maximization	gradually	spectrum	deterioration	

    1. A profit _____ objective may require a bigger initial investment than the firm can commit or wants to commit.

    2. Theoretically，total revenue is a function of price and quantity demanded and that quantity demanded depends on _____ .

    3. Thus，changing a price strategy can require dramatic _____ in the marketing mix.

    4. The pill allows patients to avoid years of painful physical _____ and lead normal lives.

    5. Firms can also effectively use price skimming when a product is well protected legally，when it represents a technological _____ ，or when it has in some other way blocked entry to competitors.

6. As long as demand is greater than supply, skimming is a(n) _____ strategy.

7. Skimming lets a company start out with a small production facility and expand it _____ as price falls and demand increases.

8. Another problem with penetration pricing is when a(n) _____ brand moves to penetration pricing to gain market share and fails.

9. A penetration strategy tends to be effective in a(n) _____. Price should decline more rapidly when demand is elastic, because the market can be expanded through a lower price.

10. Penetration pricing is at the end of the _____, opposite skimming. Penetration pricing means charging a relatively low price for a product as a way to reach the mass market.

III. Match the terms and expressions on the left with the explanations on the right.

1. status quo   a. advancing or progressing by regular or continuous degrees
2. prestige   b. the practice of charging a high price for a new product in order to make as much profit as possible before other similar products become available and prices fall
3. elasticity   c. the act or process of piercing or penetrating something
4. penetration   d. the condition or property of being elastic; flexibility
5. clot   e. a broad sequence or range of related qualities, ideas, or activities
6. spectrum   f. the existing condition or state of affairs
7. gradually   g. causing admiration because of being connected with being rich or powerful
8. skimming   h. a thick, viscous, or coagulated mass or lump, as of blood

IV. True and False statements.

1. A good understanding of the marketplace and of the consumer can sometimes tell a manager very quickly whether a goal is realistic. (　　)

2. A profit maximization objective requires a smaller initial investment than the firm can commit or wants to commit. (　　)

3. Theoretically, total revenue is a function of price and quantity demanded and that quantity demanded depends on elasticity. (　　)

4. A successful skimming strategy enables management to recover its product development or "educational" costs slowly. (　　)

5. As a product progresses through its life cycle, the firm may lower its price to successfully reach larger market segments. (　　)

6. A company's freedom in pricing a new product and devising a price strategy depends on the market conditions and other elements of the marketing mix. (　　)

V. Translate the following into Chinese.

The basic, long-term pricing framework for a product or service should be a logical extension of the pricing objectives. The marketing manager's chosen price strategy defines the initial price and gives direction for price movements over the product life cycle.

The price strategy sets a competitive price in a specific market segment, based on a well-defined positioning strategy. Changing a price level from premium to superpremium, may require a change in the product itself, the target customers served, the promotional strategy, or the distribution channels. Thus, changing a price strategy can require dramatic alternations in the marketing mix. A carmaker cannot successfully compete in the superpremium category if the car looks and drives like an economy car.

A company's freedom in pricing a new product and devising a price strategy depends on the market conditions and other elements of the marketing mix. If a firm launches a new item resembling several others already on the markets, its pricing freedom will be restricted. To succeed, the company will probably have to charge a price close to the average market price. In contrast, a firm that introduces a totally new product with no close substitutes will have considerable pricing freedom.

VI. Translate the following into English.

1. 制定正确价格的第一步是建立定价目标。
2. 对于产品和服务来说，这种长期、基本的价格结构是定价目标合理的延续。
3. 在销售组合中改变定价策略往往需要有戏剧性的变化。
4. 低价格可以获取大量充实的市场份额，从而导致生产成本的降低。
5. 当生产由于技术困难、原料短缺或税收限制等原因，不能迅速扩展时，经营者就可采取撇脂定价策略。
6. 低价格可以吸引其他的购买者进入市场。

Supplemental Reading Material

The Stages of the Buying Decision Process

Smart companies research the buying decision process involved in their product category. They ask consumers when they first became acquainted with the product category and brands, what their brand beliefs are, how involved they are with the product, how they make their brand choices, and how satisfied they are after purchase. How can marketers learn about the stages in the buying process for their product? They can think about how they themselves would act (i. e., introspective method). They can interview a small number of recent purchasers, asking them to recall the events leading to their purchase (i. e., retrospective method). They can locate consumers who plan to buy the product and ask them to think out loud about going through the buying process (i. e., prescriptive method). Each method yields a picture of the steps in the consumer buying process.

The consumer passes through five stages: problem recognition, information search, evaluation of alternatives, purchase decision, and post purchase behavior. Clearly the buying process starts long before the actual purchase and has consequences long afterward.

Five-stage Model of the Consumer Buying Process

The model implies that consumers pass sequentially through all five stages in buying a product. But this is not the case. Especially with low-involvement purchases. Consumers may skip or reverse some stages. Thus a woman buying her regular brand of toothpaste goes directly from the need for toothpaste to the purchase decision, skipping information search and evaluation. However, we will use the model because it captures the full range of considerations that arise when a consumer faces a highly involving new purchase.

Problem Recognition   The buying process starts when the buyer recognizes a problem or need. The buyer senses a difference between his or her actual state and a desired state. The need can be triggered by internal or external stimuli. In the former case, one of the person's normal needs—hunger, thirst—rises to a threshold level and becomes a drive. In the latter case, a need is aroused by an external stimulus. A person passes a bakery and sees freshly baked bread that stimulates her hunger; or she admires a neighbor's new car. Marketers need to identify the circumstances that trigger a particular need. By gathering information from a number of consumers, marketers can identify the most frequent stimuli that spark an interest in a product category. The marketer can then develop marketing strategies that trigger consumer interest.

Information Search   An aroused consumer will be inclined to search for more information. We can distinguish between two levels of arousal. The milder search state is called heightened attention. At the next level, he or she may enter active information search. Of key interest to the marketer are the major information sources to which the consumer will turn and the relative influence each will have on the subsequent purchase decision. Consumer information sources fall into four groups: personal sources, commercial sources, public sources, experiential sources.

The relative amount and influence of these information sources vary with the product category and the buyer's characteristics. Generally speaking, the consumer receives the most information about a product from commercial sources—that is, marketer-dominated sources. But the most effective information comes from personal sources. Each information source performs a different function in influencing the buying decision. Commercial information normally performs an informing function, and personal sources perform a legitimizing and/or evaluation function. For example, physicians often learn of new drugs from commercial sources but turn to other doctors for evaluation. Through gathering information, the consumer learns about competing sets of brands and their features.

Evaluation of Alternatives   How does the consumer process competitive brand information and make a final judgment of value? There is no simple and single evaluation process used by all consumers in all buying situations. There are several decision evaluation processes, the most current models of which see the consumer evaluation process as cognitively oriented. That is, they see the consumer as forming product judgments largely on a conscious and rational basis. Some basic concepts will help us understand consumer evaluation processes. First, the consumer is trying to satisfy a need. Second, the consumer is looking for certain benefits from the product solution. Third, the consumer sees each product as a bundle of attributes with varying abilities of delivering the benefits sought to satisfy this need.

Consumers differ as to which product attributes they see as most relevant as well as on the importance of weights they attach to each attribute. They will pay the most attention to the attributes that deliver the sought benefits. The market for a product can often be segmented according to the attributes that are salient to different consumer groups. The consumer develops a set of brand beliefs about where each brand stands on each attribute. The set of beliefs about a brand makes up the brand image. The consumer's brand image will vary with his or her experiences as filtered by the effects of selective perception, selective distortion, and selective retention. The consumer arrives at attitudes (judgments, preferences) toward the various brands through an attribute evaluation procedure.

Purchase Decision   In the evaluation stage, the consumer forms preferences among the brands in the choice set. The consumer may also form an intention to buy the most preferred brand. However, two factors can intervene between the purchase intention and the purchase decision. The first factor is the attitudes of others. The second factor is unanticipated situational factors. These may erupt to change the purchase intention.

In executing a purchase intention, the consumer may make up to five purchase subdecisions. He or she will make a brand decision, vendor decision, quantity decision, timing decision and payment-method decision. Purchases of everyday products involve fewer decisions and less deliberation. For example, in buying sugar, a consumer gives little thought to the vendor or payment method.

Post-Purchase Behavior   After purchasing the product consumers will experience some level of satisfaction or dissatisfaction. The marketer's job does not end when the product is bought but continues into the post purchase period. Marketers must monitor post-purchase satisfaction, and post-purchase actions.

What determines whether the buyer will be highly satisfied, somewhat satisfied, or dissatisfied with a purchase? The buyer's satisfaction is a function of the closeness between the buyer's product expectations and the product's perceived performance. If the product's performance falls short of customer expectations, the customer is disappointed; if it meets expectations, the customer is satisfied; if it exceeds expectations, the customer is delighted. These feelings make a difference in whether the customer buys the product again and talks favorably or unfavorably about the product to others. The importance of post-purchase satisfaction suggests that sellers must make product claims that truthfully represent the product's likely performance. Some sellers might even understate performance levels so that consumers experience higher-than-expected satisfaction. The consumer's satisfaction or dissatisfaction with the product will influence subsequent behavior. If the consumer is satisfied, he or she will exhibit a higher probability of purchasing the product again. Dissatisfied consumers respond differently. They may abandon or return the product. They may seek information that confirms its high value. They may take public action such as by complaining to the company, going to a lawyer, or complaining to other groups. Private actions include making a decision to stop buying the product or warning friends. Marketers can and should take steps to minimize the amount of consumer post-purchase dissatisfaction.

Discussion and Review Questions:

1. How can marketers learn about the stages in the buying process for their product?

2. What are the stages of consumer decision making?

3. What are the other influencing factors between purchase intention and purchase decision?

4. What are the influencing factors for consumers to buy again?

Unit 17

Steps in Developing Effective Communication

Text

Marketers need to understand how communication works. Communication involves the nine elements shown in the figure below. Two of these elements are the major parties in a communication—the sender and the receiver. Another two are the major communication tools—the **message** and the **media**. Four more are major communication functions—**encoding**, **decoding**, response, and feedback. The last element is noise in the system. Definitions of these elements follow and are applied to a McDonald's television ad:

Exhibit 17. 1　Elements in the Communication Process

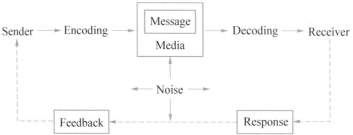

- ★ Sender: The party sending the message to another party—McDonald's.
- ★ Encoding: The process of putting thought into symbolic form—McDonald's advertising agency assembles words and illustrations into an advertisement that will convey the intended message.
- ★ Message: The set of symbols that the sender transmits—the actual McDonald's advertisement.
- ★ Media: The communication channels through which the message moves from sender to receiver—in this case, television and the specific television programs

McDonald's selects.

* Decoding: The process by which the receiver assigns meaning to the symbols encoded by the sender—a consumer watches the McDonald's ad and interprets the words and illustrations it contains.
* Receiver: The party receiving the message sent by another party—the consumer who watches the McDonald's ad.
* Response: The reactions of the receiver after being exposed to the message—any of hundreds of possible responses, such as the consumer likes McDonald's better, is more likely to eat at McDonald's next time he or she eats fast food, or does nothing.
* Feedback: The part of the receiver's response communicated back to the sender—McDonald's research shows that consumers like and remember the ad, or consumers write or call McDonald's praising or criticizing the ad or McDonald's products.
* Noise: The **unplanned** static or **distortion** during the communication process, which results in the receiver's getting a different message than the one the sender has sent—the consumer has poor TV reception or is distracted by family members while watching the ad.

This model points out several key factors in good communication. Senders need to know what audiences they wish to reach and what responses they want. They must be good at encoding messages that take into account how the target audience decodes them. They must send messages through media that reach target audiences, and they must develop feedback channels so that they can assess the audience's response to the message.

Thus, the marketing communicator must do the following: identify the target audience; determine the response sought; choose a message; choose the media through which to send the message; select the message source; and collect feedback.

Identifying the Target Audience

A marketing communicator starts with a clear target audience in mind. The audience may be potential buyers or current users, those who make the buying decision or those who influence it. The audience may be individuals, groups, special publics, or the general public. The target audience will heavily affect the communicator's decisions on what will be said, how it will be said, when it will be said, where it will be said, and who will say it.

Determining the Response Sought

Once the target audience has been defined, the marketing communicator must decide what response is sought. Of course, in most cases, the final response is purchase. But purchase is the result of a long process of consumer decision making. The target audience may be in any of six buyer-readiness stages, the stages consumers normally pass through on their way to making a purchase. The marketing communicator needs to know where the target audience now stands and to what stage it needs to be moved. These stages include awareness, knowledge, liking, preference, conviction, or purchase.

The marketing communicator's target market may be totally **unaware** of the product, know only its name, or know one or a few things about it. The communicator must first build awareness and knowledge. For example, when Nissan introduced its Infiniti automobile line, it began with an extensive "**teaser**" advertising campaign to create name **familiarity**. Initial ads for the Infiniti created curiosity and awareness by showing the car's name but not the car. Later ads created knowledge by informing potential buyers of the car's high quality and many innovative features.

Assuming target consumers know the product, how do they feel about it? Once potential buyers know about the Infiniti, Nissan's marketers want to move them through successively stronger stages of feelings toward the car. These stages include liking (feeling favorable about the Infiniti), preference (preferring Infiniti to other car brands), and conviction (believing that Infiniti is the best car for them). Infiniti marketers can use a combination of the promotion mix tools to create positive feelings and conviction. Advertising **extols** the Infiniti's advantages over competing brands. Press releases and other public relations activities stress the car's innovative features and performance. **Dealer** salespeople tell buyers about options, value for the price, and after-sale service.

Exhibit 17.2 Buyer-Readiness Stages

Finally, some members of the target market might be convinced about the product, but not quite get around to making the purchase. Potential Infiniti buyers may decide to wait for more information, or for the economy to improve. The communicator must lead these consumers to take the final step. Actions might include offering special promotional prices, **rebates**, or **premiums**. Salespeople might call or write to selected customers, inviting them to visit the **dealership** for a special showing.

Of course, marketing communications alone cannot create positive feelings and purchases for Infiniti. The car itself must provide superior value for the customer. In fact, outstanding marketing communications can actually speed the demise of a poor product. The more quickly potential buyers learn about the poor product, the more quickly they become aware of its faults. Thus, good marketing communication calls for "good deeds followed by good words".

In discussing buyer readiness states, we have assumed that buyers pass through **cognitive** (awareness, knowledge); **affective** (liking, preference, conviction); and behavioral (purchase) stages, in that order. This "learn-feel-do" sequence is appropriate when buyers have high involvement with a product category and perceive brands in the category to be highly differentiated, as is the case when they purchase a product such as an automobile. But consumers often follow other sequences. For example, they might follow a "do-feel-learn" sequence for high-involvement products with little perceived differentiation, such as aluminum siding. Still a third sequence is the "learn-do-feel", where consumers have low involvement and perceive little differentiation, as is the case when they buy a product such as salt. By understanding consumers' buying stages and their sequence, the marketer can do a better job of planning communications.

Choosing a Message

Having defined the desired audience response, the communicator turns to developing an effective message. Ideally, the message should get Attention, hold Interest, arouse Desire, and obtain Action (a framework known as the AIDA model). In practice, few messages take the consumer all the way from awareness to purchase, but the AIDA framework suggests the qualities of a good message.

In putting the message together, the marketing communicator must solve three problems: what to say (message content), how to say it logically (message structure), and how to say it symbolically (message format).

Message Content

The communicator has to figure out an appeal or theme that will produce the desired response. There are three types of appeals: rational, emotional, and moral. Rational appeals relate to the audience's self-interest. They show that the product will produce the desired benefits. Examples are messages showing a product's quality, economy, value, or performance. Thus, in its ads, Mercedes offers automobiles that are "engineered like no other car in the world", stressing engineering design, performance, and safety. Then pitching computer systems to business users, IBM salespeople talk about quality, value, improved productivity, and service.

Emotional appeals attempt to stir up either negative or positive emotions that can motivate purchase. These include fear, guilt, and shame appeals that get people to do things they should (brush their teeth, buy new tires), or to stop doing things they shouldn't (smoke, drink too much, eat fatty foods). For example, a Crest ad invokes mild fear when it claims, "There are some things you just can't afford to gamble with" (cavities). So does a Michelin tire ad that features **cute** babies and suggests, "Because so much is riding on your tires." Communicators also use positive emotional appeals such as love, humor, pride, and joy. Thus, AT & T's long-running ad theme, "reach out and touch someone", arouses strong, positive emotions.

Moral appeals are directed to the audience's sense of what is "right" and "proper". They often are used to urge people to support social causes such as a cleaner environment, better race relations, equal rights for women, and aid to the needy. An example of a moral appeal is the March of Dimes appeal: "God made you whole. Give to help those He didn't."

Message Structure

The communicator also must decide how to handle three message-structure issues. The first is whether to draw a conclusion or leave it to the audience. Early research showed that drawing a conclusion was usually more effective. More recent research, however, suggests that in many cases the advertiser is better off asking questions and letting buyers come to their own conclusions. The second message-structure issue is whether to present a one-sided argument (mentioning only the product's strengths), or a two-sided argument (**touting** the product's strengths while also admitting its shortcomings). Usually, a one-sided argument is more effective in sales presentations except when audiences are highly educated，negatively disposed，or likely to hear opposing claims. In these cases，two-sided messages can enhance the advertiser's **credibility** and make buyers more resistant to competitor attacks. The third message-structure issue is whether to present the strongest arguments first or last. Presenting them first gets strong attention，but may lead to an **anticlimactic** ending.

Message Format

The marketing communicator also needs a strong format for the message. In a print ad，the communicator has to decide on the **headline**，copy，illustration，and color. To attract attention，advertisers can use **novelty** and contrast；eye-catching pictures and headlines；**distinctive** formats；message size and position；and color，shape，and movement. If the message is to be carried over the radio，the communicator has to choose words，sounds，and voices. The "sound" of an announcer promoting banking services should be different from one promoting quality furniture.

Glossary

encoding *n.* converting data by the use of a code or a coded character set in such a manner that reconversion to the original form is possible 编码

decoding *n.* converting from code into plain text 译解

unplanned *a.* not thought out or prepared in advance；spontaneous 无计划的，未预先想到或准备的

distortion *n.* a statement that twists fact；a misrepresentation 歪曲，扭曲事实的陈述；曲解

unaware *a.* not aware or cognizant 未意识到的，不知道的

teaser *n.* an advertisement that attracts customers by offering something extra or free 优惠广告通过提供额外的或免费的东西来吸引顾客的广告

familiarity *n.* the quality or condition of being familiar 熟悉，通晓熟悉的特点或状态

extol *v.* to praise highly；exalt 高度赞扬；吹捧

dealer *n.* one that is engaged in buying and selling 商人，从事买卖的人

rebate *n.* a deduction from an amount to be paid or a return of part of an amount given in payment 折扣；部分退款，从将要支付的款子里减掉一部分或从已支付的款子里退还一部分

premium *n.* something offered free or at a reduced price as an inducement to buy something else 赠品，为刺激购买其他物品而免费赠送或减价销售的东西

dealership *n.* a franchise to sell specified items in a certain area 代理权，经销权，商品经销特许权，在某一区域内出售某特定商品的特许权

cognitive *a.* of, characterized by, involving, or relating to cognition 认识的属于、描述、包括或有关认识的，认知的

affective *a.* influenced by or resulting from the emotions 感情的，受感情影响的或由感情引起的，情感的，表达感情的

cute *a.* sweet；lovely 可爱的

tout *v.* to promote or praise energetically；publicize 吹嘘，吹捧促销或激情洋溢地赞扬；引起公众对……的注意

credibility *n.* a capacity for belief 可信程度

anticlimactic *a.* causing disappointment because something was less exciting than was expected，or happened immediately after a much more exciting event or experience 虎头蛇尾的

headline *n.* the title or caption of a newspaper article，usually set in large type 大字标题，通常用大号铅字排印的新闻报道的标题或题目

novelty *n.* the quality of being novel；newness 新奇新颖的性质；新鲜

distinctive *a.* characteristic or typical 特别的，特殊的；有特色的

Key Terms and Concepts

Message：The set of symbols that the sender transmits. 消息，信息
Media：The communication channels through which the message moves from sender to receiver. 媒体
Encoding：Encoding here，in this context，refers to the process of putting thought into symbolic form. 编码
Decoding：The process by which the receiver assigns meaning to the symbols encoded by the sender. 解码

Exercises

I. Discussion and Review Questions

1. How many elements are involved in the communication?
2. What are the communication functions?
3. What do the senders need to know?
4. Why do the senders need to develop feedback channels?
5. Please explain how to identify the target audience. Give an answer briefly.
6. What is the result of a long process of consumer decision making?
7. How many message-structure issues must be handled by the communicator?
8. What are the three types of appeals?

II. Vocabulary Review: Without referring to the text, fill in the blanks in the following sentences with the correct words from this list. You may change the tense, number, or form of the words to fit the context. Use each word only once; not all of the words on the list will be used.

| decoding | cute | dealership | unaware | extols | dealer | affective |
| anticlimactic | credibility | rebate | distortion | unplanned | tout | familiarity |

1. The marketing communicator's target market may be totally _____ of the product，know only its name，or know one or a few things about it.
2. In these cases，two-sided messages can enhance the advertiser's _____ and make buyers more resistant to competitor attacks.
3. Presenting them first gets strong attention，but may lead to a(n) _____

ending.

4. Actions might include offering special promotional prices, _____, or premiums.

5. In discussing buyer readiness states, we have assumed that buyers pass through cognitive (awareness, knowledge); _____ (liking, preference, conviction); and behavioral (purchase) stages, in that order.

6. Advertising _____ the Infiniti's advantages over competing brands.

7. Salespeople might call or write to selected customers, inviting them to visit the _____ for a special showing.

8. Four more are major communication functions—encoding, _____, response, and feedback.

9. _____ salespeople tell buyers about options, value for the price, and after-sale service.

10. So does a Michelin tire ad that features _____ babies and suggests, "Because so much is riding on your tires."

III. Match the terms and expressions on the left with the explanations on the right.

1. dealership	a. a capacity for belief
2. distortion	b. something offered free or at a reduced price as an inducement to buy something else
3. rebate	c. of, characterized by, involving, or relating to cognition
4. credibility	d. a deduction from an amount to be paid or a return of part of an amount given in payment
5. cognitive	e. a statement that twists fact; a misrepresentation
6. familiarity	f. to praise highly; exalt
7. extol	g. a franchise to sell specified items in a certain area
8. premium	h. the quality or condition of being familiar

IV. True and False statements.

1. Communication involves the nine elements shown in the figure. (   )

2. In good communication, senders don't need to know what audiences they wish to reach and what responses they want. (   )

3. The communicator also must decide how to handle three message-structure issues. (   )

4. The communicator has to figure out an appeal or theme that will produce the desired response. (   )

5. In most cases of marketing communication, the final response is not purchase. (   )

6. By understanding consumers' buying stages and their sequence, the marketer can do a better job of planning communications. (   )

Assuming target consumers know the product, how do they feel about it? Once potential buyers know about the Infiniti, Nissan's marketers want to move them through successively stronger stages of feelings toward the car. These stages include liking (feeling favorable about the Infiniti), preference (preferring Infiniti to other car brands), and conviction (believing that Infiniti is the best car for them). Infiniti marketers can use a combination of the promotion mix tools to create positive feelings and conviction. Advertising extols the Infiniti's advantages over competing brands. Press releases and other public relations activities stress the car's innovative features and performance. Dealer salespeople tell buyers about options, value for the price, and after-sale service.

Finally, some members of the target market might be convinced about the product, but not quite get around to making the purchase. Potential Infiniti buyers may decide to wait for more information, or for the economy to improve. The communicator must lead these consumers to take the final step. Actions might include offering special promotional prices, rebates, or premiums. Salespeople might call or write to selected customers, inviting them to visit the dealership for a special showing.

Of course, marketing communications alone cannot create positive feelings and purchases for Infiniti. The car itself must provide superior value for the customer. In fact, outstanding marketing communications can actually speed the demise of a poor product. The more quickly potential buyers learn about the poor product, the more quickly they become aware of its faults. Thus, good marketing communication calls for "good deeds followed by good words".

1. 销售者应知道要吸引什么样的顾客,要得到什么样的反馈。

2. 受众可能是潜在的消费者或目前的用户,即有权做出购买决定,或有权影响购买决定的人。

3. 如果广告语是用于广播的,那么营销人员就要对用词、音响和语音做出选择。

4. 购买是消费者花费很长时间所做出的决策。

5. 通常的活动包括提供特殊的促销价格、折扣和赠品。

6. 首先提出最有力的论点,会得到充分的关注,但或许会得到虎头蛇尾的结果。

Supplemental Reading Material

Marketing Strategies in the Introduction Stage

In launching a new product, marketing management can set a high or a low level for each marketing variable (price, promotion, distribution, product quality).

Considering only price and promotion, management can pursue one of the four strategies. A rapid-skimming strategy consists of launching the new product at a high price and a high promotion level. The firm charges a high price in order to recover as much profit per unit as possible. It spends heavily on promotion to convince the market of the product's merits even at the high piece. The high promotion acts to accelerate the rate of market penetration. This strategy makes sense under the following assumption: a large part of the potential market is unaware of the product; those who become aware of the product are eager to have it and can pay the asking price; and the firm faces potential competition and wants to build brand preference. A slow-skimming strategy consists of launching the new product at a high price and spending heavily on promotion. The high price helps recover as much profit per unit as possible, and the low level of promotion keeps marketing expenses down. This combination is expected to skim a lot of profit from the market. This strategy makes sense when the market is limited in size; most of the market is aware of the product; buyers are willing to pay a high price; and potential competition is not imminent. A rapid-penetration strategy consists of launching the product at a low price and spending heavily on promotion. This strategy promises to bring about the fastest market penetration and the largest market share. This strategy makes sense when the market is large, the market is unaware of the product, most buyers are price-sensitive, there is strong potential competition, and the company's unit manufacturing costs fall with the company's scale of production and accumulated manufacturing experience. A slow-penetration strategy consists of launching the new product at a low price and low level of promotion. The low price will encourage rapid product acceptance, and low promotion costs bring profits up. The company believes that market demand is highly sensitive to price but minimally sensitive to promotion. This strategy makes sense when the market is large, the market is highly aware of the product, the market is price-sensitive, and there is some potential competition.

Marketing strategies in the growth stage During the growth stage, the firm uses several strategies to sustain rapid market growth as long as possible: It improves product quality and adds new product features and improved styling. It adds new models and flanker products (i. e., products of different sizes, flavors, and so forth that protect the main product). It enters new market segments. It increases its distribution coverage and enters new distribution channels. It shifts from product-awareness advertising to product-preference advertising. It lowers prices to attract the next layer of price-sensitive buyers. The firm that pursues these market expansion strategies will strengthen its competitive position. In the growth stage it faces a trade-off between high market share and high current profit. By spending money on product improvement, and distribution, it captures a dominant position. It forgoes maximum current profit in the hope of making even greater profits in the next stage.

Marketing strategies in the maturity stage In the maturity stage, some companies abandon their weaker products. They prefer to concentrate their resources on their more profitable products and on new products. Yet by doing so they may be ignoring the high potential that many old products will have. Marketers should systematically consider strategies of market, product, and marketing-mix modification.

Market modification The company might try to expand the market for its mature brand by working with the two factors that make up sales volume: *Volume = number of brand users × usage rate per user*. The company can try to expand the number of brand users in three ways. Enter new market segments: The company can try to enter new market segments that use the demand but not the brand. Convert nonusers: The company can try to attract nonusers to the product. Win competitors' customers: The company can attract competitors' customers to try or adopt the brand. Volume can also be convincing current brand users to increase their annual usage of the brand. Here are three strategies: The company can try to get customers to use the product more frequently. The company can try to interest users in using more of the product on each occasion. And it can try to discover new product uses and convince people to use the product in more varied ways.

Product Modification   Managers also try to stimulate sales by modifying the product's characteristics through quality improvement, improvement, or style improvement. A strategy of quality improvement aims at increasing the product's functional performance—its durability, reliability, speed, taste. A strategy of feature improvement aims at adding new features that expand the product's versatility, safety, or convenience. A strategy of style improvement aims at increasing the product's aesthetic appeal.

Marketing-mix modification   Product managers might also try to stimulate sales by modifying other marketing-mix elements (prices, distribution, advertising, and personal promotion). Marketers often debate which tools are most effective in the mature stage. Some say that sales promotion has more impact at this stage because consumers have reached an equilibrium in their buying habits and preferences, and psychological persuasion (advertising) is not as effective as financial persuasion (sales-promotion deals). Other marketers argue that brands should be managed as capital assets and supported by advertising. Advertising expenditures should be treated as a capital investment, not a current expense. Brand managers, however, use sales promotion because its effects are quicker and more visible to their superiors, but excessive sales-promotion activity can hurt the brand's image and long-run profit performance.

Marketing strategies during the decline stage   In handling its aging products, a company faces a number of tasks and decisions. The first task is to establish a system for identifying weak products. To do this, many companies appoint a product-review committee with representatives from marketing, R & D, manufacturing, and finance. This committee develops system for identifying weak products. The controller's office supplies data for each product showing trends in market size, market share, prices, costs, and profits. A computer program then analyzes this information to help managers decide which products are dubious. The managers responsible for dubious products fill out rating forms showing where they think sales and profits will go with and without any changes in marketing strategy. The product-review committee examines this information and makes a recommendation for each dubious product— leave it alone, modify its marketing strategy, or drop it. Some firms will abandon declining markets earlier than others. Much depends on the presence and height of exit barriers in the industry. The lower the exit barriers, the easier it is for firms to leave the industry, and the more tempting it is for the remaining firms to stay and attract the withdrawing firms' customers. The remaining firms will enjoy increased sales and profits. The appropriate decline strategy depends on the industry's relative attractiveness and the company's competitive strength in that industry. For example, a company that is in an unattractive industry but possesses competitive strength should consider shrinking selectively. A company that is in an attractive industry and has competitive strength should consider strengthening its investment.

Discussion and Review Questions:

1. Under what assumptions does a rapid-skimming strategy make sense?

2. What strategies do marketers use in the growth stage?

3. Which aspects of strategic marketers should be systematically considered in the maturity stage?

4. As a company tries to expand the market for its mature brand, what factors will the company work with?

5. What strategies do marketers use in the decline stage?

Unit 18

The Realities of Public Relations

Text

The public relations practitioners serve as an intermediary between the organization that he or she represents and all of that organization's **publics**. Consequently, the PR practitioners have responsibilities both to the institution and to its various publics. He or she distributes information that enables the institution's publics to understand its policies.

Public relations involves research into all audiences: receiving information from them, advising management of their attitudes and response, helping to set policies that demonstrate responsible attention to them and constantly evaluating the effectiveness of all PR programs. This inclusive role **embraces** all activities connected with ascertaining and influencing the opinions of a group of people. But, just as important, public relations involves responsibility and responsiveness in policy and information to the best interests of the organization and its publics.

The complexity of PR's role prompted the Public Relation Society of America to define fourteen activities generally associated with public relations: (1) **publicity**, (2) communication, (3) **public affairs**, (4) issues management, (5) government relations, (6) financial public relations, (7) **community** relations, (8) industry relations, (9) minority relations, (10) advertising, (11) press agency, (12) promotion, (13) media relations, and (14) **propaganda**.

Another definition of public relations as "reputation management" has gained currency. The British Institute of Public Relations offers this:

Public relations is about reputation—the result of what you do, what you say and what others say about you. Public Relations Practice is the discipline which looks after reputation with the aim of earning understanding and support, and influencing opinion and behavior.

As a practical matter, good public relations involves confronting a problem openly and honestly and then solving it. In the long run, the best PR is disclosure of an active social conscience.

The Basic Principles of Public Relations

We can describe the function and role of public relations practice by stating the basic principles:

1. Public relations deals with reality, not false fronts. **Conscientiously** planned programs that put the public interests in the forefront are the basis of sound public relations policy.

2. Public relations is a service-oriented profession in which public interest, not personal reward, should be the primary consideration.

3. Since a public relations practitioner must go to the public to seek support for programs and policies, public interest is the central **criterion** by which he or she should select these programs and policies.

4. Because a public relations practitioner reaches many publics through mass media, which are the public channels of communication, the integrity of these channels must be preserved.

5. Because PR practitioners are in the middle between an organization and its publics, they must be effective communicators—conveying information back and forth until understanding is reached.

6. To expedite **two-way communication** and to be responsible communicators, public relation practitioners must use scientific **public opinion** research intensively.

7. To understand what their publics are saying and to reach them effectively, public relations practitioners must employ the social sciences—psychology, sociology, social psychology, public opinion, communications study and **semantics**.

8. Because a lot of people do PR research, the PR person must adapt the work of other, related disciplines, including learning theory and other psychology theories, sociology, political science, economic and history.

9. Public relations practitioners are obligated to explain problems to the public before these problems become crises.

10. A public relations practitioner should be measured by only one standard: **ethical** performance.

PR and Related Activities

Public relations involves many activities. People's participation in the activities of public relations and their subsequent assertion that, therefore, they are "in public relations" often cause confusion in others' understanding of what public relations is. The activities of PR practice include: press agency, promotion, publicity, public affairs, research, graphic, advertising, marketing and **merchandising** support. But public relations is something greater than just this collection of activities.

Changes in the environment for public relations can shift the emphasis from one activity to another over time. Recently, advances in technology—such as significant difference in the way the news media operate—have driven many of these shifts. Another result of these advances has been increased **globalization**, affecting both internal and external communication and significantly altering the way crises are handled. All crises now get global recognition which creates considerable urgency of appropriate organizational responses that are destined to be weighted in the world court of public opinion.

Press Agentry

Because PR's origins are associated with press agency, many people think that press agentry and public relations are the same. But press agentry involves planning activities or staging events—sometimes just stunts—that will attract attention to a person, institution, idea or product. There is certainly nothing wrong with attracting crowds and giving people something to see or talk about, provided that no deception is involved. Today's press agents are polished pros who steer clear of fraud and **puffery**, unless it is done strictly in fun and is clearly recognizable as such.

Promotion

A hazy line separates yesterday's press agentry from today's promotion. Although promotion incorporates special events that could be called press agentry, it goes beyond that into opinion making. Promotion attempts to **garner** support and **endorsement** for a person, product, institution or idea. Promotional campaigns depend for their effectiveness on the effective use of various PR tools, and in many cases more is not better. Examples of promotion are the various fund-raising drives conducted by charities, health-care groups and conservation interests. Promotion, fund raising and all the attendant drum beating constitute one variety of PR activities that may be incorporated into an overall public relations program. What makes promotion activities worthwhile is the merit of the cause. The **legitimacy** of the cause is also important from a purely pragmatic viewpoint: It won't receive media coverage if it isn't legitimate news and if it can't maintain public support.

Publicity

Because publicity is used to call attention to the special events or the activities surrounding a promotion, there is confusion about this term. Public relations is often used as a synonym for publicity, but the two activities are not the same. Publicity is strictly a communications function, whereas PR involves a management function as well. Essentially, publicity means placing information in a news medium—either in a mass media or in a specialized medium.

Publicists are writers. Use of the term public relations by institutions to describe publicity jobs is unfortunate. Publicists perform a vital function—disseminating information—but their counselors, usually at the executive level, are in a position to effect substantive management changes.

Publicity isn't always good news. In a crisis, for example, it's often important for the organization to tell its story before the news media develop it on their own. In these situations, the publicist is an inside reporter for internal and external media.

Publicity is not public relations. It is a tool used by public relations practitioners. Some writers do choose careers as information writers, but they are publicists, not public relations practitioners.

Public Affairs

Many public relations people use the term public affairs to describe their work, but this is misleading. Public affair is actually a highly specialized kind of public relations that involves community relations and governmental relations—that is, dealing with officials within the community and working with legislative groups and various pressure groups such as consumers. It is a critical part of a public relations program, but it is not the whole program.

In agencies of the government, including the military, the term public affairs is commonly used to designate a broader responsibility than public information, which consists merely of publicity—handing out information. Thus a public information officer is a publicist, whereas a public affairs person in government often has policy making responsibility. Because a rather shortsighted law precludes government use of people identified as public relations personnel, military public affairs officers often have responsibility for all facets of internal and external public relations.

Research

The foundation of good public relations strategy is research—research on publics and public opinion, as well as on the situation and circumstances that have created the environment for public opinions. Public relations people do research to identify an organization's publics and to discover what they think. This research involves asking people questions and observing their behavior. Other observations include looking at the background behind a situation or problem to find out what issues or concerns are involved and how events have affected or been affected by public opinion. Public relations practitioners must think in broad terms about research and research **methodologies**; this entails recognizing the need for research and understanding how to apply research results.

PR people do both primary and secondary research. Primary research means generating new information. Secondary research means using data others have generated to arrive at some conclusions and recommendations. Technology has made research much easier because so much information is now **accessible** by computer.

Merchandising

In contrast to marketing, merchandising is concerned with packaging of a product, an idea or perhaps even a president. Its research asks what subtle emotions play a part in acceptance of the product, what shape of package is easiest to handle, what color is likely to attract more attention or what kind of display will make people react. The answers are important to salespeople and dealers and provide a valuable supplement to the marketing and advertising research in a campaign.

Technology has changed merchandising dramatically. Today it is tied more closely to marketing and other activities such as advertising and promotion. This change is seen in the diversity of messages delivered directly to potential customers by mail—print, cassette or computer disk, as well as CD-ROM—and the direct response system of television shopping channels and ordering by computer.

Merchandising experts are strong in graphic, color, tactile response and emotional reactions to physical imagery. Their work is a frequent and vital part of the public relations milieu. However, it is not itself public relations.

Glossary

public *n.* people in general 公众

embrace *v.* to accept or include something 包括，包含

publicity *n.* attention in magazines，newspaper or TV 宣传报道

community *n.* the people who live in an area 社区

propaganda *n.* information that a government or organization spreads in order to influence people's opinions and beliefs 宣传，鼓吹

conscientiously *ad.* in a careful way that involves a lot of effort 认真地，一丝不苟地

criterion *n.* a standard that is used for judging something or making a decision about something（批评、评判）标准

semantics *n.* the meaning of words and phrases 语义学

ethical *a.* involving the principles used for deciding what is right and what is wrong 伦理的；道德的

merchandising *n.* the business of arranging and showing products in shops in a way that makes people want to buy them 商品化，商品在货架上如何摆放以吸引顾客的艺术

puffery *n.* an advertisement boasting about a product 吹捧；吹捧广告

garner *v.* to collect or obtain a large amount of something useful or important 收集

endorsement *n.* an occasion where someone gives official or public support to a particular person or thing 赞同，认可

legitimacy *n.* the fact that something is legal 合法性，正统性

methodology *n.* the methods and principles used for doing a particular kind of work 方法学；方法论；一套方法

accessible *a.* easy for anyone to obtain and use 容易接近的，容易获得的

Key Terms and Concepts

Public affairs：A special kind of public relations that involves community relations and government relations，the relations dealing with the officials within the community and working with the legislative groups and pressure groups. 公共事务

Two-way communication：The process of giving or making emotions or ideas known to someone and at the same time receiving the feedback from the people who received the message and responding accordingly. 双向沟通

Public opinion：The attitude that people in general have towards something，or thoughts of general public about something. 公共舆论

Globalization：The idea that the world is developing a single economy and culture as a result of improved technology and communications and the influence of very large multinational companies. 全球化

Exercises

I. Discussion and Review Questions.

1. What is the exclusive role played by public relations?
2. What are the criteria for a good public relations practice?
3. How can public relations be used in an integrated manner with other marketing techniques?
4. Give an example to illustrate the importance of crises management for an organization?
5. What are the major differences between publicity and advertising?
6. "To entertain a company's clients is not part of public relations." Make your comments on this remark.
7. How do you understand the idea that public relations is reputation management?

II. Vocabulary Review: Without referring to the text, fill in the blanks in the following sentences with the correct words from this list. You may change the tense, number, or form of the words o fit the context. Use each word only once; not all of the words on the list will be used.

conscience	embrace	publics	criterion	garner
disseminate	methodology	legitimacy	accessible	preclude
community	graphic	merchandising	ethical	

1. In the long run, the best PR is disclosure of an active social _____ .
2. This inclusive role _____ all activities connected with the ascertaining and influencing the opinions of a group of people.
3. A public relations practitioner should be measured by only one standard: _____ performance.
4. Since a public relations practitioner must go to seek support for programs and policies, public interests is the central _____ by which he or she should select these programs and policies.
5. Technology has made research much easier because so much information is now _____ by computer.
6. Because a rather shortsighted law _____ government use of people identified as public relations personnel, military pubic affairs officers often have responsibility for all facets of internal and external public relations.
7. But, just as important, public relations involves responsibility and responsiveness in policy and information to the best interests of the organization and its _____ .

8. Promotion attempts to _____ support and endorsement for a person, product, institution or idea.

III. Match the terms and expressions on the left with the explanations on the right.

1. community   a. an occasion when someone gives official or public support to a particular person or thing
2. endorsement   b. a series of actions intended to produce political, social or economic change
3. publicity   c. coming or happening before other things
4. ethical   d. involving the principles used for deciding what is right and what is wrong
5. campaign   e. the people who live in an area
6. emotion   f. not real but only created in your mind
7. merchandising   g. attention in magazines, newspaper or TV
8. imaginary   h. a feeling that you experience
9. charity   i. the business of arranging and showing products in shops in a way that makes people want to buy them
10. primary   j. money or food that is given to people who are poor or ill so that they can live

IV. True and False statements.

1. Public relations is about reputation—the result of what you do, what you say and what others say about you. (   )
2. Because publicity is used to call attention to the special events or the activities surrounding a promotion, there is confusion about this term. (   )
3. The research of merchandising asks what obvious emotions play a part in acceptance of the product. (   )
4. PR people usually only do secondary research. (   )
5. It is wise for institutions to use the term public relations to describe publicity jobs. (   )
6. Secondary research means using data others have generated to arrive at some conclusions and recommendations. (   )
7. Changes in the environment for public relations will not shift the emphasis from one activity to another over time. (   )
8. Publicity is not public relations but a tool used by public relations practitioners. (   )
9. Technology has never changed merchandising dramatically. (   )

V. Translate the following into Chinese.

Seeking the PR "Source Spring"

For all his influence on the field of public relations, Bernays is not its "founder". In fact, some authorities say Bernays learned public relations while serving on George Creel's Committee on Public Information, which was dedicated to gaining popular support for the United States' war effort during World War I.

Public relations probably has no single "founder", but many public relations practitioners in the United States see Ivy Lee as the first practitioner of a modern-style relations practice.

Without doubt, public relations developed faster in the United States than in other countries. Historian Alan R. Raucher attributes this to the nation's social, political, cultural and economic climate, as well as to the power of its media to render all large public institutions vulnerable to public opinion. Public relations practice also has become an important export service, as other nations have developed their own versions of the practice.

Public relations as a concept has no central, identifying founder, national origin or founding date because it focuses on efforts to influence—not only opinions but behavior. This very element has created the greatest criticism of public relations. Historians who view public relations as a significant positive influence regard it as a broker for public support of ideas, institutions and people. Others, however, contend that this entails the sacrifice of individual freedom, which is usurped by majority decision. Of course, the same tradeoff is central to the nature of democracy itself; but this does not dispose of the problem that public opinion can be misused.

VI. Translate the following into English.

1. 实际上,良好的公共关系涉及开诚布公地面对问题然后解决它。

2. 公共关系人员必须在问题成为危机前向公众解释这一问题。

3. 随着时间的推移,公共关系环境的变化可以使其工作重心从一个活动转向另一个活动。

4. 公共事务实际上是一种高度专业化的公共关系,它涉及社区和政府的关系。

5. 促销活动的有效性取决于是否能有效地使用各种公关手段。

6. 许多公关人员使用"公共事务"来描述他们的工作,但这容易引起误导。

7. 一项好的公关策略是建立在好的公关调查的基础上的。

8. 技术的发展使得商品化活动发生了巨大的变化。

Supplemental Reading Material

Identifying and Describing Publics

Every discipline seems to develop its own terminology; sometimes, the same term is used in different ways by people in different disciplines and professions. And within public relations, the distinction between an "audience" and a "public" is likewise essential to understand.

The term "public" has traditionally meant any group that has some involvement with an organization's neighbors, customers, employees, competitors and government regulators. Publics and organizations have consequences for each other: what a public does has some impact on the organization, and vice versa. You might imagine that "public" and "audience" are synonymous. But in important ways they are not.

From a public relations perspective, the term audience suggests a group of people who are recipients of something—a message or a performance. An audience is thus inherently passive. But this conflicts with the goal of most public relations programs, which is to stimulate strong audience participation. To help resolve the semantic conflict, the term "public" evolved to distinguish between passive audiences and active ones.

In public relations, the term "public" ("active audience") encompasses any group of people who are tied together, however loosely, by some common bond of interest or concern and who have consequences for an organization. The best way to understand this concept is to think of various publics that you, as an individual, might be part of.

First, you belong to a group of consumers that, no doubt, has been well-defined by marketing people. You may, for instance, be in the eighteen-to-twenty-one-year-old "college" market. This market receives a great deal of attention because—although you may not believe it—it is responsible for a vast outlay of cash. Second, you may have an organizational identity. For instance, if you belong to social or civic organization, you are a member of a public. You also belong to other publics because of your race, religion, ethnic group or national origin. You probably would not want to be thought as member of "the general public", and you are not. No one is. No such public exists. Instead, you are a member of many definable, describable publics. It is the job of public relations practitioners to identify these publics as they relate the practitioners' organization.

Discussion and Review Questions:

1. How to define the term "public" from the public relations perspective? Could the same explanation apply to "audience"?

2. What are the differences between an "audience" and a "public"? Please give your opinion.

3. What are the characteristics of consumers according to your understanding?

4. Try to define the term "consumers" according to your understanding. Give a concrete example of this term in reality.

From Business Models to E-Business Models

Text

From Business Models
to E-Business Models

The term business model is often mentioned in the print and by executives. According to one respected researcher, "A business model is the method of doing by which a company can **sustain** itself—that is to generate revenue." Another researcher suggested that a business model contains three streams: the value proposition, the value stream, and the logistical stream relating to supply chain issues. Based on current use of the term, we suggest that a business model is the method by which an organization sustains itself in the long run and includes its value proposition for partners and customers as well as its revenue streams.

A business model does not exist in vacuum. It relates to strategy in that a firm will select one or more business models as strategies to accomplish enterprise goals. For instance, if the firm is to position itself as a high-tech, innovative company, it might decide to use the Internet to connect and communicate with its suppliers and customers, as does Dell Computer, Microsoft and the like.

Presented with many opportunities, how does a firm select the best business models? The authors of *Internet Business Models and Strategies* suggest the following components as critical to appraising the fit of a business model for the company and its environment:

- Customer value. Does the model create value through its product offerings that is differentiated in some way from that of its competitors?

- Scope. Which markets does the firm serve? Are they growing? Are these markets currently served by the firm, or will they be the higher-risk new markets?
- Price. Are the firm's products priced to appeal markets and also to achieve company share and objectives?
- Revenue sources. Where is the money coming from? Is it plentiful enough to sustain growth and profit objectives over time? Many dotcom failures overlooked this element.
- Connected activities. What activities will the firm need to perform to create the value described in the model? Does the firm have these **capabilities**? For example, if 24/7 customer service is part of the value, the firm must be prepared to deliver it.
- **Implementation**. The firm must have the ability to actually make it happen. This involves the firm's systems, people, culture, and so on.
- Capabilities. Does the firm have the resources (financial, core competencies, and so on) to make the selected model work?
- **Sustainability**. The e-business model is particularly appropriate if it will create a competitive advantage over time. This means it will be difficult to imitate and the environment will be attractive for maintaining the model over time.

Traditional business models such as retailing, selling, advertising, and **auction** have been around ever since the first business set up shop. What makes a business model an e-business model is the direct connection with information technology:

E-Business Model = Business Model + Information Technology

Thus, an e-business model is a method by which the organization sustains itself in the long term using information technology, which includes its value proposition for partners and customers as well as its revenue streams. For example, the Internet allows media, music, and software firms to deliver their products over the Internet, creating new distribution models that cut costs and increase value. E-business models that take advantage of the Internet properties may be seen as part of a **subset** sometimes called Internet business models.

E-business models can capitalize on digital data collection and distribution techniques without using the Internet. For example, when retailers scan products and customer cards at the checkout, these data can become a rich source of knowledge for inventory management and promotional offers; that is e-marketing without Internet. Similarly, when these data are available through the firm's **proprietary** computer network (intranet), the firm is applying e-business without the Internet. Even though the Internet spawned the vast majority of e-business models, it is very important to remember that e-marketing and e-business models may operate outside the Internet.

Value and Revenue

As part of its e-business model, a company describes the ways in which it creates value for customers and partners. Business partners might include supply chain members such as suppliers, wholesalers and retailers, or firms with which the company joins forces to create new brands (such as Microsoft and NBC allied to create MSNBC). Firms deliver **stakeholder** value through e-business models by using digital products and processes; whether online or offline, the value proposition involves knowing what is important to the customer and partner and delivering it better than other firms. Value encompasses the customer's perceptions of the product's benefits, specifically its **attributes**, brand name, and supporting services. Subtracted from the benefits are the costs involved in acquiring the product, such as monetary, time, energy, and psychic. Like customers, partners evaluate value by determining whether the partnership provides more benefits than costs.

Value = Benefits − Costs

Information technology usually—but not always—increases benefits and lowers costs to stakeholders. E-business strategies capitalize on the Internet properties to add many general benefits, thus increasing stakeholder value. (See Exhibit 19.1) Conversely, they can also decrease value when web sites are complex, information is hard to locate, and technical difficulties interrupt data access or shopping transactions.

Exhibit 19.1   Benefits of E-Business

E-business increases benefits
- Online mass customization (different products and messages to different stakeholders)
- Personalization (giving stakeholders relevant information)
- 24/7 convenience
- Self-service ordering and tracking
- One-stop shopping

E-business decreases costs
- Low-cost distribution of communication messages
- Low-cost distribution channel for digital products
- Lowers costs for transaction processing
- Lowers costs for knowledge acquisition (e.g. research and customer feedback)
- Increases efficiencies in supply chain (through communication and inventory optimization)
- Decreases the cost of customer service

E-business increases revenue
- Increases online transaction revenues such as product, information, advertising, and subscriptions sales; or commission/fee on transaction
- Adds value to products/services and increase prices (e.g. online FAQ and customer support)
- Increases customer base by reaching new markets
- Builds customer relationships and, thus, increases current customer spending (share of wallet)

As a general rule, e-business strategies can help a firm to decrease internal costs, often improve value proposition for customers and partners. They can also increase enterprises' revenue stream, an important part of e-business models.

Menu of E-Business Models

A key element in setting strategic objectives is to take stock of the company's current situation and decide the level of **commitment** to e-business in general and e-marketing in particular. The possible levels of commitment fall along a **continuum** that is appropriately presented as a **pyramid** since few businesses occupy the top position. As a general rule, the higher the firm travels up the pyramid, the higher its level of commitment to e-business becomes, the more its strategies are integrated with information technology, and the greater impact information technology has on its organization. Also, the more strategic moves at the top, the more tactical activities at lower levels; as a result, higher levels carry more risks than lower levels for most firms.

Bear in mind that one firm's activity may be another firm's enterprise-level strategy. For example, electronic transaction ordering process (e. g. selling product on a web site) may be a small activity for a ski shop with 1% of its business from the on-line channel, but it is an enterprise-level activity for FedEx, the package delivery service company.

In consulting with CEOs worldwide, the Gartner Group poses these questions for firms prior to embarking on any e-business strategies:

1. Are the business models likely to change in my industry? If they are not, there is no reason to get involved. If they are, answering this question suggests strategic direction for the firm.

2. What does the answer to question 1 mean to my company? The answers vary by size, industry, location, and more.

3. When do I need to be ready? This involves thoughtful competitive analysis.

4. How do I get there from here? This is where e-business strategy comes in.

E-Business Models at Various Levels of Commitment

Each level of the pyramid indicates a number of opportunities for the firm to provide stakeholder value and generate revenue streams using information technology. A company can become involved in e-business at activity level, business process level, enterprise level, or through a pure play. Commitment is lower at activity level and rises with each level. The main e-business models at activity level include online purchasing, order processing, e-mail, micro-mail, content publishing, business intelligence, online advertising, online sales promotion, and **dynamic pricing** strategies. The main e-business models at business process level are customer relationship management (CRM), knowledge management (KM), **supply chain management (SCM)**, community building online, database marketing online, **enterprise resource planning (ERP)**, and mass customization. The main e-business models at enterprise level are e-commerce, portal, online broker, online agent, manufacturer's agent, and virtual mall. The final level of the pyramid is composed of the Internet pure plays. Pure plays are businesses that began on the Internet like Amazon. com and other dotcoms, even if they later added a **brick-and-mortar** presence.

An Optimized System of E-Business Models

We defined e-business as the continuous **optimization** of a firm's business activities through digital technology. Regardless of commitment level, this means that firms usually combine traditional business and e-business models. Some firms adopt only one or two of these processes, which shows commitment at the business process level. The best examples of players at enterprise level are click-and-mortar enterprises such as Dell, Amazon, Dangdang. com, and JD. com and many brick-and-mortar operations that have successfully migrated online. These businesses face unique challenges since customers view them as unified businesses and expect a high degree of coordination between online and offline operations. Thus, a customer would like to be able to access the same Amazon online account whether from his home computer late at night or from the local office—and he can. The danger at the enterprise level is that the established corporate culture might squash e-commerce initiatives or slow them down with the best intentions. To avoid these problems, many businesses have spun off their e-commerce operations as wholly owned subsidiaries or pure plays so they can compete without the weight of the parent business, while this strategy may be successful, reuniting the parent and child operations can be difficult.

A fully optimized e-business that uses the Internet to sell is the sum of multiple e-business activities and processes: e-commerce, business intelligence, customer relationship management, supply chain management, and enterprise resource planning as represented in the following equation:

$$EB = EC + BI + CRM + SCM + ERP$$

Glossary

sustain *v.*   to supply with necessities and support 维持;支撑,承担

capability *n.*   the quality of being capable (physically or intellectually or legally) 能力;本领;潜在能力

implementation *n.*   the act of implementing (providing a practical means for accomplishing something); carrying into effect 执行;实施

sustainability *n.*   the property of being sustainable 持续性;永续性;能维持性

auction *n.*   the public sale of something to the highest bidder 拍卖;竞卖;竞拍

subset *n.*   a set contained within another set 子集

proprietary *a.*   protected by trademark or patent or copyright; made or produced or distributed by one having exclusive rights 所有的;专利的;私人拥有的

stakeholder *n.*   someone who has an interest in a company's or organization's affairs 利益相关者

attribute *n.*   an abstraction belonging to or characteristic of an entity 属性;特质

commitment *n.*   the act of binding yourself (intellectually or emotionally) to a course of action 承诺,保证;委托;承担义务

continuum *n.*   a continuous non-spatial whole or extent or succession in which no part or portion is distinct or distinguishable from adjacent parts 连续体

pyramid *n.*   a massive monument with a square base and four triangular sides 金字塔;棱锥体

optimization *n.*   the act of rendering optimal 最优化;最佳化状态

Key Terms and Concepts

Business model: A business model is the method by which the organization sustains itself in the long run and includes its value proposition for partners and customers as well as its revenue streams. 商务模式

E-business model: An e-business model is a method by which the organization sustains itself in the long term using information technology, which includes its value proposition for partners and customers as well as its revenue streams. For example, the Internet allows media, music, and software firms to deliver their products over the Internet, creating new distribution model that cuts costs and increases value. E-business models that take advantage of the Internet properties may be seen as part of a subset sometimes called Internet business models. 电子商务模式

Stakeholder: Stakeholder here refers to a party that has an interest in an enterprise or project. The primary stakeholders in a typical corporation are its investors, employees, customers and suppliers. However, modern theory goes beyond this conventional notion to embrace additional stakeholders such as the community, government and trade associations. 利益相关者

Dynamic pricing: Dynamic pricing refers to a pricing strategy that applies different price levels for different customers and situations. For example, a first-time buyer or someone who hasn't purchased for many months may receive lower prices than a heavy user, or prices may drop during the lower demand periods. The Internet allows firms to price items automatically while users view pages on the web sites. 动态定价

Supply Chain Management（SCM）: The term supply chain management（SCM）was developed during the 1980s to express the need to integrate the key business processes, from end users to original suppliers. Original suppliers are those that provide products, services, and information that add value for customers and other stakeholders. The basic idea behind SCM is that companies and corporations involve themselves in a supply chain by exchanging information about market fluctuations and production capabilities. 供应链管理

Enterprise Resource Planning（ERP）: Enterprise Resource Planning utilizes ERP software applications to improve the performance of organizations' resource planning, management control and operational control. ERP software is multi-module application software that integrates activities across functional departments, from product planning, parts purchasing, inventory control, and product distribution, to order tracking. ERP software may include application modules for the finance, accounting and human resources aspects of a business. 企业资源规划系统

Optimization: Optimization is an act, process, or methodology of making something （as a design, system, or decision）as fully perfect, functional, or effective as possible. 最优化

Brick-and-mortar operations: Here in this context, it refers to traditional offline physical store operations as opposed to online operations. 实体(店)经营

Exercises

I. Discussion and Review Questions

1. How does e-business strategy relate to strategy on the corporate level?
2. Define e-business/marketing strategy and explain how it is used.
3. How does an e-business model differ from a traditional business model?
4. What is the formula for determining value according to the text?
5. What are the four levels of commitment to e-business? Give examples of each level of commitment.
6. What is customer relationship management（CRM）and why do companies create strategies in this area?

7. How is e-commerce defined?

8. What is an Internet pure play? List some examples.

9. Why is it important for an e-business model to create value in a way that is differentiated from the way competitors create value?

10. According to text and your experience as a customer and your examination of Amazon.com site, what strategic objectives do you think are appropriate for this e-business?

II. *Vocabulary Review: Without referring to the text, fill in the blanks in the following sentences with the correct words from this list. You may change the tense, number, or form of the words to fit the context. Use each word only once; not all of the words on the list will be used.*

attribute	auction	capabilities	commitment	continuum
implementation	optimize	optimization	pyramid	proprietary
stakeholder	subset	sustain	sustainability	

1. Each level of the pyramid indicates a number of opportunities for the firm to provide _____ value and generate revenue streams using information technology.

2. By definition, a data mart is a(n) _____ of a data warehouse designed for specific group of users or a particular subject area.

3. Traditional business models such as retailing, selling, advertising, and _____ have been around ever since the first business set up shop.

4. As a general rule, the higher the firm travels up the pyramid, the higher its level of _____ to e-business becomes, the more its strategies are integrated with information technology, and the greater impact information technology has on its organization.

5. The possible levels of commitment fall along a(n) _____ that is appropriately presented as a pyramid since few businesses occupy the top position.

6. We defined e-business as the continuous _____ of a firm's business activities through digital technology. Regardless of commitment level, this means that firms usually combine traditional business and e-business models.

7. Similarly, when these data are available through the firm's _____ computer network (intranet), the firm is applying e-business without the Internet.

8. Environment, natural resources, climate change, remaining poverty, and growing inequality. These issues all affect the _____ for growth.

9. Value encompasses the customer's perceptions of the product's benefits, specifically its_____ , brand name, and supporting services.

10. _____ means that the firm must have the ability to actually make it happen. This involves the firm's systems, people, culture, and so on.

III. Match the terms and expressions on the left with the explanations on the right.

1. business model

2. brick-and-mortar operations

3. pure plays

4. e-business model

5. dynamic pricing

6. mass customization

7. optimization

8. subset

a. businesses that began on the Internet like Amazon. com and other dotcoms, even if they later added a brick-and-mortar presence

b. a method by which an organization sustains itself in the long term using information technology, which includes its value proposition for partners and customers as well as its revenue streams

c. a pricing strategy that applies different price levels for different customers and situations

d. a set whose members are members of another set

e. the use of flexible computer-aided manufacturing systems and online information to produce custom output. Those systems combine the low unit costs of mass production processes with the flexibility of individual customization

f. an act, process, or methodology of making something (as a design, system, or decision) as fully perfect, functional, or effective as possible

g. the method by which an organization sustains itself in the long run and includes its value proposition for partners and customers as well as its revenue streams

h. traditional offline physical store operations as opposed to online operations

IV. True and False statements.

1. A business model does not exist in vacuum. It relates to strategy in that a firm will select one or more business models as strategies to accomplish enterprise goals. (　　)

2. What makes a business model an e-business model is the direct connection with information technology: E-Business Model ＝ Business Model ＋ Information Technology. (　　)

3. E-business models must capitalize on digital data collection and distribution techniques using the Internet. (　　)

4. Even though the Internet spawned the vast majority of e-business models, it is very important to remember that e-marketing and e-business models may operate outside the Internet. (　　)

5. According to the text, information technology can always increase benefits and lower costs to stakeholders. (　　)

6. As a general rule, e-business strategies can help a firm to decrease internal costs, often improve value proposition for customers and partners. They can also increase enterprises' revenue stream, an important part of e-business models. (　　)

7. A company can become involved in e-business at activity level, business process

level, enterprise level, or through a pure play. Commitment is lower at activity level and rises with each level. (　　)

8. The main e-business models at business process level are customer relationship management（CRM）, knowledge management（KM）, supply chain management（SCM）, community building online, database marketing online, enterprise resource planning（ERP）, and mass customization. (　　)

Menu of E-Business Models

A key element in setting strategic objectives is to take stock of the company's current situation and decide the level of commitment to e-business in general and e-marketing in particular. The possible levels of commitment fall along a continuum that is appropriately presented as a pyramid since few businesses occupy the top position. As a general rule, the higher the firm travels up the pyramid, the deeper its level of commitment to e-business becomes, the more its strategies are integrated with information technology, and the greater impact information technology has on its organization. Also, the more strategic moves at the top, the more tactical activities at lower levels; as a result, higher levels carry more risks than lower levels for most firms.

Bear in mind that one firm's activity may be another firm's enterprise-level strategy. For example, electronic transaction ordering process (e.g. selling product on a web site) may be a small activity for a ski shop with 1% of its business from the online channel, but it is an enterprise-level activity for FedEx, the package delivery service company.

In consulting with CEOs worldwide, the Gartner Group poses these questions for firms prior to embarking on any e-business strategies:

1. Are the business models likely to change in my industry? If they are not, there is no reason to get involved. If they are, answering this question suggests strategic direction for the firm.

2. What does the answer to question 1 mean to my company? The answers vary by size, industry, location, and more.

3. When do I need to be ready? This involves thoughtful competitive analysis.

4. How do I get there from here? This is where e-business strategy comes in.

E-Business Models at Various Levels of Commitment

Each level of the pyramid indicates a number of opportunities for the firm to provide stakeholder value and generate revenue streams using information technology. A company can become involved in e-business at activity level, business process level, enterprise level, or through a pure play. Commitment is lower at activity level and rises with each level. The main e-business models at activity level include online purchasing, order processing, e-mail, micro-mail, content publishing, business intelligence, online advertising, online sales promotion, and dynamic pricing strategies. The main e-business models at business process level are customer relationship management（CRM）, knowledge management（KM）, supply chain management（SCM）, community building online, database marketing online, enterprise resource planning（ERP），and mass customization. The main e-business models at enterprise level are e-commerce，portal，online broker，online agent，manufacturer's agent，and virtual mall. The final level of the pyramid is composed of the Internet pure plays. Pure plays are businesses that began on the Internet like Amazon. com and other dotcoms，even if they later added a brick-and-mortar presence.

VI. Translate the following into English.

1. 商务模式不是存在于真空中。它关系到企业的战略，企业可以选择一种或多种商务模式作为战略来实现企业目标。

2. 无论是线上还是线下，价值主张就是了解什么是对客户和合作伙伴最为重要的，并且传递比其他公司更好的产品或服务。价值包括客户对产品益处的感知，特别是对产品的特性、品牌和所提供服务的理解。

3. 与客户类似，合作伙伴会通过比较合作所带来的利益是否高于成本来评判其价值。

4. 相反的，当网站过于复杂，信息难以查找，技术难题干扰了数据的获取和交易的进行时，价值会降低。

5. 依据动态定价，公司对不同的客户群，甚至可根据每个客户制定不同的价格。通过拍卖的形式进行在线议价，是一种由买家而非卖家发起的动态定价方式。

6. 知识管理是一个综合体。它包括企业数据库内容、用于系统创建的技术以及将数据转化成有用信息和知识的过程。

Supplemental Reading Material

Customer Relationship Management Metrics

Online marketers use numerous metrics to measure the Internet value in delivering CRM performance—among them are ROI，cost savings，revenues，customer satisfaction，and especially the contribution of each CRM tactic to these measures. Recall that all online marketing performance measures assess specific tactics from different perspectives，and that the metrics of choice depend on the firm's goals and strategies. Here we present a few of the common metrics used to track customers' progress through the consumer life cycle. See Exhibit 19. 2 below.

Exhibit 19. 2 CRM Metrics by Customer Life Cycle Stage

Target
● Recency，frequency，monetary analysis（RFM）—identify high-value customers.
● Share of customer spending—proportion of revenues from high-value customers as compared to low-value customers.

(continued)

Acquire

- New customer acquisition cost.
- Number of new customers referred from partner sites.
- Campaign responses—click-throughs, conversations, etc.
- Rate of customer recovery—proportion of customers who drop away that the firm can lure back using various offers.

Transact

- Prospect conversation rate—percent of visitors to site that buy.
- Customer cross-sell rate from online to offline, and the reverse.
- Services sold to partners.
- Sales of a firm's products on partner web sites.
- Average order value (AOV)—dollar sales divided by number of orders for any given period.
- Referral revenue—dollars in sales from customers referred to the firm by current customers.
- Sales leads from Internet to closure ratios.

Service

- Customer satisfaction ratings over time.
- Time to answer incoming message/e-mail from customers.
- Number of complaints.

Retain

- Customer attrition rate—proportion of customers who don't repurchase in a set time period.
- Percentage customer retention—proportion of customers who repeat purchase.

Grow

- Lifetime value (LTV)—net present value of the revenue stream for any particular customer over a number of years.
- AOV over time—increase or decrease.
- Average annual sales growth for repeat customers over time.
- Loyal program effectiveness—sales increase over time.
- Number of low-value customers who moved to high value.

Armed with this and other information about what makes customers value the firm's products, firms attempt to increase conversion and retention rates, reduce defection rates, and build AOV and profits per customer over time (acquire, retain, grow). For example, FTD.com, the florist, worked hard in 2002 to improve its CRM metrics over those in 2001. In the second quarter, it successfully increased orders year-to-year from 514,000 to 624,000, increased AOV from $57.00 to $58.93, and reduced marketing costs by 8% from 8.3 to 7.67.

In addition to performance improvements, many firms use some of these methods to identity the least profitable customers and minimize interactions with them. The point is not to treat some customers poorly but to try to minimize the time invested in serving low-profit customers.

One very important CRM metric that deserves more discussion is customer lifetime value (LTV). Shown in Exhibit 19.3, is adaptation of an LTV calculation from the Peppers and Rogers Group. This calculation assumes that the firm has 1,000 customers in the first year, each spending an average of $35.9. In the second year, 60% of the customers are retained, and due to clever cross- and up-selling, they each spend $75.90 in that and subsequent years. The second to last column includes the net present value of each year's net profits, calculated at 15%. Finally, the 10-year LTV of each customer is displayed. The numbers may look smaller than expected because this calculation realistically discounts revenues to its present value. Note that the LTV increases after the fifth year due to the higher retention rate in the later years. Even with this high retention rate assumption (60% to 80%), notice how few customers are left in year 10. This calculation demonstrates the benefits of retaining customers over time and the need for building share of wallet. It also shows that no matter how good a firm is at retaining customers, new customer acquisition is still an important activity.

Exhibit 19.3   Customer Lifetime Value (LTV)

Year	Total Customer	Retention Rate	Total Revenue ($)	Net Profits ($)	NPV at 15% ($)	10-Year LTV ($)
1	1000	60%	35,900	5,900	5,900	66.94
2	600	65%	45,540	27,540	23,948	118.12
3	390	70%	39,601	17,901	13,536	129.15
4	273	75%	20,721	12,531	8,239	138.35
5	205	78%	15,541	9,398	5,373	143.35
6	160	79%	12,122	7,330	3,645	145.45
7	126	80%	9,576	5,791	2,504	146.81
8	101	80%	7,661	4,633	1,742	146.81
9	81	80%	6,129	3,706	1,212	146.81
10	65	80%	4,903	2,965	843	146.81

Discussion and Review Questions:

1. What metrics are used to measure the Internet value in delivering CRM performance?

2. What are the targets of Customer Relationship Management Metrics?

3. What can be acquired from Customer Relationship Management Metrics?

4. How to understand "Transact" in Exhibit 19.2? Give a concrete example of this term in reality.

5. How to define lifetime value? Give a concrete example of this term in reality.

The Emergence of E-Marketing

Text

As the growth of Google.com shows, some marketing principles never change. Markets always welcome an **innovative** new product, even in a crowded field of competitors, as long as it provides **customer value**. Also, Google's success shows that customers trust good brands and that well-crafted marketing mix strategies can be effective in helping newcomers enter crowded markets. Nevertheless, organizations are scrambling to determine how they can use information technology profitably and to understand what technology means for their business strategies. Marketers want to know which of their time-tested concepts will be enhanced by the Internet, databases, wireless mobile devices, and other technologies. The rapid growth of the Internet and subsequent bursting of the dot-com bubble has marketers wondering, "What next?". This Unit attempts to answer these questions through careful and systematic examination of successful **e-marketing** strategies in light of proven traditional marketing practices.

What Is E-Marketing?

E-marketing is the application of information technologies for:

● Transforming marketing strategies to create more customer value through more effective **segmentation**, targeting, **differentiation** and positioning strategies;

● More efficiently planning and executing the conception, distribution, promotion, and pricing of goods, services and ideas;

● Creating exchanges that satisfy individual consumers and organizational objectives.

This definition sounds a lot like the definition of traditional marketing. Another way to view it is that e-marketing is the result of information technology applied to traditional marketing. E-marketing affects traditional marketing in two ways. First, it increases efficiency in traditional marketing functions. Second, the technology of e-marketing transforms many marketing strategies. The transformation results in new business models that add customer value and/or increase company profitability.

What Is E-Business?

E-business is important, powerful and unstoppable. But what is it, exactly? IBM coined the term e-business and the Gartner Group **fleshed** it **out** to mean the continuous optimization of a firm's business activities through digital technology. **Digital technologies** are things like computers and the Internet, which allow the storage and transmission of data in digital formats (1's and 0's). In this book we use the term digital technology and information technology interchangeably. E-business involves attracting and retaining the right customers and business partners. It permeates business processes, such as product buying and selling. It includes digital communication, e-commerce, and online research, and it is used by every business discipline. **E-commerce** is the subset of e-business focused on transactions.

The Big Picture

Easy, inexpensive, and quick access to digital information transforms economies, governments, societies, and businesses. Digital information enhances economies through more efficient markets, more jobs, information access, communication globalization, lower barriers to foreign trade and investment and more. However, the Internet's impact is not evenly distributed across the globe. The approximately 530 million users connected to the Internet worldwide represent just 8.5% of the global population. In fact, developed nations hold only 15% of the world's population but account for 88% of all Internet users (see www. weforum. org). One estimate puts U.S. Internet users at 182 million, representing 64% of the population (Nielsen/ NetRatings). At the same time, stories abound about **indigenous** peoples in remote locations gaining health, legal, and other advice or selling native products using the Internet. Clearly, the Internet is having a huge impact.

A networked world creates changes that some see as undesirable. Societies change as global communities based on interests form, and worldwide information access slowly decreases cultural and language differences. Some say that the existence of a truly global village will have the effect of removing cultural differences and that this is not good. Furthermore, easy computer networking means that work and home boundaries are blurring. Although this makes working more convenient, it may encourage more workaholism and less time with family. Yet another issue is the digital divide. This is the idea that Internet adoption occurs when folks have enough money to buy a computer, the literacy to read what is on Web pages, and the education to be motivated to do it. Internet critics are justifiably concerned that class divisions will grow, preventing the upward mobility of people on lower socioeconomic levels and even entire developing countries. Meantime, governments are working to solve some of these problems, but they have other important worries, such as how to collect taxes and tariffs when transactions occur in cyberspace in a borderless world.

In the business world, the digital environment is enhancing processes and activities across the entire organization. Disciplines work together in cross-functional teams using computer networks to share and apply knowledge for increased efficiency and profitability. Financial experts communicate shareholder information online, file required government statements, and invent new ways to value risk, return, and capital investments in dotcom firms that have high sales and few profits. Human resources personnel use the Net for electronic recruiting and training; an increasing number are managing organizational knowledge and work flow through corporate Web portals. Production and operation managers can adjust manufacturing based on the Internet's ability to give immediate sales feedback—resulting in truly just-in-time inventory and building products to order.

Strategists at top corporate levels are **leveraging** the Net to apply the firm's knowledge in building and maintaining a competitive edge. Digital tools allow **execs** easy access to data from their desktops and show results of the firm's strategies at the click of a mouse. In a 2002 survey of thousands of U. S. top executives, at least half mentioned important e-business benefits of building better-quality customer relationships, finding more business partners and other development opportunities, and building better brand visibility (Exhibit 20.1). This study emphasizes the importance of marketing and logistics functions, because all of these benefits (except for partner development) are typically marketing responsibilities.

Exhibit 20.1 The Most Important Benefits of E-Business to U. S. Executives

Benefit	%Mentioning
Better-quality customer relationships	61
More business development opportunities	50
Better brand visibility	50
Drive fat from supply chain	42
Reduce time-to-market	33
Increase customer quantity	25

Glossary

innovative *a.* being or producing something like nothing done or experienced or created before 革新的；创新的

customer value a measure of the difference between what a customer pays for a product or service, and the value they get from it 顾客价值

segmentation *n.* the act of dividing or partitioning; separation by the creation of a boundary that divides or keeps apart 分割；割断

differentiation *n.* a discrimination between things as different and distinct 分化，区别

flesh out to make fat or plump 充实

indigenous *a.* originating where it is found 本土的；土著的

leverage *v.* to use so as to obtain an advantage or profit 利用；举债经营

exec *n.* executive 执行者，经理主管人员

Key Terms and Concepts

E-marketing: The practice of marketing by means of the Internet. 网络营销

E-business：A business that uses the internet to sell goods or services，especially one that does not also have stores or offices that people can visit or phone. 电子业务

E-commerce：Commerce conducted electronically(as on the Internet).电子商务

Exercises

I. Discussion and Review Questions

1. What is e-business?
2. What is e-marketing?
3. What does easy computer networking mean?
4. What does Google's success show?
5. Do you think a true e-business model will emerge? Why?
6. What changes does a networked world create? Give some examples.

II. Vocabulary Review: Without referring to the text, fill in the blanks in the following sentences with the correct words from this list. You may change the tense, number, or form of the words to fit the context. Use each word only once; not all of the words on the list will be used.

| flesh out | indigenous | leverage | e-marketing-strategies | digital technologies |
| enhancing processes | leveraging | innovative | segmentation | differentiation |

1. At the same time，stories abound about _____ peoples in remote locations gaining health，legal，and other advice or selling native products using the Internet.

2. This book attempts to answer these questions through careful and systematic examination of successful _____ in light of proven traditional marketing practices.

3. _____ are things like computers and the Internet，which allow the storage and tramsmission of data in digital formats（1's and 0's).

4. Strategists at top corporate levels are _____ the net to apply the firm's knowledge in building and maintaining a competitive edge.

5. In the business world，the digital environment is _____ and activities across the entire organization.

6. Markets always welcome a（n) _____ new product，even in a crowded field of competitors，as long as it provides customer value.

7. E-marketing means applying information technologies for transforming marketing strategies to create more customer value through more effective_____

_____ , targeting, differentiation and positioning strategies.

III. Match the terms and expressions on the left with the explanations on the right.

1. innovative	a. the act of dividing or partitioning
2. segmentation	b. a discrimination between things as different and distinct
3. differentiation	c. being or producing something like nothing done or experienced or created before
4. flesh out	d. originating where it is found
5. indigenous	e. fall in prices
6. leverage	f. to make fat or plump
7. shakeout	g. to use parts of something to repair something else
8. cannibalize	h. to use so as to obtain an advantage or profit
9. astutely	k. a stock broker's business; a fee or commission charged by a broker to act as intermediary between buyer and seller
10. brokerage	j. in a shrewd manner

IV. True and False statements.

1. Marketers want to know which of their time-tested concepts will be enhanced by the Internet, databases, wireless mobile devices, and other technologies. (   )

2. Digital technologies are things like computers and the Internet, which allow the storage and transmission of data in digital formats. (   )

3. E-business does not involve attracting and retaining the right customers and business partners. (   )

4. A networked world creates changes that some see as undesirable. (   )

5. Digital tools do not allow execs easy access to data from their desktops and show results of the firm's strategies at the click of a mouse.

V. Translate the following into Chinese.

As the growth of Google.com shows, some marketing principles never change. Markets always welcome an innovative new product, even in a crowded field of competitors, as long as it provides customer value. Also, Google's success shows that customers trust good brands and that well-crafted marketing mix strategies can be effective in helping newcomers enter crowded markets. Nevertheless, organizations are scrambling to determine how they can use information technology profitably and to understand what technology means for their business strategies. Marketers want to know which of their time-tested concepts will be enhanced by the Internet, databases, wireless mobile devices, and other technologies. The rapid growth of the Internet and subsequent bursting of the dot-com bubble has marketers wondering, "What next?".

A networked world creates changes that some see as undesirable. Societies change as global communities based on interests form, and worldwide information access slowly decreases cultural and language differences. Some say that the existence of a truly global village will have the effect of removing cultural differences and that this is not good. Furthermore, easy computer networking means that work and home boundaries are blurring. Although this makes working more convenient, it may encourage more workaholism and less time with family. Yet another issue is the digital divide. This is the idea that Internet adoption occurs when folks have enough money to buy a computer, the literacy to read what is on Web pages, and the education to be motivated to do it.

E-business involves attracting and retaining the right customers and business partners. It permeates business processes, such as product buying and selling. It includes digital-communication, e-commerce, and online research, and it is used by every business discipline. E-commerce is the subset of e-business focused on transactions.

VI. Translate the following into English.

1. 谷歌的成功表明顾客信任好的品牌，好的营销组合战略可以有效地帮助新顾客进入纷繁复杂的市场。

2. 市场营销人员需要知道因特网、数据库、无线移动设备及其他技术能提升哪些经过长时期实践检验的营销理念。

3. 电子业务包括挖掘和保留合适的客户群和合作伙伴。

4. 有些人认为网络世界也产生了许多不尽如人意的改变。

5. 电子商务是电子业务中侧重交易的一个子集。

Supplemental Reading Material

E-marketing in Contest

Tough Times

The first generation of e-business was like a gold rush. New start-ups and well-established businesses alike created a Web presence and experimented a lot. Many companies quickly attracted huge sales and market share, but only a handful brought anything to the bottom line. In early 2000 one estimate listed 21 firms with 12-month sales growth between 100% and 500%—but all had negative profits. Notable in that list were CDNow, Lycos, Double Click, E* Trade, and Amazon.com. Since January 2000, however, over 500 Internet firms have shut down in the United States alone. Having gone through the boom and the bust in developed nations (the Internet is still booming in many emerging economies), we are now firmly entrenched in what Gartner Group calls the *trough of disillusionment* (Exhibit 20.2). According to Gartner, the disillusionment is based 30% on the technology recession and 70% on disappointment with e-business results. This is a time when marketers return to their traditional roots and rely on well-grounded strategy and sound marketing practices. During the dot-com shakeout from 2000 – 2002, there was much industry consolidation. Some firms, such as Levi Strauss, stopped selling online both because it was not efficient and because it created *channel conflict*. Other firms merged, with the stronger firms acquiring smaller ones, although in at least one case an e-business firm took over a traditional firm: AOL purchased Time-Warner. All of this is typical in a maturing market environment.

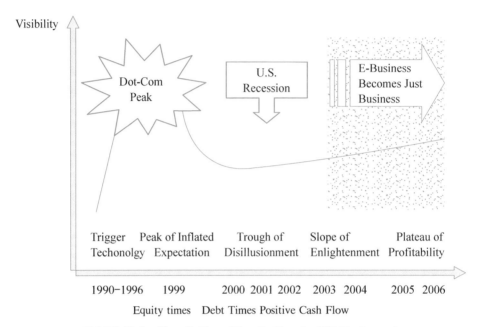

Exhibit 20. 2   There Is Hope After the Trough of Disillusionment

Scorce: Adapted from Raskino and Andren of Gartner Research (2001).

Gartner Group predicts that a true e-business model will emerge, and by 2008 the "e" will be dropped, making electronic business just part of the way things are done. This sounds plausible, although the timing is uncertain. Some say that "E-business has become just business. E-commerce has become just commerce. The new economy has become just the economy". Others say that this is far from the truth—for them, e-business will always have its own models, concepts, and practices. Time will tell.

An example of a firm that has already gone through the entire cycle is Charles Schwab, which allowed e.Schwab.com to cannibalize the larger brick-and-mortar securities firm in 1998. Dubbed "eat your own DNA" by former CEO Jack Welch of General Electric, Schwab astutely pitted the online and offline business models against each other and allowed the most profitable methods to win. The e.Schwab model resulted in lower prices, incorporation of successful e-marketing strategies, and faster-growing accounts and assets. For this brokerage firm, e-business is just business.

Just where does e-marketing fit into this picture? To answer that, we describe a framework for understanding e-marketing's role in the business environment.

Environment, Strategy, and Performance (ESP)

E-marketing flows from the organization's overall e-business strategies and selected business models. As depicted in Exhibit 20.3, it starts with the business environment, where legal, technological, competitive, market-related, and other environmental factors external to the firm create both opportunities and threats. Organizations perform SWOT analyses to discover what strengths and weaknesses they have to deploy against threats and opportunities. This SWOT analysis leads into e-business and e-marketing strategy. Firms select e-business strategies and e-business models, and then marketers formulate strategy and create e-marketing plans that will help the firm accomplish its overall goals. The final step is to determine the success of the strategies and plans by measuring results. **Performance metrics** are specific measures designed to evaluate the effectiveness and efficiency of the e-business and e-marketing operations. This is so important in today's e-business climate that media reports seem to be full of references to ROI (return on investment) and other measures of success for e-business strategies and tactics featured in the model.

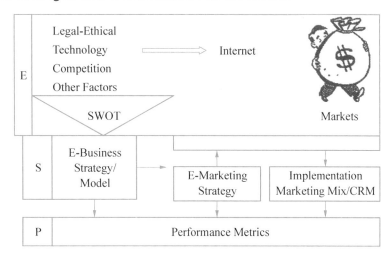

Exhibit 20.3   E-Marketing in Context: The ESP Model

The ESP model might just as easily depict a brick-and-mortar business process—by removing a few "e's". This underscores the idea that e-businesses are built on sound practices and proven processes but with important e-transformations and e-marketing practices, as discussed here.

Discussion and Review Questions:

1. Try to explain e-marketing's role(s) in the business environment.

2. What is the difference(s) between "e-business has become just business" and "e-commerce has become just commerce"?

3. What is your opinion on "e-business will always have its own models, concepts, and practices"?

4. Please use SWOT to analyze why firms lead to e-business strategies and e-business models.

5. Try to explain what the ESP model is and give a concrete example of this model in reality.

Key to Exercises

Unit 1

I. （略）

II.

1. generalize　2. memoirs　3. classical，behavioral，management science　4. integrate　5. contingent
6. dynamic　7. conflicts　8. compromised　9. interdependent　10. popularity　11. reliance，sufficient
12. insights

III.

1. g　2. h　3. b　4. a　5. f　6. e　7. d　8. c

IV.

1. T　2. F　3. T　4. T　5. T　6. F　7. F

V.

为什么要学习管理

　　学习管理的重要性体现在两个方面。首先，我们的社会依赖于专门的机构和组织来提供我们想要的商品和服务。这些组织由一个或多个被称为"经理"的人的决定所引导和控制。在以市场为基础的经济中，管理人员根据不同的甚至是竞争性的目的分配社会资源。管理者有权力和责任去构建安全或不安全的产品，寻求战争或是和平，建立或破坏城市，或者是清理或污染环境。经理给我们创造了条件，给我们提供了获取就业机会、收入、生活方式、产品、服务、卫生保健和知识的环境。已经很难找到一个既不是经理也不会受到经理决策的影响的人。

　　第二，没有受过管理者培训的人也经常可以发现自己在管理中的职位。许多人目前接受过教师、会计师、音乐家、销售人员、艺术家、医生或律师的培训，总有一天他们会像经理人那样谋生。而他们将要管理的是学校、会计师事务所、管弦乐队、销售组织、博物馆、医院和政府机构。美国是一个组织化社会，其中大约1 600万组织机构必须有经理人。

　　国家未来的成功在于管理生产力，使它能够应对环境的变化，并妥善管理员工。这些挑战将需要受过良好教育、知识渊博且勤劳的人，他们可以决定管理生涯对于他们个人的价值。我们认为，对于一个男人或女人，管理工作是一种最刺激和最值得做的事业。

VI.

1. The modern era of management began early in the 20th century when classical theorists，economists，and industrial engineers offered a classical approach to increase the productivity of individuals and organizations.

2. A management theory that emphasizes employee satisfaction may be more helpful in dealing with a high employee turnover than with delays in production.

3. Even today，a great deal of what we know about management comes from the autobiographies and memoirs of men and women who are or have been practicing managers.

4. Although these approaches evolved in historical sequence，later ideas have always replaced early ones.

5. During the last 30 years or so，there have been attempts to integrate the three approaches to

management—classical，behavioral，and management science.

6. In this situation，a compromise is necessary for the overall system to achieve its objective.

7. Rigid plans，clearly defined jobs，autocratic leadership，and tight controls have at times resulted in high productivity and satisfied workers.

8. The contingency approach seeks to match different situations with different management methods.

Unit 2

I. （略）

II.

1. strive   2. pervasive   3. entails   4. automotive   5. tactical   6. affordable   7. fostering
8. peers   9. conform   10. analogues

III.

1. g 2. f 3. e 4. h 5. c 6. b 7. a 8. d

IV.

1. T   2. F   3. T   4. T   5. F   6. F

V.   **管理职能和流程**

在 20 世纪初期,法国工业家亨利·法约尔提出管理者的五个管理职能:计划、组织、指挥、协调和控制。在 20 世纪 50 年代中期,一本管理类教科书第一次使用规划、组织、人员配备、指挥和控制的职能框架。大多数管理教科书(本书也不例外)仍继续围绕着管理职能,尽管它们已经浓缩成了四个非常基本和重要的职能:计划、组织、领导和控制。让我们简要地定义下这些管理职能所包括的内容。

如果你没有特别的目的地,你可以走任何道路。然而,如果你有特定的目的地,那么你必须计划最佳的途径。因为组织的存在是为了实现某种特定的目的,必须有人能够清晰地定义可以达到成功的目的和手段。管理者就是这个人。计划职能包括定义目标的过程,建立策略来实现这些目标,制定计划来整合和协调活动。

管理者需要负责安排工作来实现组织的目标,我们称之为组织职能。它涉及的过程包括确定哪些任务要做,谁去做,任务是如何分组,谁向谁报告,需要作出哪些决策。

每个组织都包括很多员工,管理工作就是通过组织员工来完成组织的目标。这就是领导职能。当管理者要激励下属或者影响个人或团队工作时,他们需要选择最有效的沟通渠道,或以任何方式去处理员工行为问题,这就是领头人。

最后一个管理职能是控制。在目标设置和计划制定后,确定结构安排,雇佣员工,训练和领导员工,评估进展是否按计划完成。要确保工作按规定完成,经理必须监控和评估表现。实际表现必须与预先设定的目标作比较。如果出现重大偏差,那么这就是管理的工作了,使这些出现偏差的表现重回正轨。这个监控、对比和修正的过程是我们所说的控制功能。

现实中的管理并不像这些管理职能描述的这样简单。管理活动并不会如经理计划、组织、领导和控制的那样有简单的、固定的起点或终点。管理者在工作时,经常发现自己同时在执行规划、组织、领导和控制的职能,也许甚至没有严格按照顺序执行。如果从过程的角度来看待这些管理者的管理职能可能更现实一些。管理过程中有一系列正在进行的决策和工作活动,管理者确保它们如计划、组织、领导和控制的一样。这意味着,作为经理人,他们的工作活动通常是一个连续的方式,就是所谓的一个过程。对这个职能实现的过程最普遍接受的说法是,经理所要做的就是清晰化和简化计划、组织、领导和控制的过程。

VI.

1. Of course，having a vision is no guarantee of success.

2. A mission statement often focuses on the market and customers that the company serves.

3. These managers are the strategists who develop the plans that guide the organization toward its goals.

4. All the skills required to communicate with other people，work effectively with them，motivate them，and lead them are interpersonal skills.

5. In order to transform vision to reality，managers must define specific goals and objectives.

6. The best organizational goals are specific，measurable，relevant，challenging，attainable，and time limited.

Unit 3

I. （略）

II.

1. operating environment   2. Corporate-level strategy formulation   3. Business-level strategy formulation
4. Functional-level strategy formulation   5. Strategy implementation   6. situation analysis
7. environmental determinism

III.

1. d 2. b 3. g 4. e 5. c 6. f 7. h 8. a

IV.

1. T 2. F 3. F 4. F 5. T 6. T

V.

 如上节所述,战略制定形成了组织及其各个层级的行动计划。另一方面,战略执行,表示一种决策模式和执行计划需要的行动。战略实施包括为达成组织最终目标所需的职能战略、系统、结构和程序。职能战略描述每个职能必须进行的具体行动,从而使总体战略转化为行动。组织系统是为了收集、分析和传递信息。组织结构反映了人员和工作的组织方式,包括决定工作小组、团队和部门的内部关系与构成。组织程序,比如标准操作程序,是为了建立跨组织的协调性并提升效率。随着时间的推移,战略实施可能因为组织追求新战略而需要改进这些因素。

VI.

1. In the immediate post-WWII era, U.S. companies dominated the global economy due to technological superiority and because the infrastructures of many countries were badly damaged during the war.

2. The broad environment forms the context in which the organization and its operating environment exist, and includes sociocultural forces, global economic forces, technological change, and global political and legal forces.

3. A strategy can be thought of in two ways: (1) as a pattern that emerges in a sequence of decisions over time and (2) as an organizational plan of action that is intended to move an organization toward the achievement of its fundamental purposes.

4. Strategic control refers to the processes that lead to adjustments in strategic direction, strategies, or the implementation plan, when necessary.

5. Restructuring typically involves a renewed emphasis on the things an organization does well, combined with a variety of tactics to revitalize the organization and strengthen its competitive position.

Unit 4

I. (略)

II.

1. Managers 2. Organization 3. planning 4. leading 5. human skills 6. conceptual skills
7. Organizational behavior 8. Political science 9. Workforce diversity 10. Total quality management
11. Reengineering

III.

1. f 2. g 3. a 4. c 5. b 6. e 7. d

IV.

1. T 2. T 3. F 4. F 5. T 6. F

V.

 组织行为学(常简称为 OB)是研究组织中的个体、群体和结构对组织行为的影响的科学,目的在于应用这类知识以提高组织的效率。这句话很长,我们来分析一下。

 组织行为学是一门科学。这表明组织行为学是由一套知识体系构成的一个独特的专业领域。组织行为学研究什么呢? 它研究组织行为的三个决定性因素:个体、群体和组织结构。而且,组织行为学收集关于个体、群体和组织结构对行为影响的信息,应用这些信息使组织工作更有效率。

 简言之,组织行为学是关于组织中人们的行为以及这些行为如何影响组织的绩效的科学。因为组织行为学特别关注与雇佣相关的情况,所以它强调行为与职业、工作、缺勤、员工流动率、生产率、人力绩效与管理的关系。

VI.

1. Recognition of the importance of developing managers' interpersonal skills is closely tied to the need for organizations to get and keep high-performing employees.

2. The people who oversee the activities of others and who are responsible for attaining goals in these organizations are managers.

3. The planning function encompasses defining an organization's goals, establishing an overall strategy for achieving those goals, and developing a comprehensive hierarchy of plans to integrate and coordinate activities.

4. When managers motivate employees, direct the activities of others, select the most effective communication channels, or resolve conflicts among members, they are engaging in leading.

5. One common thread runs through the functions，roles，skills，and activities approaches to management：Each recognizes the paramount importance of managing people.

6. Managers will need to shift their philosophy from treating everyone alike to recognizing differences and responding to those differences in ways that will ensure employee retention and greater productivity，while，at the same time，not discriminating.

Unit 5

I. （略）

II.

1. inputs，outputs   2. production   3. marketing   4. finance   5. cooperative teamwork
6. financial objectives

III.

1. d   2. c   3. a   4. b

IV.

1. T   2. F   3. T   4. T   5. F   6. T

V.

　　生产系统会使用所投入的资源——原材料、人员、机器、建筑、技术，现金及其他资源——并将这些资源转化成产出——产品和服务。这个转化过程是所谓生产的核心，是一个生产系统的主要活动。由于生产运作管理经理(我们简称为业务经理)负责生产系统，因此他们主要关注的是与转化过程或生产相关的活动。

　　尽管生产、营销、财务在达成各自的职能目标时是各自独立作用的，但在实现组织目标时是相互结合、共同作用的。想要在动荡的商业环境中实现组织的盈利、生存和增长的目标，需要这些主要的企业职能之间的相互合作。尽管生产经理、营销经理、财务经理有许多相似之处，但他们所做出的决策可能截然不同。

　　西部的快速开发和移民定居，创造了人们对诸多产品的需求，以及将产品转移到匮乏地区的手段。内战前的一段时间诞生了大型铁路运输业——美国第二大产业。铁路线大大延伸，同时开发了许多新的领土，随着 20 世纪的到来，有效而又经济的交通系统，在全国范围内投入运营。

VI.

1. Because managers in production and operations management（POM），whom we shall simply call operations managers，manage the production system，their primary concern is with the activities of the conversion process or production.

2. Whereas production，marketing，and finance act independently to achieve their individual functional goals，they act together to achieve the organization's goals.

3. While managers in production，marketing，and finance have much in common，the decisions that they make can be distinctly different.

4. The rapid exploration and settlement of the West created the need for numerous products and a means to deliver them to the product-hungry settlers.

Unit 6

I. （略）

II.

1. innovative   2. mechanization，standardization   3. analytic   4. optimizing   5. navigational
6. carousels   7. outmaneuver   8. hazardous   9. exotic   10. medieval

III.

1. c   2. h   3. f   4. e   5. g   6. b   7. d   8. a

IV.

1. F   2. T   3. F   4. T   5. F

V.

智能工厂和美国制造业的复兴

　　这一工业复兴背后的力量是微处理器，单片计算机设备控制一切机械包括从烤面包机到汽车引擎。在一些工厂如摩托罗拉，微处理器处理客户订单、指引机器人和控制装配线。然而，这不是干涉，机器人自动化常与弹性制造系统(FMS)相结合。人类发挥核心作用，作出瞬间决策和执行精密装配工作，那些是机器人所不擅长的。

　　摩托罗拉的车间和其他类似的设施是建立在训练有素的员工团队和敏捷的计算机系统上的。这个想法并不是为了生产成千上万相同的产品，而是为了定制那些能尽量满足每一位客户需求的产品。因为，当你做小批量甚至个别单位产品时，你会发现信息流是如此重要，所以在这些工厂中软件已经比机器更重要了。

IBM生产经理把微处理器称作全球市场中的"美国的秘密武器"。事实上,一些日本的大规模自动化工厂几年前还令人感到敬畏,如今看起来似乎已处于劣势。不仅仅是它们的复杂性会产生各种各样的操作问题,而且它们也难以应对日益增长的定制产品需求。美国的工厂依靠这个秘密武器运作得如何成功,最显著的迹象就是大量参观者造访美国的工厂想探明这个秘密武器的底细。

VI.

1. Production is the transformation of resources into goods or services that people need or want.
2. Companies pursue these objectives in order to maintain competitive advantage.
3. Although industrial robots may seem exotic,like some science fiction creation,they are quite common and are really nothing more than smart tools.
4. Producers can outmaneuver less agile competitors by moving swiftly into profitable new fields.
5. Using computers to aid design and engineering saves time and money because revising computer designs is much faster than revising hand-drafted designs and building physical models.

Unit 7

I.（略）

II.

1. coordinate　2. incentive　3. eliminate　4. simulations　5. inventory　6. interchange
7. establish　8. executives　9. principles　10. holdups　11. obsolete

III.

1. d　2. g　3. e　4. a　5. f　6. h　7. c　8. b

IV.

1. T　2. T　3. F　4. T　5. F　6. T

V.
准时系统

准时系统(JIT)是一种日益普遍的方法管理操作,包括库存控制和生产计划。类似于制造资源规划(MRP),准时系统目标是准确数量的材料在其所需要的精确的时间到达。一个制造商生产刚好够完成订单的产品,可以消减成品库存。工人在生产线上可以立即处理这些前一站完成的零件或材料,根据工作系统生产而不是大规模生产。制造商仅在需要物资送达时才下订单,而不是提前订购,由此实现原材料零库存。因此,这样可以减少浪费和提高质量。

在20世纪50年代,准时系统在日本演进,当时对日本汽车的需求很低,没有厂家能适用大规模生产的规则。二战后的日本企业也缺乏资本和存储空间。因此,他们在努力减少库存,同时减少了资金和存储空间。丰田的丰田英二告诉他的员工要消除一切浪费,他所说的浪费是指任何超过可以增加产品价值的最低数量的设备、材料、零件、空间和时间。丰田的这种指令就是准时生产系统,它的特点是多功能团队合作、弹性生产、小批量的生产、严格的生产控制、快速设置、一致的生产水平、预防性维护和可靠的供应商网络。当所有这些因素·同生效时,制造商实现了精益生产——也就是说,用较少的资源做更多的事。

VI.

1. Not having an adequate supply of inventory can delay production and result in unhappy customers.
2. So many companies today are seeking new ways of managing inventory.
3. Managers use computer programs to calculate when certain materials are needed,when they should be ordered,and when they should be delivered so that they won't cost too much to store.
4. The price scanners found at the checkout counters of many stores are part of perpetual inventory systems.
5. Every time a product is purchased,the scanner deletes that particular item from the computer system's inventory data.
6. That's why more and more companies are changing the way they purchase and handle the materials they use to produce goods and services.

Unit 8

I.（略）

II.

1. volatility　2. equity　3. barometer　4. Incentives　5. perquisites

III.

1. f　2. a　3. e　4. d　5. b　6. h　7. c　8. g

IV.

1. F　2. T　3. F　4. T　5. T

V.

　　企业的第二个重要的决策是筹资决策。财务经理在这方面关心的是资产负债表右边的组成。如果观察各行业中混合融资的公司,你会发现明显的区别。一些公司有相当多的负债,然而有些公司几乎没有负债。是雇佣的融资经理不同所产生的影响吗? 如果是,为什么? 而且,在某种程度上,是否有一种确定比例的混合融资可以被视为最佳选择?

　　除此之外,股利分配政策被视为公司的融资决策不可或缺的一部分。派息比率决定了可以留存在公司的盈利。公司保留大量当前收益意味着将用更少的现金支付当前的股息。作为一种股权融资的手段,支付给股东的股息价值必须与失去留存收益的机会成本保持平衡。

　　一旦确定混合融资的比例,财务经理必须决定如何用最佳方法获得资金。必须理解获取短期资金、签订长期租赁合同、商议债券或股票价格的含义。

VI.

1. The financial manager plays a dynamic role in a modern company's development.

2. In an economy, efficient allocation of resources is vital to optimal growth in that economy; it is also vital to ensuring that individuals obtain satisfaction of their highest levels of personal wants.

3. The decision function of financial management can be broken down into three major areas: the investment, financing, and asset management decisions.

4. Two companies may have the same expected earnings per share, but if the earnings stream of one is subject to considerably more risk than earnings stream of the other, the market price per share of its stock may well be less.

5. Whether your business career takes you in the direction of manufacturing, marketing, finance, or accounting, it is important for you to understand the role that financial management plays in the operations of the firm.

6. When economic wants are unfulfilled, this misallocation of funds may work to the detriment of society.

7. Dividend policy must be viewed as an integral part of the firm's financing decision.

8. In addition, a company will be more or less risky depending upon the amount of debt in relation to equity in its capital structure.

9. Once the mix of financing has been decided, the financial manager must still determine how best to physically acquire the needed funds.

10. Frequently, profit maximization is offered as the proper objective of the firm.

Unit 9

I. (略)

II.

1. international corporation　2. accounting information　3. groupware products　4. encounter
5. headquarters　6. subsidiary　7. specifications　8. networks　9. legitimate

III.

1. g　2. a　3. e　4. b　5. h　6. f　7. d　8. c

IV.

1. F　2. T　3. T　4. F　5. T　6. T

V.

　　技术给跨国公司提供更多管理企业的有利工具。协作是全球公司面临的主要问题。信息技术提供了许多改善沟通及协作的方法,比如电子邮件和传真。群组软件产品的出现对跨国公司来说是非常重要的。这些系统让不同地区的工人创造出了一种共享、电子化的工作氛围。经理人可以在许多方面使用信息技术来设计全球组织结构。我们可以看到技术在跨国公司的设计和运营中扮演着至关重要的角色。

　　当国外的分部和总部不能相协调时,首要的问题是管理在当地地区的发展。国外的分公司可能在重复开发世界其他地方正在进行的工作,而分公司可能缺乏有才华的员工,导致构思设计出来的系统水准低下。总公司和分公司协作和管理的问题是追求国际企业战略的中心问题。

　　作为任何跨国公司都会遇到的问题,语言和文化差异也可能对在全球范围内发展信息技术产生挑战。时差问题可能使得世界不同地方的沟通变得困难,尽管传真和电子邮件在很大程度上缓解了这一问题。一些公司加强由不同国家的代表组成的联合发展团队,以避免在任何单一国家或以任何单一语言形成的系统会出现的问题。国外的分公司可能更愿意接受一个由跨国文化团队所开发的国际化系统。

VI.

1. Coordination is a major problem for the global firm.

2. We can see that technology plays a crucial part in the design and operation of international firms.
3. The question of headquarters – subsidiary coordination and management is a central one in pursuing an international corporate strategy.
4. Time differences can also make communication difficult for different parts of the world，though fax and e-mail have eased this problem considerably.
5. Foreign subsidiaries may be more willing to adopt an international system developed by a cross-cultural team.

Unit 10

I.（略）

II.

1. flexible 2. consequences 3. facilitator 4. dictatorship 5. pervasiveness 6. incarnations
7. customized

III.

1. c 2. a 3. d 4. b 5. i 6. g 7. f 8. e 9. h

IV.

1. T 2. T 3. F 4. T 5. T 6. F

V.

一个单一的企业可能同时涉及多个供应链,对于不同的供应链,其期望和要求的知识是不同的,认识到这一点很重要。

当一个组织与一家供应商或一家客户进入长期互利协作关系时,该组织应该知道这一安排会影响供应链的其他部分。

广而言之,一个组织在尝试整合供应链时可以寻求三种主要方法。一种方法是通过纵向一体化,这样一个组织在一个供应链中可以拥有众多成员;确实,20 世纪 20 年代的福特汽车公司就拥有伐木和轧钢厂并严谨地控制其经销商。第二种可能协调供应链的办法就是利用不同参与方之间的正式合同。协调供应链的第三种办法就是利用不同组织间为寻求共同的目标或目的而签订的非正式协议,并由供应链中最大的组织来控制。

许多不同的活动也可以由第三方物流提供者来执行,最常见的包括派送系统的开发、电子数据交互能力以及合并运输。而且,一些第三方物流提供商已经开始提供所谓的附加服务——如产成品装配、产品包装、产品整修等等,已经远远超出了传统提供的服务内容。

VI.

1. An individual firm can be involved in multiple supply chains at the same time，and it's important to recognize that expectations and required knowledge can vary across supply chains.
2. A variety of different activities also can be performed by third-party logistics providers.
3. When an organization enters into a long-term agreement with a source or customer, the organization must keep in mind how this arrangement could affect the rest of the supply chain.
4. Broadly speaking, organizations can pursue three primary methods when attempting to integrate their supply chains.
5. A third method of supply-chain coordination involves informal agreements among the various organizations to pursue common goals and objectives.

Unit 11

I.（略）

II.

1. utilization 2. advisory 3. catalyst 4. expanding 5. Career 6. appraisal

III.

1. j 2. d 3. c 4. f 5. b 6. g 7. i 8. h 9. a 10. e

IV.

1. F 2. T 3. F 4. F 5. F

V.

每项人力资源管理的功能都需要有效的研究。这种研究可以被用来确定哪些属于有所作为的雇员,或者用于确定与工作相关的事故的原因。在人力资源研究中使用了许多定量分析方法。工作环境变得越来越复杂,及时且准确的信息迅猛地增长,(人力资源管理的)此功能将变得日益重要。

人力资源管理的功能不是相互独立和截然不同的,它们是高度相关的。管理者必须认识到,他们在某个范围内决策可能影响另一个范围的决策。管理还必须识别出这些影响可能是什么。例如,当一个公司在强调销售队伍的招聘和培训时却忽略了提供足够的报酬,他们就是在浪费时间、精力和财力。此外,如果管理者确实关心职工福利的话,他必须确保一个安全健康的工作环境。额外的福利之一,可以是保持公司工会自由。当我们详细介绍每个主题时,人力资源管理功能间的内在联系将变得更加显而易见。

VI.

1. Human resource planning (HRP) is the process of systematically reviewing human resource requirements to ensure that the required numbers of employees, with the required skills, are available when they are needed.

2. Recruitment is the process of attracting such individuals in sufficient numbers and encouraging them to apply for jobs with the organization.

3. Selection is the process through which the organization chooses, from a group of applicants, those individuals best suited both for open positions, and for the company.

4. Through performance appraisal, employees are evaluated to determine how well they are performing their assigned tasks.

Unit 12

I. (略)

II.

1. information 2. technique, function 3. Exploratory 4. conclusive 5. characteristics
6. Accuracy 7. cause 8. observe 9. third 10. statistical

III.

1. i 2. b 3. d 4. f 5. j 6. g 7. c 8. e 9. h 10. a

IV.

1. F 2. F 3. T 4. F 5. T

V.

前面我们讨论了市场营销研究在管理方面的好处。当然,要通过营销研究获得这些好处就需要经费。进行营销研究既需成本也有效益。在任何决策条件下,管理者都必须识别可选的行动方案,然后衡量每种选择的价值与成本之比。决策无需研究即可做出定论还是必须进行研究之后才能做出定论,管理者应思考三个问题:(1)从盈利或回报率来说,此项调查研究值得吗? (2)通过营销研究所获得的信息将提高营销决策的质量从而保证补贴开销? (3)对可用资金来说,研究预算是否最佳?

VI.

1. The determination of the need for marketing research centers on (1) time constraints, (2) the availability of data, (3) the nature of the decision to be made, and (4) the value of the research information in relation to costs.

2. Organizations engaged in international business often find that data about business activity or population characteristics found in abundance when investigating the United States are nonexistent or sparse when the geographic area of interest is a developing country.

3. A routine tactical decision that does not require a substantial investment may not seem to warrant a substantial expenditure for marketing research.

4. In general, the more strategically or tactically important the decision, the more likely research will be conducted.

Unit 13

I. (略)

II.

1. array 2. mobility 3. anticipated 4. assessment 5. augmenting 6. dissatisfied 7. affinity
8. monitor 9. compare

III.

1. g 2. a 3. h 4. e 5. b 6. c 7. d 8. f

IV.

1. T 2. T 3. F 4. T 5. F 6. F

V.

因此,消费者的购买决策常常会基于一些判断,这些判断来源于营销所提供的价值。客户的购买满意度取决于产品的性能和购买者的预期。客户可能会有不同程度的满意度。如果产品的真实性能低于预期,客户将会不满意。如果产品性能达到了预期,客户将会满意。如果性能超过预期,客户将会非常满意或高兴。

但是买家如何形成他们的期望呢? 期望是基于客户过去的购买经验,朋友和同事的意见,营销人员和竞争对手的信息和承诺。营销人员必须小心制定正确的预期水平。如果他们设置的预期过低,他们可能会满足那些购买者但未能吸引足够多的买家。相反,如果他们把期望值提得太高,买家可能要失望了。例如,假日酒店在几年前做了一个被称为“没有意外”的活动,他们承诺提供持续无障碍的住宿和服务。然而,假日酒店的客人们仍然遇到了很多问题,这个活动过高的期望设置只会让客户更加不满意。假日酒店不得不取消这个活动。

不过,如今一些相当成功的公司正在提高期望程度,同时也履行了与之相匹配的性能。这些公司满足了客户。例如,本田宣称,“我们的客户非常满意的一个原因是我们没有满意”。信诺宣称“我们永远不会满意,直到你100%满意。”这些公司设定的目标高,因为他们知道,当一般程度满意的顾客得到一份更好的报价的时候仍会轻易地切换供应商。例如,美国电话电报公司(AT&T)的一项研究显示,70%的客户说他们对产品或服务感到满意时仍会愿意更换到竞争对手那边。相比之下,高度满意的顾客不会轻易转变。一项研究显示,75%高度满意的丰田买家中,其中约75%的顾客打算再次购买丰田产品。因此,客户的愉快心理与某产品或服务产生了情感关联时,这不仅仅是一种理性偏好,更是一种较高的客户忠诚度。

VI.

1. Today's customers face a vast array of product and brand choices, prices, and suppliers.

2. It can try to increase total customer value by strengthening or augmenting the product, services, personnel, or image benefits of the offer.

3. Expectations are based on the customer's past buying experiences, the opinions of friends and associates, and marketer and competitor information and promises.

4. Customer satisfaction with a purchase depends on the product's performance relative to a buyer's expectations.

5. Total customer cost includes the buyer's anticipated time, energy, and psychic costs.

6. If a product's performance falls short of expectations, customers will be dissatisfied.

(略)

Unit 14

I. (略)

II.

1. harmonize 2. designated 3. tailored 4. logistics 5. counterparts 6. interact 7. stock up
8. replenishment 9. docks 10. teamwork

III.

1. f 2. c 3. e 4. a 5. h 6. g 7. d 8. b

IV.

1. T 2. F 3. T 4. T 5. F 6. T

V.

多数企业内部,多种多样的供应链活动被分配至许多不同的职能单元中去,如营销、销售、财务、制造和采购。这就造成多数时候,每一个职能单元在最优化自己供应链活动表现的同时,却忽略了其他职能单元的供应链活动。但是,运输、存货、仓储和订单处理等活动是相互作用、相互影响的,而且它们之间的关系经常是负向影响。比如,较低的存货水平从缺货、延期交货、特殊生产运行和昂贵的快速货运方面降低了存货成本。因为物流活动涉及重大的平衡取舍,因此多职能单元的决策必须要协调合作才能取得更好的总体供应链表现。

综上所述,整合供应链管理的目标就是权衡企业的所有供应决策。跨职能单元间相近的工作关系可以通过以下几种方式实现。一些企业会建立临时供应链委员会,委员会由负责不同的物流活动的经理组成,这些经理时常会通过会议来制定提升总体供应链绩效水平的政策。企业也可以创造出一些连接不同职能单位的供应链活动的职位,比如,宝洁公司内部有一个“供应管理经理”职位,其负责的就是针对每一个产品类别的所有的供应链管理活动。此外,许多企业内部也会设立一个跨职能单元的副总裁以负责供应链管理活动。根据一位供应链专家所讲,实际上,3/4的主要批发商和零售商以及1/3的主要制造商内部都会设立副总裁及以上级别的负责供应链管理的高管。重点在于企业要以一个合理的成本协调其供应活动和营销活动来创造更高的市场满意度,至于供应链管理在企业内部处于什么地位则是次要考虑的问题。

VI.

1. Today, more and more companies are adopting the concept of integrated logistics management.

2. The goal of integrated logistics management is to harmonize all of the company's distribution

decisions.

3. The success of each channel member depends on the performance of the entire supply chain.
4. They must also work with other channel members to improve whole-channel distribution.
5. Channel partnerships may also take the form of information sharing and continuous inventory replenishment systems.
6. Each supply point reorders automatically when its order point is reached.

Unit 15

I. （略）
II.
1. frills 2. millennium 3. premium 4. thrust 5. suffices 6. entrants 7. patronize 8. intangible
9. Headquartered
III.
1. e 2. a 3. h 4. b 5. c 6. f 7. d
IV.
1. F 2. F 3. T 4. T 5. F 6. T 7. T 8. F
V.

　　大多数实体产品往往具有相对较高的搜索属性,消费者可以在购买之前确定其特点,比如颜色、风格、形状、价格、舒适性、硬度和气味。其他产品和一些服务,比较之下,可能只有在购买以后或者在使用期间才能确定其特点,比如,味道、耐磨损性、操作便捷性、噪音和个性化。此外,还有一些信用属性,这些特点甚至在消费者购买以后也难以衡量。以信用属性为主的服务包括手术、会计、技术维修等专业服务。

　　服务营销人员能通过特定服务满足消费者的需求,帮助消费者克服在购买服务之前的犹豫不安,告诉消费者购买期间和交付以后能够获得什么服务。在体贴和善待顾客方面有很好声誉的公司将获取现有顾客的信任并得益于正面的口碑。

VI.

1. Many complain about how difficult it is to make a profit，how hard it is to find skilled and motivated employees，or how difficult to please customers have become.
2. Around the world，the service sector of the economy is going through a period of almost revolutionary change in which established ways of doing business continue to be shunted aside.
3. A service is an act or performance offered by one party to another. Although the process may be tied to a physical product，the performance is essentially intangible and does not normally result in ownership of any of the factors of production.
4. In most countries，the service sector of the economy is very diverse，comprising a wide array of different industries that sell to individual consumers and business customers as well as to government agencies and nonprofit organizations.
5. Services marketing function is much broader than the activities and output of the traditional marketing department，requiring close cooperation between marketers and those managers responsible for operations and human resources.
6. When the firm rents out usage of its physical，human，or intangible assets，time becomes an important denominator；in particular，determining the relevant costs requires time-based calculations.

Unit 16

I. （略）
II.
1. maximization 2. elasticity 3. alternations 4. deterioration 5. breakthrough 6. attainable
7. gradually 8. prestige 9. price-sensitive market 10. spectrum
III.
1. f 2. g 3. d 4. c 5. h 6. e 7. a 8. b
IV.
1. T 2. F 3. T 4. F 5. T 6. T
V.

　　最基础又长期的针对商品或服务的定价框架应该是定价目标的合理延伸。营销经理选定的价格策略确定了最初的价格,也给今后产品生命周期中的价格变化指明了方向。

　　根据明确的定位策略,价格策略可以在特定细分市场上制定具有竞争优势的价格。将产品的定价由最优价格调整至超优价格可能得需要产品自身的改变，或者说目标客户、促销策略、分销渠道的改变。因此，价格策略的变动对营销组合可能会产生巨大变动。一家汽车制造商如果制造的汽车看起来和驾驶起来就像一辆经济型轿车，那它和属于超豪华车系列的汽车制造商竞争肯定不可能成功。

一家企业在给新产品定价和设计价格策略时享有的自由度取决于市场条件和营销组合中的其他元素。如果一家企业推出的新产品和市场现已存产品高度类似，那它的定价自由空间将被限制住。为了成功，这家企业很可能会对该新品收取和市场平均价格相近的一个价格；与此相反的是，一家企业推出了一个在市场上完全没有替代的新产品时，其将会拥有广阔的自由定价空间。

VI.

1. The first step in setting the right price is to establish pricing goals.
2. The basic, long-term pricing framework for a good or service should be a logical extension of the pricing objectives.
3. Changing a price strategy can require dramatic alternations in the marketing mix.
4. The low price is designed to capture a large share of a substantial market, resulting in lower production costs.
5. Managers may follow a skimming strategy when production cannot be expanded rapidly because of technological difficulties, shortages, or constraints imposed by the skill and time required to produce a product.
6. Low prices can draw additional buyers to enter the market.

Unit 17

I. （略）

II.

1. unaware 2. credibility 3. anticlimactic 4. rebates 5. affective 6. extols 7. dealership 8. decoding 9. Dealer 10. cute

III.

1. g 2. e 3. d 4. a 5. c 6. h 7. f 8. b

IV.

1. T 2. F 3. T 4. T 5. F 6. T

V.

假设目标顾客知道了产品，那他们对产品的感受如何？一旦潜在购买者知道了英菲尼迪，尼桑公司的营销者想要的就是使这些潜在购买者对英菲尼迪的情感经历几个阶段，变得越来越强烈。这些情感变化的阶段包括：①喜爱：对英菲尼迪产生好感；②偏爱：相比于其他车来说，更喜爱英菲尼迪；③确信：相信英菲尼迪是对他们来说最好的车。英菲尼迪的营销者可以使用一系列促销组合工具来创造潜在消费者对于英菲尼迪的好感度和确信度：广告可以告诉消费者英菲尼迪较之于其他竞争品牌的优势。新闻发布会和其他公共活动可以强调车辆的创新特性和表现；也可以通过经销商销售人员向消费者提供关于选择、性价比和售后服务的信息。

最后，一些目标市场用户可能被产品所说服，但还没有进行直接购买的欲望。潜在购买者可能还在等待更多信息，或者等待其经济状况提升。此时，和消费者的沟通将会使得这些消费者跨出最后一步，沟通策略包括提供特别的促销价格、折扣、保险等。销售人员可能会给选中的顾客致电或者写邮件，邀请他们参加经销商的特别展出。

当然，仅仅是营销沟通还不能够创造出对品牌的好感或者对英菲尼迪的购买行为。汽车本身也需要为消费者提供优质的产品价值，事实上，出色的营销沟通活动可以加速劣质产品的消亡。潜在购买者对劣质产品了解得越快，就能越快认识到劣质产品的缺点。因此，优秀的营销沟通活动需要"好话带来好业绩"。

VI.

1. Marketers need to know what customers they wish to reach and what responses they want.
2. The audience may be potential buyers or current users, those who make the buying decision or those who influence it.
3. If the message is to be carried over the radio, the communicator has to choose words, sounds, and voices.
4. Purchase is the result of a long process of consumer decision making.
5. Actions might include offering special promotional prices, rebates, or premiums.
6. Presenting the strongest arguments first gets strong attention, but may lead to an anticlimactic ending.

Unit 18

I. （略）

II.

1. conscience 2. embraces 3. ethical 4. criterion 5. accessible 6. precludes 7. publics 8. garner

III.

1. e 2. a 3. g 4. d 5. b 6. h 7. i 8. f 9. j 10. c

IV.

1. T 2. T 3. T 4. F 5. F 6. T 7. F 8. T 9. F

V.

寻找公共关系的"源泉"

伯尼斯在公共关系领域很有影响,但他不是公共关系的创始人。实际上,一些权威人士声称伯尼斯在供职于乔治·克里尔委员会的公共信息部门时学会了公共关系,在一战期间,此机构致力于为美国的战争寻求广泛的支持。

公共关系可能没有单独的创始人,但美国很多公共关系从业者把艾维·李当作现代公共关系的第一个实践者。

毫无疑问,公共关系在美国比在其他国家发展得更快。历史学家艾伦 R. 罗彻认为这是因为美国有较好的社会、政治、文化和经济氛围,并且美国媒体的力量可以使所有的大型公共机构受制于公众的观点。公共关系的实践已经变成了一项重要的出口服务,同样,其他国家也已经发展了适合当地的公共关系实践。

公共关系作为一个概念没有确定的创始人,没有确定的来源国家和创建日期,是因为它聚焦于其影响——不仅是观点,而且是行为。这一特别的因素已经招致了对公共关系的极大批评。那些认为公共关系具有重要的积极影响的历史学家把公共关系看作是为观点、机构和人民寻求公众支持的中间人。然而,其他人认为这需要牺牲个人自由,这种个人自由被大多数人的决定所霸占。当然,这样的权衡对民主的本质极为重要,但这并不能解决公众意见被误用的问题。

VI.

1. As a practical matter, good public relations involves confronting a problem openly and honestly and then solving it.
2. Public relations people must tell their own stories to the public before a problem turns into a crisis.
3. Changes in the environment for public relations can shift the cmphasis from one activity to another over time.
4. Public affairs are actually a highly specialized kind of public relations that involves community relations and governmental relations.
5. The effectiveness of promotional campaigns depends on their effective use of various PR tools.
6. Many public relations people use the term public affairs to describe their work, but this is misleading.
7. A good public relations strategy is based on research.
8. The development in technologies has changed merchandising dramatically.

Unit 19

I.（略）

II.

1. stakeholder 2. subset 3. auction 4. commitment 5. continuum 6. optimization 7. proprietary
8. sustainability 9. attributes 10. Implementation

III.

1. g 2. h 3. a 4. b 5. c 6. e 7. f 8. d

IV.

1. T 2. T 3. F 4. T 5. F 6. T 7. T 8. T

V.

电子商务模式菜单

制定战略目标的一个关键因素是要评估公司当前的情况,并且确定一般意义上的电子商务以及具体而言的电子营销的承诺实施水平。可能的承诺实施水平呈现出一种金字塔式的持续下降,因为鲜有企业占据榜首位置。一般而言,企业在金字塔所处地位越高,对电子商务的承诺实施水平越高;同时,企业战略集成了越多的信息技术,该战略对组织的影响越大。战略举措的实施发生在企业的最上层,战术性的活动更多的是发生在企业的底层。因此,对大多数企业来说,实施高水平的电子商务比低水平的电子商务包含着更大的风险。

值得注意的是,一家企业的底层的活动可能是另一家企业的顶层的战略。例如,电子交易订货流程(如在网上销售产品)对于一个只有 1% 的业务是通过网上渠道的滑雪用品商店可能只是很小的一个业务活动,但对于快递服务公司联邦快递(FedEx)来说,这可能就是整个企业级的活动。

在向世界范围的首席执行官们(CEOs)进行咨询后,Gartner Group 提出了任何电子商务战略开始实施之前都要提出的问题:

1. 我所在的行业的商业模式可能改变吗？如果不能，就没有理由介入了。如果能，回答这个问题就为企业提供了战略方向。

2. 第一个问题的回答对我的公司意味着什么？这个答案会因为规模、行业、地位等的不同而有差异。

3. 我什么时候需要做好准备？这需要进行全面深入的竞争分析。

4. 我们怎样才能从现在的这种状态达到所需要的那种状态？这就是电子商务的开端。

不同承诺实施水平的电子商务模式

对金字塔的不同层级的企业来说，都有大量的机会能够给股东和利益相关者提供价值，利用信息技术产生收入流。公司可以在活动层面、业务流程层面、企业层面，或者是以纯粹的电子商务形式（pure play）参与电子商务活动。承诺实施在具体活动层面较低，随着承诺实施水平的提高而提高。活动层面的主要电子商务模式包括在线购买、订单处理、电子邮件、微信、内容发布、商业智能、网络广告、网上促销，以及动态定价策略。业务流程层面的主要电子商务模式是顾客关系管理（CRM）、知识管理（KM）、供应链管理（SCM）、在线社区建设、数据库网络营销、企业资源规划（ERP），以及大规模定制。企业层面的电子商务模式是电子商务、门户网站、在线经纪人、网络代理人、代理商和虚拟网上商场。金字塔的最后一个层级是由互联网中的参与角色构成。这些纯粹的电子商务玩家是指那种从网上开始运营的企业，如亚马逊（Amazon.com）及其他网络公司（dotcoms），尽管后来它们都增加了实体店（brick-and-mortar）的形式。

VI.

1. A business model does not exist in vacuum. It relates to strategy in that a firm will select one or more business models as strategies to accomplish enterprise goals.

2. Whether online or off-line, the value proposition involves knowing what is important to the customer and partner and delivering it better than other firms. Value encompasses the customer's perceptions of the product's benefits, specifically its attributes, brand name, and supporting services.

3. Like customers, partners evaluate value by determining whether the partnership provides more benefits than costs.

4. Conversely, e-business can also decrease value when web sites are complex, information is hard to locate, and technical difficulties interrupt data access or shopping transactions.

5. With dynamic pricing, a firm presents different prices to various groups of customers, even at the individual level. Online negotiation through auctions is one type of dynamic pricing initiated by the buyers instead of sellers.

6. Knowledge management is a combination of a firm's database contents, the technology used to create the system, and the process of transformation of data into useful information and knowledge.

Unit 20

I. （略）

II.

1. indigenous 2. e-marketing strategies 3. Digital technologies 4. leveraging 5. enhancing processes
6. innovative 7. segmentation

III.

1. c 2. a 3. b 4. f 5. d 6. h 7. e 8. g 9. j 10. k

IV. 1. T 2. T 3. F 4. T 5. F

V.

谷歌的成长发展说明一些营销原理从来不曾变化。对于一项创新产品，只要它能为顾客提供价值，即使已有众多竞争者，市场也总是乐于接受的。谷歌的成功表明顾客信任好的品牌，好的营销组合战略可以有效地帮助新竞争者进入纷繁复杂的市场。然而，企业组织纷纷争相确定如何更好地利用信息技术获得收益，确定技术对企业战略而言意味着什么。市场营销人员需要知道因特网、数据库、无线移动设备及其他技术能提升哪些经过时间检验的营销理念。面对飞速发展的因特网及其后爆发的.com经济泡沫，市场营销人员总是会问："接下来会是什么？"

有一些人认为网络世界也产生了许多不尽如人意的改变。社会随着基于利益的全球社区的形成而变化，世界范围内的信息获取渠道逐渐减少了文化及语言差异。有人说，真正的地球村的存在会消除文化差异，而这是不好的。而且，方便的电脑网络意味着工作和家庭的界限已经日渐模糊。虽然这使工作变得更加方便，但这可能促成更多工作狂，更少与家人相处的时间。然而另一问题是数字鸿沟。当大家有足够的钱购买电脑时，当有能力能够读懂网页上的信息时，以及有足够的教育刺激时，安装网络的想法也就出现了。

电子商务包括挖掘和保留合适的客户群和合作伙伴，这贯穿于业务流程之中，如产品的购买和销售。

电子业务还包括数字通信、电子商务以及每个业务单位都用到的在线调查。电子商务是电子业务中侧重交易的一个子集。

VI.

1. Google's success shows that customers trust good brands and that well-crafted marketing mix strategies can be effective in helping newcomers enter crowded markets.

2. Marketers want to know which of their time-tested concepts will be enhanced by the Internet，databases，wireless mobile devices，and other technologies.

3. E-business involves attracting and retaining the right customers and business partners.

4. A networked world creates changes that some see as undesirable.

5. E-commerce is the subset of e-business focused on transactions.